STRATEGIC FINANCIAL PLANNING
FOR THE 1990s

Strategic

Financial

Planning

for

the 1990s

B. O'NEILL WYSS, CFP

Scott, Foresman and Company

Glenview, Illinois   London

ISBN 0-673-38588-4

Copyright © 1990 B. O'Neill Wyss.
All Rights Reserved.
Printed in the United States of America.

Library of Congress Cataloging-in-Publication Data
Wyss, B. O'Neill.
    Strategic financial planning for the 1990s
/ B. O'Neill Wyss.
        p.   cm.
    ISBN 0-673-38588-4
    1. Finance, Personal.
2. Investments.   3. Estate planning.
    I. Title.
    HG179.W97   1990
    332.024—dc20   89-24306
                                    CIP

1 2 3 4 5 6 MPC 94 93 92 91 90 89

Scott, Foresman professional books are
available for bulk sales at quantity discounts.
For information, please contact Marketing
Manager, Professional Books Group, Scott,
Foresman and Company, 1900 East Lake
Avenue, Glenview, IL   60025.

DEDICATION

Much of the credit for the writing of this book goes to my wonderful wife, Mary, who was patient with me through the countless hours I spent in its preparation. She sacrificed her own time to do tasks that I ordinarily would have done at home.

I would also like to thank the professionals in the financial planning industry who reviewed and verified the accuracy of the technical aspects of the book. Among these special people is my brother Emert, who is a tax attorney specializing in estate planning.

Finally, I would like to dedicate my book to the development and improvement of the financial planning industry. This book is meant to serve both the consumer who needs to plan for the 1990s and my colleagues in the financial planning field, who will be able to sharpen their knowledge and skills, and become more successful in helping their clients.

May all of you benefit from reading this book.

CONTENTS

SECTION IV
Special Financial Situations | 237

FINANCIAL PLANNING OVERVIEW

Do you remember the long lines of cars that formed at gasoline pumps during the mid and late 1970s? If you were old enough at the time to drive a car, you'll probably never forget them.

Do you remember the unprecedented jump in the prime interest rate to over 20 percent and the ensuing inflation rate that peaked in the high teens during the early 1980s? It's almost amusing now to think that some people actually believed the days of 4 percent inflation were gone forever. But obviously, they weren't. In the past several years, inflation has fallen into the low single digits, although during the third quarter of 1989 the prime rate stood at 10.5 percent, which has slowed down the rate of economic growth.

Finally, I'm sure you'll never forget "Black Monday," October 19, 1987, when the stock market fell 508 points to record its worst one-day loss in history. Just when we thought that economic storms were a thing of the past, we find that Congress and the Federal Reserve must act jointly to solve our deficit and monetary problems, lest they affect our financial markets.

But despite all of its apparent ills, the American

economy has always rebounded. Now that we have a new administration in the White House under President George Bush, we can look ahead to the 1990s. One of the goals of this administration is to stabilize the U.S. dollar and reduce the federal budget deficit. Hopefully, home mortgage interest rates will remain at reasonable levels, and inflation will stay in the single digits.

Meanwhile, Congress in 1986 passed the broadest tax reform bill in recent memory. Under the Reagan administration, deregulation opened up all kinds of investment opportunities, and it would seem that tax reform is the best example of deregulation the administration could offer. By most economic apperances (rising corporate earnings, low unemployment, and lower inflation), America seems to be doing well again.

But what about you? Are you taking advantage of these good economic times by investing for your future? Or are you like many confused Americans who hesitate to invest in good economic times as though we were experiencing periods of stock market turbulence?

Perhaps you fear bad times will return. No one knows for sure what will happen, and the opinions of economists vary. Some say the end of good times is nowhere in sight. Others say that the effects of the 1987 stock market crash will lead us into a recession in the early 1990s. Wouldn't it be nice if someone had a crystal ball and could tell us exactly what will happen? Perhaps your uncertainty has caused you to hesitate and become discouraged about investing. The fear of what tomorrow will bring could make you decide to postpone your investment plans for another day, in hopes that tomorrow will bring the answers to your questions.

As a certified financial planner, I have to tell you that such a "tomorrow" will never come: no day offers you all the answers. Investors must take the best information they have, make informed decisions, and hope that their investments will achieve their financial objectives.

Furthermore, no matter how much you know about financial planning, you won't begin to improve your long-term financial situation until you start investing. Jobs that pay significantly more than the average wage earner can spend are few and far between. But most jobs do provide sufficient income for a person to build financial security over the course of a career, provided he or she knows how to go about it.

Unfortunately, the average American, who doesn't know much about investing, will tend to leave the issue of post-retirement security in the hands of Uncle Sam, through the payment of social security. Consequently, he or she will experience a shortfall in the income needed to secure a comfortable retirement.

Good economic times or bad, the United States has a grim retirement problem. Ninety-five percent of the retired people living in the richest nation in the world are barely breaking even. This is not because they made bad investments, but because, like the average American, they made no investments at all. Instead, they procrastinated!

This one single factor, procrastination, causes many Americans to fail financially. Even people who are lucky enough to have money to invest, and some with more money than they know what to do with, are still so fearful that they postpone taking action. Until a person knows the benefits of investing, it's very unlikely that he or she will understand enough about the nature of economics to profit from good or bad markets. If you want to profit from both, you must know what to do and when.

This book will help you understand what investing is all about. It contains information that every American adult can use throughout his or her life. Even though the outlook for Social Security has become brighter in recent years, every one of us must be concerned with contributing our part to our future well-being. After all, it's very likely that if we do not contribute for ourselves, what is done for us (if anything) won't be sufficient to provide for us in our retirement years. With the cost of education rising faster than the rate of inflation each year, Americans with families must invest quickly and successfully to meet these expenses. Likewise, current and future medical advancements make it more imperative than ever to invest for retirement because you are likely to live longer than you might think.

To invest wisely, you must not only understand the concepts of financial planning and learn new investment techniques for the 1990s, but you must also be able to put them into practice. Among other things, this book is designed to help you prepare a budget, determine your personal net worth, calculate your insurance needs, and plan for education and retirement. It also gives you ways to cope with specific financial problems that will become more prevalent in the 1990s.

For those areas in which you need more personal advice, you should consult a knowledgeable, competent financial planner. Financial planners are qualified in a number of areas to guide you in making the right financial decisions. A competent financial planner can take into consideration your personal situation and map a financial strategy that may lead to financial independence. Some financial planners are even certified, or trained, in a number of special areas, and can address some of your more specific problems.

However, to acquire a working knowledge of what these professionals do—and what you must do to ensure that you have a chance of reaching your financial goals—this book has been prepared. It is designed both to help people who know little to nothing about investing and to give experienced investors some new strategies for improving the returns on their portfolios.

In this book, I will explain why individuals should invest for the 1990s, the reasons why many people end up just breaking even, the concepts of compounded growth, how you can find money to invest, and how lump-sum investing can make up for lost time. I will point out the hazards associated with the ever-changing investment markets, and how you can minimize your risks and maximize your returns. I will explain the benefits of the International Retirement Association, because, even though it was a casualty of tax reform, it still remains a good investment strategy for millions of taxpayers. I have also included information on various corporate retirement plans that, depending on your personal situation, may help you toward financial independence.

Perhaps you've made some bad investments. It's not too late to profit from them. I'll examine this problem, too, along with some ideas on planning for your children's college educations and estate protection for your heirs.

Living in America is quite a privilege. We enjoy the highest standard of living in the world. But it costs a lot to enjoy such a high standard of living. Many people live from hand to mouth, just barely paying their bills. They feel that having any money left over at the end of the month to invest is a status symbol in itself—a distinguishing factor between the rich and the middle-class. No matter how high your lifestyle is now, it's likely to drop suddenly and rudely if, when your income stops, you have made no investments to provide you with additional income over and above Social Security and a possible pension.

Through investing, you can have any type of future you are willing to work toward. Naturally, if you can afford only limited monthly investments, you may have difficulty accumulating one million dollars. But that doesn't mean that you can't be financially self-sufficient some day. Such a goal doesn't require brilliance so much as it calls for discipline and persistence, traits that you can develop.

Are you excited about the future? I certainly hope

so. We are about ready to enter the '90s, and if you thought things changed quickly during the '80s, fasten your seat belt and prepare for some unbelievable events. Financial institutions and their markets will change even more drastically. Most institutions, such as banks, savings and loan institutions, credit unions, retailers, and brokerage firms will be competing head to head for your savings dollars, and they will spend millions in advertising to get control of your money.

With the mass confusion which lies ahead, you will need a lot of investment know-how just to survive the evils of inflation and higher taxes. Let's face it, no one in this world will provide for your financial security more carefully and more thoughtfully than you. So don't let yourself down. Read on and prepare to journey forth into the 1990s.

I

WHY YOU NEED FINANCIAL PLANNING TODAY

1

WHY YOU MUST PLAN AND INVEST FOR YOUR FUTURE

How did you find today? When you opened your eyes in bed this morning, there it was, just waiting for you. Was it a good day, filled with pleasant occasions and opportunities? Or was it a not-so-good day, fraught with hassles, disappointments, and setbacks? Whatever happened to you today can be attributed to one of two factors.

The first is fate. If fate was responsible for the events of your day, such events would have occurred under any circumstances, no matter what you may have done or failed to do to bring them about or to avoid them. If fate was cruel, you can't blame yourself; it wasn't your fault. But, if fate was kind, I hope you enjoyed it—even fate will throw you a juicy bone from time to time—but you can't take credit.

So much for fate. This book doesn't deal too heavily with chance. Instead, we are going to focus on the second category of events, those which happen by design. These are events that are influenced by our past actions.

Perhaps you received a letter from a friend today, in response to a letter you wrote. Maybe you received a raise at work, a reward for your past production. Any party invitations you received obviously resulted from the fact that the host or hostess enjoyed your company in the past and wants to see you again.

On the other hand, maybe today didn't go so well. If you missed an important deadline at work, it may be because you didn't use time to your best advantage. If you didn't receive any letters from friends, it may be because you haven't mailed any to them. And if your dog bit you when you arrived home, he might have been repaying you for having locked him out in the rain this morning. The point is that, with the exception of whatever fate dealt you, most of your day was directly influenced by the actions of your past. In the end, we stand solely responsible for whatever pleasure or pain we experience. If we want to be financially comfortable in the future, we must make—and carry through—financial planning now.

FINANCIAL PLANNING

Chances are you have probably heard the term *financial planning* many times. It has been used in various contexts all across the country. Insurance agents use it in the context of insurance planning. Stockbrokers refer to it as investment planning. Accountants use it for tax planning. Attorneys use it for estate planning. Nothing is wrong with any of these specialized uses of the term because each one comprises an integral part of the total financial planning picture.

What is our simple definition of *financial planning*? It is actually composed of five areas, each of which will probably affect you at some point in your life.

1. **Insurance Planning**, also known as "protection planning," involves protecting your family or estate against unexpected catastrophes.
2. **Investment Planning** is a method to effectively manage money and make it work toward accomplishing your financial goals.
3. **Retirement Planning** involves all the sources of income you will need for a happy retirement and ways of making those sources work effectively.
4. **Tax Planning** is popular with people who want to save on their income taxes and use these savings for other purposes.
5. **Estate Planning** helps to preserve the hard-earned assets you build up during the working (accumulation) years of your life and enables you to pass them on to your heirs.

This book emphasizes investment planning because you need to know how to invest your hard-earned savings to accomplish your financial goals of protection, investment, retirement, tax savings, and estate preservation. You will have a much better understanding of the term "financial planning" when you use it in this context.

WHAT IS INVESTING?

All the things you do in life are investments. When you want to land a new job, preparing for the interview is an investment in your career. When you want new friends, spending time getting to know them is an investment in your social life. When you actively seek recreation or pleasure of any sort, you are making an investment in your peace of mind and emotional well-being. Even sleep is an investment in your physical, mental, and emotional state. All of your actions are investments that you make to improve your present or future. If the future doesn't turn out the way you planned, you can either blame fate for dealing you a bad hand or blame yourself for making bad investments.

Once you understand this, you should realize that you have the power to become financially self-sufficient at some point in your future, if you're willing to make the proper financial investments. As you've undoubtedly heard it said, it takes money to make money. If you don't put your money to work properly, you cannot expect to have money in the future over and above what you earn in your day-to-day profession.

We all know that there are risks involved in investing, just as there are risks we take in everyday living. You could lose your money through no fault of your own. Economic circumstances can lead to negative re-actions in any type of market. Unfortunately, we tend to dwell on negative things, more than we should perhaps, and these thoughts can get us into trouble. Any investment program you develop for the 1990s should emphasize long-term strategies. That means you should plan a ten-year program in order to show successful results.

In the final analysis, the person who becomes wealthy can either thank fate (e.g., an unexpected windfall such as a lottery winning or an inheritance) or the fact that he or she made some good investments in the past. By the same token, the person who winds up poor can either blame fate or his or her own ill-planned or non-existent investments. There is no other peg upon which the hat of blame can be hung.

You may achieve whatever financial status you'd like in life—from security in your retirement years to independent wealth—if you're willing to take the time and make the investments that will yield such status. More important to such a goal than having great sums of money to invest is having sufficient discipline, knowledge, and patience to follow a plan in order to achieve your objectives.

Don't Feel Outclassed!

Some people think investing is out of their league, a game designed exclusively for the wealthy. They act— or don't act—on the belief that the world of investment is a playground for tough, money-grabbing tightwads, not a place for people of average means. They avoid making investments, partly from fear and lack of understanding and partly to avoid being identified with money-grabbers. But investing is not just a wealthy person's pastime. It's for anyone who would seek a brighter future.

What will tomorrow bring for you? If you're a young person who lives in an apartment with a spouse, the future may bring children who will eat their share of food, wear out their share of clothes, break their share of toys, contract their share of illnesses (all minor, I hope), and spend their share of money in general. Eventually, of course, your apartment may become too small, so the future may present the need for a more spacious residence. As your children grow, so will your need for automobiles. A second, third, or even a fourth car may be necessary. Of course, there is always college or technical school to be considered after your children are graduated from high school. Again, you're going to need money. In summary, you can plan on spending at least a quarter of a million on each child you raise in the years ahead.

Someday, you and your spouse also might enjoy doing something for yourselves. After all, it is your life, and you've got every right to enjoy it, too. Does travel sound appealing? Even if your trips are limited to this continent, travel can require substantial funding.

Then, one day, if fate smiles on you and you avoid the paths of speeding automobiles, you'll get old and retire. Perhaps Social Security and your pension will pull you through in the style to which you've become accustomed, but that's not likely. And if you suffer ill health and require extended medical attention, you'll need even more additional income.

All these situations may present themselves in the lives of average people, those who never desire to be extraordinarily wealthy. It takes a great deal of money just to live as an average American citizen. Money-grabbing may not seem like a pleasant way of life to you, but you had better start grabbing for all the money you can get. You're going to need it.

MONEY

Common sense tells us that nothing can take the place of life, good health, and a sound body. But make no mistake: Money can make life significantly more pleasant.

The quality of your life often depends on your ability to bring your plans to reality. Whether or not you realize or abandon your plans often boils down to a matter of money. With enough money, you can buy what you want in the future. With insufficient funds, you can only buy what you can afford.

You can't do anything to change the past, or even the way today turned out. But you can indeed do something to alter the course of your future. You should start planning immediately if you haven't been satisfied with your past financial situation, or your future will likely be a repeat performance of the past, and possibly even worse.

There Is No Free Lunch

Everything you want out of life will cost something. If you want a slim, trim body, the price is exercise and a sensible diet. On a regular basis, you have to sweat and strain while subjecting yourself to the rigors of aerobics to diminish your poundage. You have to make a habit of passing up jelly doughnuts and second (if not first) helpings of fattening foods. If you want to excel in your area of professional expertise, you have to make a mental investment that involves time and concentration on studies. If you want to enjoy an emotional relationship with someone—a friend, spouse, or child—the cost is the risk of your feelings and a certain degree of emotional vulnerability. If you want to own a home or any other material possession, it will cost you money.

That's the bottom line, right? Money may not be the end-all and be-all, but it will certainly help you acquire many of the best things in life. You must have money—either a little or a lot—depending on what you want out of tomorrow.

Here's a fact you should know before you read any further: Working for a living is fine for holding body and soul together. But most of today's money will be applied toward today's debts. Successful investors realize that tomorrow's paychecks will help take care of tomorrow's needs, but inflationary pressures mean that additional income will be needed to cover the higher costs of living.

RETIREMENT

At some time in the future, possibly during the 1990s, you might like to retire. Even if you don't want to quit, chances are that, when you reach a certain age, your employer will retire you whether you like it or not. Unless you have made sound investments, you will have no income, save for a pension and Social Security, which was not set up to provide for all of your financial needs at retirement.

You can't expect the government to take care of you. When Uncle Sam issues you an income check during retirement, it's backed by funds that were taken from someone else (through taxes). Did you know that an average taxpayer works five months of the year just to support Uncle Sam and his many dependents? More than likely, you are one of the people from whom Uncle Sam has been taking money regularly for years. However, when it comes time for you to withdraw money from the system, the amount of your monthly Social Security check will not provide for your total financial needs. Therefore, you must have your own investment plan to make up for the funds you will need to enjoy a comfortable retirement.

Let's face reality. The trend in corporate America is growing toward early retirement. Many companies in the 1990s will subscribe to the theory that early retirement saves them money that can be used for expansion and increased profits.

The average early retirement age today is 59, but the trend toward an even earlier handshake is coming. What would you do if your company suddenly offered you an incentive to retire at age 55? Would you be ready financially to accept the offer? Would the income from your personal investment program, along with income from a pension program, be enough to supplement regular earnings from your employer? Whether or not you can accept the company's request may hinge on how well you managed the money you saved during your working career.

Major corporations all across the country are offering senior employees incentives for early retirement. These people have both blue collar and white collar positions. Depending on their net worths and asset structures, they can usually shift their investments around to prepare for what should be one of the happiest times in their lives. But many people are unable to accept an attractive incentive and take early retirement because they did not plan ahead.

Social Security

The U.S. government is not going to change Social Security laws to allow people to retire early. Currently, full payments from the system are allowed beginning at age 65. Smaller, pro-rata payments are granted no earlier than at age 62. Since the government is trying to build Social Security reserves for the future, allowing people to withdraw retirement benefits earlier than age 62 is practically out of the question. From the Social Security standpoint, the government would like to see people work longer and delay collecting benefits for as long as possible. In fact, it is quite possible that the age when recipients can begin to collect full benefits may go up.

The person who is offered early retirement at age 55 will not collect Social Security benefits for seven more years, at the earliest. If the company does not offer an attractive incentive package, the only thing the retiree can fall back on is an investment program that should have been initiated many years before.

Unless you work for a large company that can afford to offer an attractive early retirement program, you may have to accept a lower standard of living. People who wait to begin their own retirement program in today's fast-moving society are flirting with disaster.

After all is said and done, the fact remains that you must pay for whatever you want out of life. One thing is certain: Having the money to pay your bills tomorrow will depend on the investments you make today. This means that you'd better start investing for your future now. If you do this, you'll have a good chance of achieving self-sufficiency in the 1990s. On the other hand, if you invest nothing, your only hope will lie with fate.

CHAPTER SUMMARY

1. With the exception of occurrences linked to fate, today is the product of your yesterdays.
2. Financial planning is an easy concept to understand when broken down into its component parts: insurance, investments, retirement, tax, and estate planning.
3. Even if you don't want to be wealthy, you'll need a lot of money just to remain average. Some typical needs for the average American family (beyond paying day-to-day bills) include raising children, funding college educations, purchasing a home, traveling, and building the necessary funds for retirement and old age.
4. There is no free lunch. Everything a person wants out

of life will cost something. If the price is money, the person who wants something had best have enough cash to acquire it.

5. Money is what you will need to acquire the essential things in life. You will also need extra funds during retirement to pay for tomorrow's debts.

6. The government alone will not support you during retirement. Social Security was not designed to take care of all your financial needs.

7. Your only hope of getting what you want out of life lies with investing for your future. You must save and invest to financially survive the 1990s.

2

HOW YOU CAN BENEFIT FROM CHANGING ECONOMIC CONDITIONS

If you could take a trip to any place in the United States, where would you go? Would your first choice be Hawaii, California, or Florida? Or would you prefer Colorado, New England, or one of our famous national parks? Chances are, one of the last places you would want to visit is Washington, D.C., our nation's capital, where all policies are made which will affect your future. But stop and think about it. This could be one of the most fascinating adventures you could ever take. You might even be able to vote more intelligently once you have an insight of what goes on in our nation's capital. The events which transpire affect each of us in our day-to-day living.

Subsequently, you have probably read and heard about our country's budget deficit, trade deficit, and the Gross National Product. You have also heard terms like CPI, inflation, taxes, and the prime interest rate. But what do these mean when it comes to planning for your future financial success? The results of the way in which these items take shape or perform over many years can mean success or failure for your long-range planning. Sometimes even your immediate plans can be altered by one horrendous day, such as Black Monday.

Let's examine some of the more important indicators we hear or frequently read about, and look at the effect they have on your financial planning.

STOCK MARKET ACTIVITY

The Dow Jones Industrial Average (DJIA) is composed of 30 major companies whose stock is held by both institutions and individuals. This index is price-weighted so that moves in high-priced stocks exercise more influence than those of lower-priced stocks. This indicator reflects the action of the overall stock market, that, in turn, anticipates future business activity.

Figure 2.1 shows the activity of the DJIA for 1987. The DJIA rose 782 points from 1,927.31 on January 2, 1987, to a high of 2,709.50 on August 21, 1987. Then a decline set in which culminated in the 508-point drop on Black Monday, October 19, 1987. But surprisingly enough, the DJIA actually ended on December 31, 1987, at 1,938.83, 11.52 points above where it began on January 2. So even though investors took a beating in October, those who kept their stocks recovered to near January prices. Thus, there is no way to predict with certainty what the DJIA will do in any given year.

Another way to measure stock prices is with Standard & Poor's 500 Stock Index (S&P 500), illustrated on Figure 2.2. This index is composed of 500 stocks from NYSE, AMEX, and OTC exchanges and is more useful

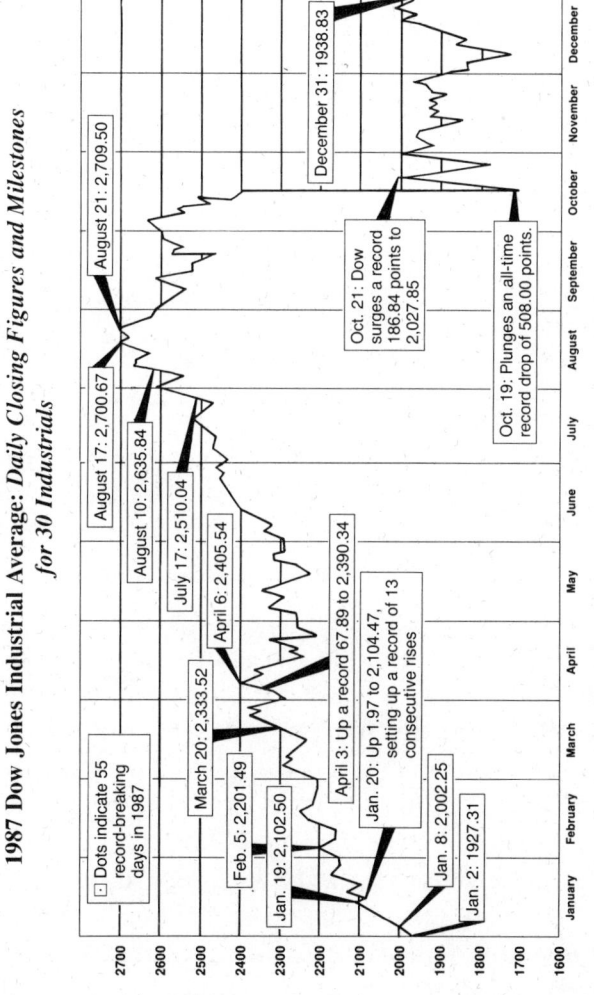

Figure 2.1.

1987 Dow Jones Industrial Average: *Daily Closing Figures and Milestones for 30 Industrials*

Source: Copyright, 1988, St. Louis Post-Dispatch, reprinted by permission.

Figure 2.2.
Stock Prices and Interest Rates

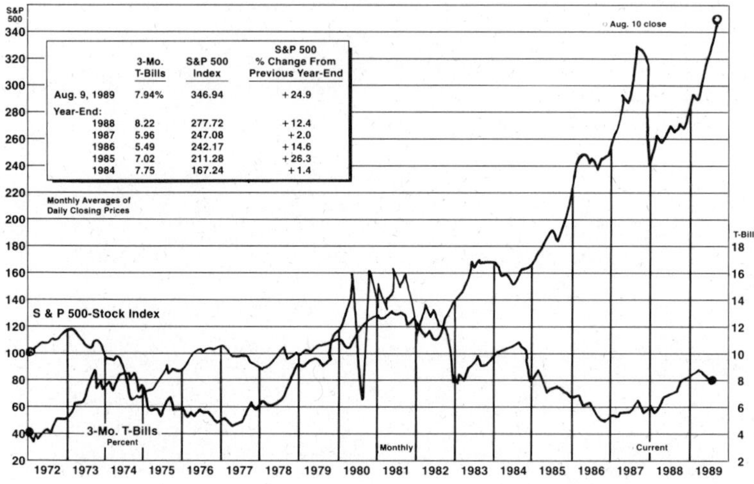
S&P 500
Aug. 10 close
3-Mo. T-Bills
S&P 500 Index
S&P 500 % Change From Previous Year-End
Aug. 9, 1989 7.94% 346.94 +24.9
Year-End:
1988 8.22 277.72 +12.4
1987 5.96 247.08 +2.0
1986 5.49 242.17 +14.6
1985 7.02 211.28 +26.3
1984 7.75 167.24 +1.4
Monthly Averages of Daily Closing Prices
S & P 500-Stock Index
3-Mo. T-Bills
Percent
Monthly
Current
T-Bills
1972 1973 1974 1975 1976 1977 1978 1979 1980 1981 1982 1983 1984 1985 1986 1987 1988 1989

Source: Compliments of Standard & Poor's Outlook, *8/16/89*.

than the DJIA because it is broader. The stocks are market-value weighted, that is, the price of each stock is multiplied by the number of shares outstanding. The S&P 500 helps predict the direction of the economy and the market. Since the market tends to anticipate future economic conditions, this is a good leading indicator. Figure 2.2 shows activity since 1971, which gives a long-term perspective. Generally speaking, to get good total returns from stocks, you must be prepared to hold them for the longer term. However, this figure clearly shows that an investor who bought into the market right after the October 1987 crash would have made an excellent return after just 21 months.

Figure 2.3.
Consumer Price Indexes: 1970 to 1986

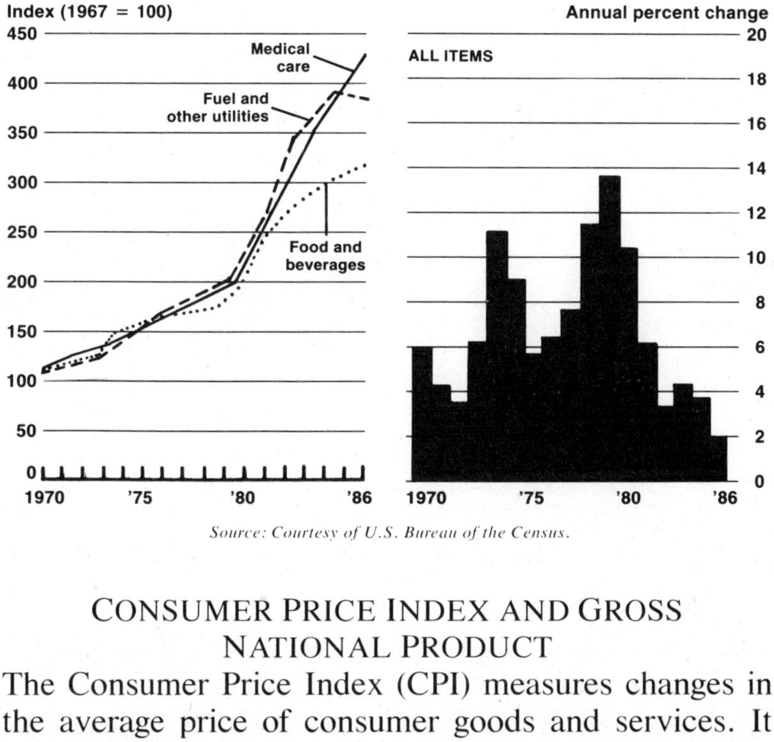

Source: Courtesy of U.S. Bureau of the Census.

CONSUMER PRICE INDEX AND GROSS NATIONAL PRODUCT

The Consumer Price Index (CPI) measures changes in the average price of consumer goods and services. It also predicts the direction of inflation and changes in the purchasing power of your money. Figure 2.3 graphs the CPI from 1970 thru 1986, where inflation rates varied widely. The years 1987 and 1988 averaged between 4 and 4½ percent. The higher the CPI, the less purchasing power consumers will have. A high CPI tends to nega- tively affect the stock market, as it did between 1976 and 1980. This generally leads to higher interest rates, which

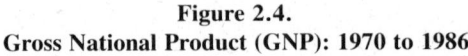

Figure 2.4.
Gross National Product (GNP): 1970 to 1986

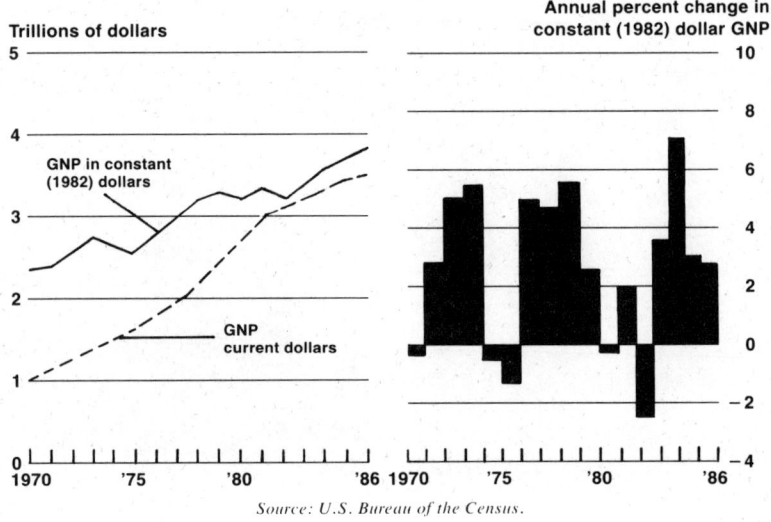

Source: U.S. Bureau of the Census.

in turn have a negative impact on bonds. A lower CPI will generally have a positive effect on the economy, as it did after 1980, creating more growth with higher stock and bond prices.

The Gross National Product (GNP) is the measurement of total goods and services produced in the U.S. on an annual basis. Because inflation can distort the accuracy of this figure, you must subtract the CPI from the GNP in order to get the real rate of economic growth. Figure 2.4 shows the GNP in trillions of dollars and in percentage terms. General business trends and economic activity are forecast by changes in the real GNP.

INTEREST RATES

Interest rates measure the amount of money paid by a borrower to use funds for a specific period of time. Figure 2.5 illustrates the level of interest rates since 1970. When conventional new home mortgage rates increase, as they did between 1978 and 1982, housing starts decrease, resulting in a slow-down in economic activity. Likewise, rising interest rates, as with three-month treasury bills, also cause an increase in the demand for short-term government paper and certificates of deposit (CDs). When more money is parked in these short-term investments, less money is available for the goods and services that expand the economy (GNP).

On the other hand, Figure 2.5 also shows how decreases in the level of interest rates helped to fuel economic growth since mid-1982. Lower mortgage rates resulted in a jump in demand for new homes. More money began to circulate in the economy as treasury bill rates dropped. When banks charged less interest on their loans to preferred customers, better known as the prime rate, more business expansion took place, resulting in a higher GNP.

To slow down economic growth and keep inflation in check, the Federal Reserve had increased interest rates on three-month treasury bills since the fourth quarter of 1986 (Figure 2.2). During the second quarter of 1989,

Figure 2.5.
Interest Rates: 1970 to 1986

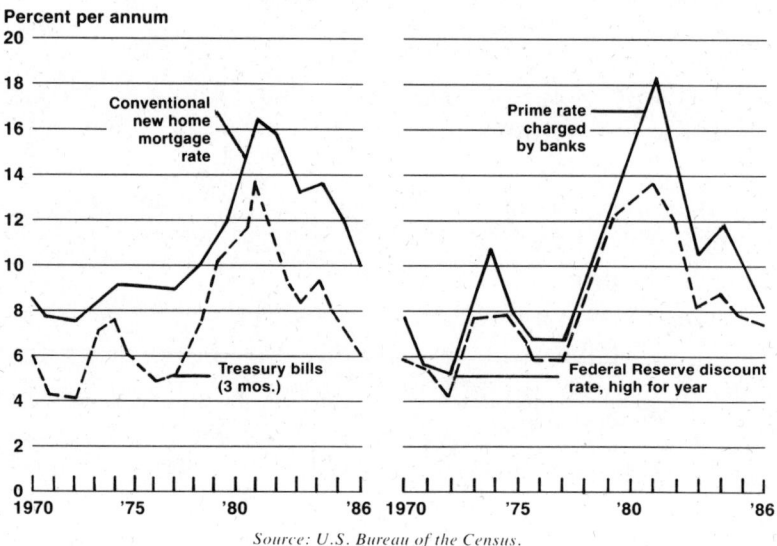

Source: U.S. Bureau of the Census.

rates on three-month treasury bills were over 9 percent. However, short-term rates as of August 1989, had already peaked and started to decline since the Federal Reserve was confident that inflation would not get out of hand during the last half of 1989.

THE FEDERAL BUDGET DEFICIT

The Federal budget deficit, illustrated in Figure 2.6, is a result of the government spending vastly more money than it receives in revenues. Even though tax revenues

Figure 2.6.
The Budget Deficit (In billions of dollars)

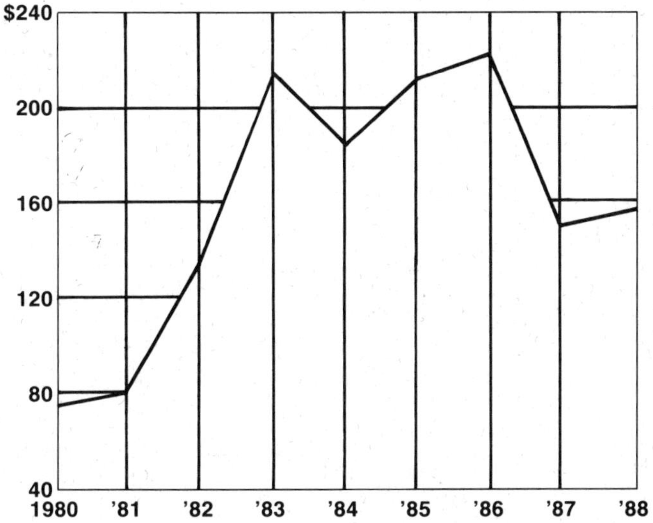

Source: U.S. Bureau of the Census.

have grown, government spending has grown at a much faster clip. To pay its bills, the U.S. Treasury sells bills, notes, and bonds to the public. The total of these debt securities is called the national debt.

Figure 2.6 illustrates how the deficit actually grows during recessionary periods (1980, '81, and '82), because shrinking tax revenues, lower incomes, and falling corporate profits reduce the government's tax base. At the same time, spending does not shrink; in fact, it tends to rise as more people qualify for welfare programs. When economic recovery took place in 1983, '84, and '85, it progressed at only a modest pace. We are probably experiencing recession level deficits now because we never really recovered from the last two recessions.

Since 1985, the budget deficit has been reduced, but still remained at a staggering $150 billion at the end of 1988. This deficit hangs like an albatross around the president's neck, hindering his movements in every direction. It is so on the minds of the American people that it has become a defense issue, a foreign policy issue, a health-care issue, and an education issue.

The new Bush administration will make every attempt to attack this problem as soon as possible because failure to address it could eventually cause a loss of confidence among foreign investors who help keep our economy rolling. The result could be a plummeting dollar, more rising interest rates, and ultimately a recession sometime during the 1990s.

How will the government reduce the budget deficit? Hopefully, it will do so through tax reduction policies (similar to the Tax Reform Act of 1986), giving people more money to save and invest. Revenues lost from a tax cut may be made up by economic expansion of the GNP as more goods and services are consumed. If the new administration pursues a policy of cutting government spending (e.g., lowering military expenditures), the budget deficit may go down as the rest of the economy catches up over the next decade. This, in turn, would be extremely encouraging for those stock market investors who own a piece of corporate America.

THE TRADE DEFICIT

Even though the United States has been blessed with one huge economic system which includes agriculture, petroleum, mining, and manufacturing, all connected with a good transportation system, we have become more integrated with the world economy over the last several decades. The Arab Oil Embargo of 1973 was but a grim reminder that our days of economic isolation are over. As countries recovered from World War II, world trade grew rapidly, and the United States imported and exported an increasing number of goods.

The difference between the value of exported goods and the value of imported goods is called the trade balance. When the country exports more than it imports (in terms of products), we have a trade surplus. The country enjoyed a trade surplus until mid-1970, when we decided to invest our surplus cash abroad. We built plants, lent to foreign governments, and purchased foreign securities. This process allowed the world economy to experience tremendous growth.

In the late 1970s, the country started to run a deficit in trade activities. We spent more on imports than we earned from exports. Even though money we were paying to the Arabs for oil was being recycled back into the United States in the form of investments, we were suddenly running a staggering trade deficit.

By 1984, many foreign governments were deciding not to purchase American grain, machinery, and electronics because the cost had about doubled in only a few years. The strong dollar was pricing us out of world markets. When the value of the dollar fell in 1985, '86, and '87, other countries were able to purchase more U.S. goods and gradually reduce our trade deficit.

The existing trade deficit will not go away overnight. But if we can continue to keep interest rates down, foreign countries will buy our goods and services in the 1990s rather than invest their dollars in U.S. government securities which would increase our budget deficit. If we increase our exports, we will also have more money to circulate in the U.S. for economic expansion and internal growth. This would bode well for investors in real assets, such as stocks and real estate.

THE ECONOMIC OUTLOOK IN THE 1990S

We will witness some dynamic changes during the next decade. By better understanding the forces that drive our economic system, you will be able to make more timely investment decisions, even before these changes actually occur. Thus, you will be able to accumulate wealth much faster than people who are not aware of these important economic trends.

As of this writing, these major trends are likely to develop in the coming years.

We Are Overdue for a Recession

We have completed seven years of business expansion through August of 1989. The rise of short-term interest rates has increased savings, slowed down the economy, and warded off the threat of higher inflation. If the Federal Reserve does not lower interest rates in the second half of 1989, we could easily enter into a mild recession. This could take place in the early 1990s, but shouldn't last very long. Because of the steady demand for goods and services which make up about two-thirds of our GNP, the continuing creation of new jobs, and the currency in circulation, a recession will be much shorter than those of the past.

Interest Rates May Decline

When the Federal Reserve sees signs that its tightened monetary policy is slowing economic growth in 1989, it will begin to lower interest rates. How fast and how low interest rates will decline is yet to be determined. Investors can make money during a recession by purchasing government bonds and locking in longer-term interest rates. For example, owners of long-term bonds could see capital gains of up to 42 percent if interest rates dropped to as low as 6 percent on long-term government bonds. The various types of bonds you can own are detailed in Chapter 7.

Stock Prices Could Decline in Anticipation of a Coming Recession

Even though interest rates have begun to decline in the third quarter of 1989, the economy could still encounter a recession in early 1990. Depending on whether it is perceived as a mild or severe recession, stock prices would react accordingly.

Stock Prices Would Recover as Interest Rates Decline
Investors will move funds into equities as interest rates for savings decline. Corporations will benefit as their borrowing costs decline, resulting in higher profits in the mid 1990s. This will usher in more takeovers by foreign investors, which will push stock prices even higher. Also, there is a very good likelihood in the early 1990s that the Japanese will begin to shift away from their overly inflated stock market and invest cash into under-valued U.S. equities. A combination of these factors will reap high rewards for patient investors in quality U.S. stocks.

Taxes Will Increase to Reduce the Federal Budget Deficit
Congress will continue to spend money on programs for drug abuse, the bailout of insolvent financial institutions, environmental problems, and improving our educational system. In order to raise new revenues, excise taxes will be collected on gasoline, cigarettes, and alcohol. At the same time, Congress may pass another tax reform act in the early 1990s to raise more revenues from corporations and individuals. Those investors who have tax-favored investments, such as municipal bonds and annuities, will be able to keep more money for themselves and thus increase their net worths.

CHAPTER SUMMARY

1. You can benefit from changing economic conditions by understanding various economic terms and the way in which the economy actually functions.

2. Stock market activity is measured by the Dow Jones Industrial Average (DJIA) and the Standard & Poor's 500 Stock Index (S&P 500). A study of these indicators will show the general trend of market activity.
3. The Consumer Price Index (CPI) determines the rate of inflation, which in turn affects the rate of economic growth (GNP).
4. The level of interest rates set by the Federal Reserve will determine how the economy expands or how it contracts.
5. The Federal Budget Deficit and Trade Deficit have become serious problems, since they mean we have spent more than we have received in revenues. The Bush administration has vowed to reduce these problems during the 1990s.
6. As of this writing, interest rates have begun to drop and the stock market has surpassed its all-time high. If federal reserve policy works to keep inflation in check and economic growth stable, owners of common stock will reap big rewards as we progress into the 1990s.

3

HOW TO AVOID MISTAKES AND OVERCOME FEARS IN PLANNING FOR YOUR FUTURE

Are there any good reasons you should plan for the 1990s? Let's explore the issue. Suppose that on the day you retire, all of your past debts are paid. No more mortgage payments for you. Your life insurance policy is paid up, and your children are grown. Your only financial obligations are limited to what it will take to keep you fed, clothed, comfortable, entertained, taxed, and in good health. Of course, your automobile will still need an occasional set of tires as well as periodic repair, and your house will also require a degree of upkeep. But if you're lucky, such maintenance will be at a minimum.

So what will you use to pay your bills? There's only one thing that your creditors will accept—money. Where will it come from?

Not to worry, you may say. You work for a company that will pay you a pension when you retire. Well, you must remember several things. You'll get that pension only if the company is solvent at the time you retire. Even though you may work for a solid, reputable company, similar companies have been known to bite the financial dust during troubled economic times.

After the stock market crash of 1987, many top companies announced they would purchase (buy back) shares of their common stock in the open market because the shares had suddenly become cheap. Included among these were such well-known firms as Citicorp, Merrill Lynch, Alcan Aluminum, and Delta Air Lines. How risky is this type of strategy?

Some companies, mainly smaller, capitalized firms, are exposed to more economic risk and could be hurt in a recession. These companies should be saving cash in the event of a potential economic slowdown, not reducing shareholder equity and corporate cash with buy-backs, because they may need to use their excess cash in order to absorb unexpected losses or even reduce their debt. So remember, nothing in life is guaranteed to last forever, including the company you work for.

Furthermore, depending on how old you are and how long you've been with the company, you might find that, by the time you retire, the pension plan will have been eliminated in favor of an employee-savings plan with contributions added by management. This could set you back to square one. You must have your own personal investment program because there is no guarantee you'll get a pension. Obviously, it's better to get the pension and not need it, than to need it and not get it.

Even if you're fortunate enough to receive pension payments, they may not take care of all of your post-retirement financial needs. And monthly Social Security benefits won't take care of your financial needs either. Pension and Social Security. Would you bet your financial future that you'll get both? If you don't have your own alternate plan working for you, that's exactly what you're doing—gambling with your future.

But let's assume that you do receive both sources of income, that the combined benefits from both are just enough to cover your monthly expenses, and that there were no cost of living adjustments. If that's the case, you'll fare just fine, won't you? For a while, perhaps. But you'll eventually encounter trouble, all because of the ravages of inflation, which are expected to be with us well into the 1990s, and possibly forever.

INFLATION

Let's take a look at what inflation can do to a fixed income cash flow during the next decade. Let's suppose that Mr. and Mrs. Johnson's fixed income amounts to $1,500 per month, or $18,000 per year. Their monthly expenses total $1,400 per month. That means that they'll have $100 per month to save. At the end of a year's time, barring any major financial problems, they should have about $1,200 set aside for the future.

But although inflation was running between 4 and 5 percent at the time of this writing, it has also been known to jump to as high as 18 percent, as it did in the early 1980s. Since an average of 7 percent is recommended for financial planning purposes, let's assume that inflation this year will be 7 percent. With the Johnson's monthly expenses currently totaling $1,400 per month, that figure, adjusted by a 7 percent increase, can be used to predict what they'll be paying next year for the same services.

$1,400 — monthly expenses
× .07 — inflation factor
$98 — next year's monthly increase

Add $98 to $1,400, and you'll discover that the Johnsons next year will be paying $1,498 for monthly services and goods that cost them only $1,400 this year. Of course, because they're on a fixed income, they will still only have $1,500 per month to spend. So instead of saving $100 per month, or $1,200 per year, the Johnsons will only be able to set aside $2 per month, or $24 per year, thanks to inflation.

After another year at 7 percent inflation the Johnsons will be in trouble.

$1,498 — revised monthly expenses
× .07 — new inflation factor
$104.86 — new revised increase

Now, the Johnsons will be paying $1,602.86 per month for the same goods and services, but they only have $1,500 per month income. They have the savings from the two previous years, which total $1,200 for the first year and $24 for the second. At the end of a year's time, the additional $104.86 per month will total $1,258.32, $34.32 more than they have saved. If they can find someone to chip in thirty-five bucks or so, they can deplete their savings and still stay on good terms with their creditors.

If they were to die at this point (or at least find a way to stop eating), their financial story would end happily. However, they will probably be lucky enough to live on, so they'll be in more trouble. Another year will have passed, and now the monthly services that they paid $1,602.86 for last year will cost—at 7 percent inflation—$1,715.06. Remember, their fixed income amounts to only $1,500 per month.

In order to make ends meet, the Johnsons will have to steadily decrease the amount of goods and services they enjoy or find a way to acquire more income. If they happen to be a young married couple, they will never be able to buy the needed goods and services to raise a family. This becomes an even more serious problem if the Johnsons are retired, since a major portion of their income from wages will have ceased. So even if you're lucky enough to receive a pension and Social Security when you reach retirement age, you will also need other sources of income. Otherwise, you may have to learn to survive on fewer than three meals per day.

THE PROBLEM OF POVERTY

Mr. and Mrs. Johnson didn't plan to finish their lives in poverty. But they did, because they didn't plan for their retirement. Mr. and Mrs. Johnson aren't at all unique. In fact, they are part of a growing majority of retired citizens. Some statistics indicate that as many as 95 percent of retired people today are in the same financial shape—just lucky enough to break even.

A milder term to describe this precarious situation is "broke." The word *broke* could apply even to you. What if your total retirement income happened to be $30,000 per year (that's just $2,500 per month). Would you be able to pay all your bills and still save for future needs? On top of that, Uncle Sam will require you to pay a chunk of taxes out of your $30,000 income. So don't just think of poverty as a slum in the inner city. It happens to people every day!

Although you might prefer the path to financial security, you won't get there if you're walking down the road to poverty. You may not be able to avoid the blows of fate, but here are seven roads to poverty you can avoid:

1. Living for the moment and failing to save money
2. Not having a definite plan to follow
3. Not setting goals for yourself
4. Not buying insurance
5. Neglecting to invest
6. Not being patient enough
7. Procrastinating

Living for the Moment and Failing to Save Money
There's nothing wrong with enjoying the pleasures of life. That's part of what makes life worth living. But if you enjoy the pleasures at the expense of a solid financial future, you're likely to grow to be bitter.

Young married couples who are deeply in debt often have good jobs and earn substantial incomes between the two of them, but succumb to the temptation to spend, especially if they have few responsibilities.

In order to be successful, young married people in particular must set aside a certain percent of their monthly earnings to build a savings program. They must pay themselves first before paying their monthly debts. When their savings reach a certain amount, they should invest the money in order to build security for their future. When and if they begin to raise a family, it will become even harder to save money, unless they have developed the discipline to save regularly and have rising incomes to maintain their initial financial program.

Table 3.1 shows the amount of money that would exist at some future time if you added $1 per year and it grew at various interest rates. For example, an annual contribution of $1 invested at an interest rate of 6 percent (after inflation and taxes) for 25 years would grow to $54.86, $25 of this in contributions and $29.86 in interest.

Likewise, if you save and invest $500 per month or $6,000 per year for the next 30 years, at a net interest rate of only 6 percent after inflation and taxes, your nest egg will grow to an incredible $474,348 ($6,000 times a factor of 79.058 in Table 3.1). You could even use these funds before retirement as you save for specific purposes, such as buying a car, investing in a home, or paying for your child's college tuition. The important point is that establishing the discipline to save and invest will

Table 3.1
Future Worth of $1.00 Invested Annually

Years Hence	1%	2%	3%	4%	5%
1	1.000	1.000	1.000	1.000	1.000
2	2.010	2.020	2.030	2.040	2.050
3	3.030	3.060	3.091	3.122	3.152
4	4.060	4.122	4.184	4.246	4.310
5	5.101	5.204	5.309	5.416	5.526
6	6.152	6.308	6.468	6.633	6.802
7	7.214	7.434	7.662	7.898	8.142
8	8.286	8.583	8.892	9.214	9.549
9	9.369	9.755	10.159	10.583	11.027
10	10.462	10.950	11.464	12.006	12.578
11	11.567	12.169	12.808	13.486	14.207
12	12.683	13.412	14.192	15.026	15.917
13	13.809	14.680	15.618	16.627	17.713
14	14.947	15.974	17.086	18.292	19.599
15	16.097	17.293	18.599	20.024	21.579
16	17.258	18.639	20.157	21.825	23.657
17	18.430	20.012	21.762	23.698	25.840
18	19.615	21.412	23.414	25.645	28.132
19	20.811	22.841	25.117	27.671	30.539
20	22.019	24.297	26.870	29.778	33.066
25	28.243	32.030	36.459	41.646	47.727
30	34.785	40.568	47.575	56.805	66.439

Source: Personal Finance, 5th ed. Boston: Allyn and Bacon, 1978.

6%	7%	8%	9%	10%	12%
1.000	1.000	1.000	1.000	1.000	1.000
2.060	2.070	2.080	2.090	2.100	2.120
3.184	3.215	3.246	3.278	3.310	3.374
4.375	4.440	4.506	4.573	4.641	4.770
5.637	5.751	5.867	5.985	6.105	6.353
6.975	7.153	7.336	7.523	7.716	8.115
8.394	8.654	8.923	9.200	9.487	10.089
9.897	10.260	10.637	11.028	11.436	12.300
11.491	11.978	12.488	13.021	13.579	14.776
13.181	13.816	14.487	15.193	15.937	17.549
14.972	15.784	16.645	17.560	18.531	20.655
16.870	17.888	18.977	20.141	21.384	24.133
18.882	20.141	21.495	22.953	24.523	28.029
21.051	22.550	24.215	26.019	27.975	32.393
23.276	25.129	27.152	29.361	31.772	37.280
25.673	27.888	30.324	33.003	35.950	42.753
28.213	30.840	33.750	36.974	40.545	48.884
30.906	33.999	37.450	41.301	45.599	55.750
33.760	37.379	41.446	46.018	51.159	63.440
36.786	40.995	45.762	51.160	57.275	72.052
54.865	63.249	73.106	84.701	98.347	133.334
79.058	94.461	113.283	136.308	164.494	241.333

reap tremendous rewards. It will also help you to achieve your financial goals.

Income drawn from this amount would be an excellent supplement to a pension and/or Social Security payment at retirement. Financial security is within your reach if you have the discipline to stick to a well-developed plan that takes into consideration your income and spending needs. Then you can determine just exactly how much you will need to reach a specific goal or objective.

The old fable of the ant and the grasshopper illustrates this clearly. The ant worked hard every day to store food and provisions for the winter, while the grasshopper fiddled in the spring, slept in the summer, danced in the fall, and wept in the winter. Therefore, being cold, broke, and hungry is no way to end life. Realize the lesson that the grasshopper learned too late—that it is best to prepare for the days of necessity. If you don't, you may just live long enough to suffer dearly for your ignorance.

Not Having a Definite Plan to Follow

Just as you need a goal to inspire or motivate yourself to build financial security, you also need a plan that will take you where you want to go. You not only have to set aside a certain amount of money every month toward your investment goal, but you also must choose the investments that will produce the desired results.

Many people fail for this reason. They didn't have any problem setting aside money each month, but after it accumulates in liquid accounts to substantial sums, they fail to transfer part of it to lucrative investments designed to fit their temperaments and needs. In conjunction with this, you must invest where it will provide returns greater than the combined effect of taxes and inflation. If you fail to take these two realities into consideration, you may indeed fail to reach your goals.

Not Setting Goals for Yourself

Merely desiring financial success isn't enough. You must decide what you want out of life that money can buy: a new house, a college education for your children. Then you've got to keep that dream in mind and strive to help it become a reality.

To achieve anything in life, you must have a clearly defined goal. Vague goals aren't sufficient. A goal to retire early isn't enough. You must envision the pleasures you will enjoy when you don't have to go to work every day. If travel is one of your desires, you must see yourself traveling wherever you want to go.

Post pictures of your goal in your home or office for inspiration. For example, if you'd like to travel the world when you reach retirement, put up pictures of Big Ben, the Eiffel Tower, the Sphinx, the Alps, and other spots that might be on your route. If your goal is a Jaguar, a Cessna airplane, or a recreational vehicle, get photographs of those, too.

Perhaps you may desire to do nothing more than go fishing every day for the rest of your life. If that's what you want, then envision it. Be motivated by it to invest your money so that one day you can punch that time clock for the last time and start every day from then on by tossing a line into a creek, pond, lake, or ocean, whichever suits your fancy.

Make sure your goal is attainable and not a bubble that can be burst. For example, many people form a goal of retiring after age 60, but their financial worlds are turned upside down when they suddenly get an early retirement offer that they can neither afford to accept nor refuse. Realistically speaking, these people had goals, but unforeseen obstacles made them unattainable. To avoid major headaches later on, plan to retire at age 55, independent of Social Security, and make a personal investment plan that will strive to achieve that goal.

Of course, you may enjoy your work and have no plans to retire. That's fine, too. You don't have to quit work just because you don't need the money. The same principle is involved with fishing. Which offers the greater appeal—to fish every day because you have to put food on the table, or to fish every day because you darn well please?

Not Buying Insurance

Failing to save, to establish a plan, or to set goals aren't the only pitfalls into which an investor may plunge. There is also improper insurance planning.

Life insurance is essential. It is designed to provide protection for a family in the event that the chief wage earner dies before financial self-sufficiency is achieved.

This protection is offered through various plans by the life insurance industry.

There are many excellent types of plans, each applicable to a particular individual circumstance. For example, **whole life** lets you invest in a savings fund along with giving you protection. **Universal life** lets you raise or reduce premiums and the amount of coverage on your life. **Variable life** lets you switch your savings among money-market, stock, bond, or gold funds. The applicability of life insurance plans are explained in Chapter 6.

Another method for protecting yourself, which is popular with people who are on a limited budget who want to accumulate funds for a specific purpose, is **term life** insurance. Term insurance offers pure protection only, for a subsequently smaller premium. The difference one would have paid into a higher premium policy can be invested in a special annuity savings plan to accumulate interest on a tax-deferred basis (as of this writing). Annuities are examined more thoroughly in a later chapter.

Besides special insurance coverages, such as **mortgage** insurance, **liability** insurance, **property and casualty** insurance, and **medical** insurance, young Americans must obtain **disability** insurance. Disability insurance is often overlooked, but statistics show that the younger you are, the more likely you are to become disabled as a result of an accident or injury. If this type of insurance is not provided through your employer, you will need a disability policy, especially if you are raising a family.

Insurance planning is one of the most important things you do in your overall financial planning, even before you invest a penny. You can obtain help by working with a professional who is familiar with risk management and who can recommend the right coverage for your particular circumstances at a cost you can afford.

Neglecting to Invest

Many older Americans were raised to save but not to invest, and this has come back to haunt them at retirement. Their children, who are now in their 40s and 50s, have learned this same philosophy. Middle-aged Americans must understand the importance of investing for the 1990s in order to have a fighting chance of overcoming the effects of inflation and taxes and achieving their financial goals. It's true that investing involves risks. But to get ahead in life, unless you are already financially independent, you must take some risks by putting your money where it has the opportunity to offset inflation and taxes.

Most Americans believe that George Bush, despite his campaign promises, will have to raise taxes in some form or another. Even if Mr. Bush opposes tax increases, Congress will have to come up with ways to start decreasing the federal budget deficit now at a staggering $150 billion. So chances are that, sometime during the 1990s, you will pay higher federal and state income taxes.

Not Being Patient Enough

Some people become impatient when their long-term financial goals are not met within a very short period of time. What causes this unfortunate shift in thinking? A number of things can affect your patience: an unexpected firing or layoff, reading a negative newspaper article, an upsetting conversation with a well-meaning friend, or some legitimate reason that can cause a change in thinking.

You must remember to be patient when working toward a long-term financial goal, such as saving for the purchase of a home, funding a college education, or building income for retirement. Once you have implemented a plan to achieve your objectives, you must not abandon it without a legitimate reason. Of course, you should never set up a plan that is inflexible to changing economic or personal circumstances. You must be able to adjust your portfolio, but not for purely emotional reasons.

Procrastinating

Unfortunately, because American lifestyles tend to be easy or sometimes very hectic, we tend to put off planning for our financial futures and just expect it to "fall into place" later on. However, this very seldom happens, unless of course we are fortunate enough to inherit a windfall or happen to be part of a wealthy family.

This makes procrastination the most difficult habit to overcome. Perhaps you may have heard the saying:

Procrastination is my sin,
It brings me constant sorrow.
I really shouldn't practice it,
Perhaps I'll start tomorrow.

One way to overcome procrastination, at least in your financial life, is to take this self-analysis quiz.

1. Do I have adequate insurance coverage in all areas where I must be protected?
2. Am I complacent with the yields I'm receiving on my savings, certificates of deposits, and money-market accounts?
3. Have I been satisfied with the performance of my investment portfolio over the last few years?
4. Are my investments well diversified to give me a feeling of security?
5. Do I have a complete retirement plan adequate to fulfill all my future retirement needs?
6. Am I saving the maximum amount of taxes by taking advantage of tax-free, tax-deferred, or tax-sheltered income?
7. Am I comfortable with the amount of taxes I'm now paying?
8. Have I been adequately informed about changes in the tax laws that will affect my financial future?
9. Is my estate plan designed to minimize fees and the amount of taxes my heirs will have to pay?
10. Am I receiving the proper guidance in the management of all my financial affairs?

If you answered no to any one of these questions, it's time to stop procrastinating and to take action on the areas you need to correct. Don't forget, procrastination will lead to many things when it comes to planning for your financial future—disappointment, self-pity, helplessness, anger, and frustration.

OVERCOMING FEARS OF TAKING RISKS

No one except a daredevil likes to take unnecessary risks. Most of us are concerned with preservation or doing things which will lead to more security. Why take unnecessary chances when you don't have to?

Many people have that same attitude when it comes to investing their money. They have worked long and hard to achieve the status they now enjoy. Likewise, seeing what happened to the stock market in October 1987 and feeling the negative effects which followed were enough to make anyone want to bury his or her money in the ground, even if they did not own stock. Because negative events in the economy always merit front-page headlines and positive events are usually listed on the back page, many Americans tend to be negative in their financial thinking and fail to take positive action.

When it comes to making investment decisions, we must, of course, consider any negative effect that our actions could cause. This means evaluating the risks involved. To better understand the fears you will encounter when taking risks with your money, you need to examine the risks and discover ways you can overcome your fears so that you can make more rational decisions.

Fear No. 1—Possible Loss of Capital

This is probably the most common fear of all. Whenever you move money from a guaranteed savings account to an investment that involves risks, you stand to lose some or all of your principal. Most people treat money as a serious matter, so what money they have is not available for risk-taking.

But in order to get ahead in life, no matter what your profession, you have to take risks. When you get up in the morning, you could fall down the stairs and break your neck. When you get into your car to drive to work, you risk having a serious accident and being injured or killed. Any time you eat food, especially away from home, you stand a chance of ingesting bacteria that could cause you serious health problems. Depending on where you live, you probably breathe polluted air every day. These are risks you have come to accept as part of daily life, and the risk of investing money to improve your future financial life is no different. To ease your fear of taking this risk, understand the purpose of your investment program and follow it with confidence.

Fear No. 2—Lack of Knowledge

Not only is lack of knowledge one of the reasons why people fail financially, but it also causes people to fear making an investment. Many people know that they should be doing something constructive with their money, but have put off taking action because there are so many things to know about investing. They feel it's impossible for anyone but a professional to understand everything.

The best way to overcome this fear is to educate yourself as much as possible. This can take the form of reading books, attending seminars, and watching educational television programs such as *Wall Street Week* on PBS-TV. I feel that it is important to educate clients so that they will understand more about investing and will therefore feel comfortable in making investment decisions. This will be discussed in greater detail in Chapter 13.

Fear No. 3—Fear of Making a Change

A person who has no objective cannot possibly feel comfortable in making decisions. Without a personal goal, you can easily fear making changes with your money.

An excellent way to overcome this is to list your personal financial goals and set a deadline for accomplishing each one. Then you can create an investment program to achieve your objectives.

Fear No. 4—Reoccurrence of Past Failures

How many times have you been ready to make a decision, when memory of a past failure has stopped you from proceeding? Just because you have made mistakes in the past is no reason to stop working on accomplishing your current financial objectives. Look at Alexander

Graham Bell—he made many mistakes and went through constant trial and error before he invented a working telephone.

The best way to overcome this fear is to be persistent! You must learn from the mistakes of the past, put them behind you and press on toward future achievements. If you doubt your own judgment, seek the advice of a knowledgeable investment planner.

Fear No. 5—Concern About What Others Think and Say
A widow who recently came to me wanted to make some important investments, but had been hesitant to do so because a friend had spoken negatively of investing. First of all, I told her that everything she did would be confidential. Then I explained that her friend had no business getting involved in the investment plan, which was specifically designed to accomplish her objectives.

You should become educated enough to make your own investment decisions. But you may sometimes want an attorney, accountant, or close relative to be involved in the decision, and you may feel you need their approval before you implement a plan. This is a good idea when your advisors or relatives have specific knowledge or expertise to share, or when their future well-being will be affected by your decision. But keep in mind that the final decision is still yours, and yours alone.

Fear No. 6—Fear of Being Outclassed
Just because you are not an expert or associated with highly successful financial people does not mean you

should avoid making investments. You don't have to personally know Carl Icahn, H. Ross Perot, or Louis Rukeyser to have a successful financial program. As long as you can trust in your financial planner, you can become very successful.

You can also invest your money with professional money managers through mutual funds (discussed in Chapter 8). By studying their track record, you will know if you are involved with winners or losers. If you are unfamiliar with this area and need special help, let a knowledgeable investment planner help you pick the right investments to suit your needs and objectives.

Fear No. 7—Lack of Self-confidence

Do you lack self-confidence when it comes to making investment decisions? Hopefully not, because it probably means you lack self-confidence in other areas as well. This could result from personal problems or other types of fears discussed earlier. In order to be successful at anything you do, you must have confidence in your ability to make the right decisions and stand behind them. After all, you are the master of your own destiny, and you will make the right investment decisions.

Fear No. 8—Questionable Potential Return

All investments are different—some have a guaranteed return and some have variable returns. You owe it to yourself to examine both types and see how each can fit into a successful investment plan. Chances are, one or the other will not accomplish your objectives alone. You will probably need a program that allocates a certain percentage to each type in order to accomplish your goals. It is also important to go with the program that makes you feel the most comfortable.

By examining these fears and taking steps to overcome them, you will take an important step along the road to financial success. By now, you should realize what fear or combination of fears that are keeping you from taking action. By all means, seek professional help if needed, and don't be afraid to overcome your fears so that you can control your life and ultimate financial destiny.

CHAPTER SUMMARY

1. If your plan for retirement consists exclusively of a promised pension and Social Security benefits, you're betting your future financial security on shaky odds.
2. Even if you win such a bet, inflation will effectively and steadily reduce the spending power of your fixed income. You must have your own investment plan to be successful.
3. To avoid poverty you must live by these rules.
   a. Save for the future.
   b. Plan for the future.
   c. Set attainable goals.
   d. Establish a good insurance program.
   e. Invest.
   f. Be patient.
   g. Never procrastinate.

4. The fears you will encounter when it comes to taking risks with your money include:
   a. possible loss of capital
   b. lack of knowledge
   c. fear of making a change
   d. reoccurrence of past failures
   e. concern about what others think and say
   f. fear of being out-classed
   g. lack of self-confidence
   h. questionable potential return
5. By recognizing and overcoming these fears, you will remove a major obstacle which keeps you from attaining financial success.

4

INVESTMENT PHILOSOPHIES

Now that you understand the need to invest and are motivated to start by familiarizing yourself with the financial benefits reserved exclusively for investors, you must go one step further and acquaint yourself with the potential hazards of investing.

No competent swimming instructor would ever teach a person how to dive without first teaching him or her to know the depth of the waters into which he or she is about to plunge. If the waters proved to be extremely shallow, the person's swimming career, not to mention his or her life, could come to a paralyzing halt. It wouldn't matter how inviting the waters may have looked, the damage would be done.

The same is true with investing. If you buy large quantities of a stock that seems attractive on the surface, your status as an investor may be compared to that of the naive diver. This strategy is sometimes alluring to investors who feel a particular stock could jump in value very quickly. But such short-term gambling can lead to disaster. Most successful investments into the stock market require a great deal of forethought, study, and patience.

Furthermore, the chances of building financial security on just one stock are infinitesimally small. True, concentration in a stock that's destined to rise can make you a fortune. But few people know for certain that a stock will rise, and they are usually those individuals connected to the fortunes of specific companies (insiders or friends of people who work directly for the company). Therefore, concentration in a stock that's doomed to plunge in value can wipe you out in a hurry.

DIVERSIFICATION

Are you willing to risk substantial sums of money on a whim? More importantly, can you afford such a bold venture? Before you answer, understand that all the careful forethought, study, and analysis in the world can't guarantee your success. Factors that influence the rise and fall of stock prices occur daily, even hourly. Market cycles (the time it takes for stock prices to go from high to low to high again) that traditionally lasted five to seven years in the 1950s and 1960s lasted three to five years in the 1980s. Likewise, with leveraged buyouts and company takeovers becoming more prevalent in the 1990s, barring any legislation from Congress to prohibit this type of activity, market cycles may grow as short as months or even days. Investing is a risky business. Once the die is cast, an investor will be more or less at the mercy of future developments which can occur very suddenly.

But even though investments are risky, many of them still pay off. So how do you increase your chances of selecting the more lucrative investments? Simple. Instead of investing all your money in one investment category, you must invest it in several areas. In other words, you increase the number of investments that you buy, and you buy a smaller amount of each type.

This is called **diversification**, and it's a process with which you've likely been familiar long before you ever considered the need for investing. For example, when you were in high school, did you devote all your attentions to one particular girl or boy in hopes of landing her or him as a "steady"? If you did, you concentrated your efforts to win the security that (you hoped) a lasting relationship might offer. On the other hand, you may have played the field. Instead of zeroing in on just one person, you may have divided your interests among several people. If you did, then you diversified your interests.

Now let's look at the results. If you concentrated your efforts on one person you either won the prize or you didn't. You either had a date every Saturday night or none at all. If the steady relationship broke off, you were suddenly left with an empty social calendar. On the other hand, if you spread out your interests you may not have had a date every weekend, but you likely were out having a good time more often than you stayed at home. If one particular date went sour, your social calendar changed very little.

Concentration into the proper investment can make you rich, but concentration in a bad investment can make you poor. Both for the average and experienced investor—and especially for the beginning investor—I heartily recommend diversification.

INVESTMENT GOALS

Many people believe that investing means separating themselves from cash that they won't use until they become old and gray. Of course, some funds should be invested for that very purpose, but not all of your goals need be long-term. After all, life is to be enjoyed in every phase, because there is no guarantee that you'll even live to retire. What a shame it would be if you sacrificed all of your life, only to have it end before you could enjoy the fruits of your investments.

But successful investors don't enjoy the present at the expense of the future. Although you could die prematurely, medical advancements in recent years and into the next decade may also add many years to your life. So you'll find it necessary to eat and stay warm during those years as well.

To derive the maximum benefit from your investments, you must plan accordingly. You, as the investor, must decide what you want out of life, and make those things your goals. There are three kinds of goals that relate to investing.

Short-term Goals

These are goals you would like to achieve within the next five years. Hopefully, retirement will not fall among your short-term goals, but investing for a supplement to pension and Social Security benefits wouldn't be out of the question for a short-term goal either.

Your short-term goals might include accumulating sufficient capital for a down payment on a first (or a second) home, taking an extended family vacation, or buying a new car or other relatively high-cost item. Depending on your own financial situation, another short-term goal might be to invest in order to provide for your parents' post-retirement income. The possibilities are many, indeed, depending on your age and your personal financial situation.

Sometimes, a short-term goal may be an intent that should have been developed in the past as an intermediate goal but, for one reason or another, wasn't planned. For example, I once helped a client who had received a $33,000 inheritance. She wanted to invest toward her daughter's college education. This required conservative investing, because her daughter was a high school senior. Through careful planning with all her assets, we were able to provide enough supplemental income to put the girl through four years of college.

Intermediate-term Goals
These are goals you'd like to accomplish during the second half of the next decade, after the first five years have elapsed but before the next ten years are over. Such goals may include college educations for your children, overseas travel for you and your spouse, or special

acquisitions suited to your personal needs or desires at some future date. Again, such goals may vary, depending on your age and personal financial situation.

As an example, a 52-year-old gentleman who had accumulated $100,000 in cash and securities came to me ten years ago. His goal was to retire in eight years and then work as a consultant on a part-time basis. We reviewed his portfolio of speculative stocks and made changes to include better quality investments which provided greater income and stability. Available cash was invested more conservatively to lower taxes and build retirement capital. This client is now retired, takes occasional trips with his wife, and works on a retainer fee as a consultant. His intermediate goals were accomplished through proper planning strategies.

Long-term Goals

These are goals you'd like to achieve at some point after the next ten years have elapsed. Of course, the ultimate long-term goal is planning for your retirement. In retirement planning, better financial results are obtained if the goal is developed at least ten years before the retirement date. Most preferably, a retirement plan should be formulated twenty or even thirty years before the anticipated date.

In today's uncertain economic climate, the more time you have to let money accumulate, the better off you are. You must make allowances for unforeseen fluctuations in the value of your portfolio, including time to recover and get back on track. For example, if you have children below the age of 8, you should have a long-term plan to build capital for covering rising college expenses. If something unexpected happens (such as the 1987 stock market crash), you will have time to recover and build the investment values up once again.

Other long-term goals might include purchasing a retirement condominium, taking an around-the-world tour, or financial security that will not only tend to all your material needs, but also to those of your heirs. Obviously, goals differ from person to person. Decide what you want out of life and when you want it. Then you'll be well on your way to developing a set of goals that can offer direction for your entire life.

STRATEGY

Merely setting short-, intermediate-, and long-term goals is not enough. You must estimate the cost of what you want in the year you plan to get it. For example, suppose your short-term goal is to acquire enough capital for a 10 percent down payment on a home that would sell for $100,000 today. If you were buying that home today, your down payment would be $10,000. But after five years of 7 percent annual inflation, the same home would sell for at least $140,000 and, since real estate tends to appreciate at 10 percent per year, it might go for as much as $160,000. So a 10 percent down payment for this home would range between $14,000 and $16,000. Therefore, you would have to develop an investment strategy that would yield $14,000 to $16,000 within five years.

Of course, such a strategy would depend on how

much capital you choose or can afford to invest and on the interest rate that is necessary to reach the desired goal. The higher the interest rate, the faster the goal can be achieved. But the higher the interest rate, the higher the risk. Investments are like motorists; the faster they go, the greater are the chances they won't survive to reach their destinations.

Investment Speed

If your goal is to raise $16,000 in five years for a down payment on a home, and you chose an investment that pays 10 percent interest, you need to invest $10,000 today. But if you already had $10,000 to invest, you would likely go ahead and buy the home today.

What happens if you don't have a lump sum of $10,000 to invest today? Let's suppose that you can invest $200 per month (or $2,400 per year) toward this short-term goal. At 15 percent interest compounded (and paying taxes on profits out of your paycheck or some other source), you would have $18,608 in five years. Then you could go ahead and buy your house and have a little pocket change left over.

If you could only afford to invest $150 per month, you could still reach your goal in five years, provided you were willing to invest your money in a more risky venture. Of course, the potential return increases along with the higher risk. If your investment survives the risk, you can accomplish your goal for less money. However, if you lose your investment, you're back at square one, with an additional period of your life behind you.

Most investment failures result from trying to build fortunes too fast. It's much like the speeding motorist; he or she may reach the destination more quickly than the motorist who obeys speed laws, but the speeding motorist will take more risks during the trip, and the chances of an accident are greater for the speeder than for the law-abiding motorist.

Just as most investment failures result from attempts to build quick fortunes, the opposite applies with equal force. Most successful fortunes have been built slowly, but surely. The paradox here is that the more time you have to invest, the more aggressively you can afford to pursue your investment goals because you can ride out stock market crashes and other unexpected setbacks. Over short periods of time, you may not want to risk your capital because you won't have time to recover. Of course, sometimes the long shot is the only chance you have for financial security, as in the following example.

Suppose you're 55 years old and have made no financial plans for retirement. Suddenly, you receive an inheritance of $50,000. At 10 percent compounded return (and assuming taxes are paid from your salary, not your interest income), you will have $129,687 in ten years, when you are 65. But that won't be a great deal more than your original investment in terms of actual spending power. At 15 percent compounded return, the total would be $202,277. That's better, but at 20 percent compounded return, the sum in a decade could amount to $309,586. Would the reward be worth the risk? It would depend on your needs at retirement. But one thing is certain, if you need a high return in a relatively short period of time, you won't get it without taking a chance.

Before you chart an investment course, determine whether the reward is worth the risk. Your own personal investment speed will depend on your estimated future needs and the risk you're willing to take. If you must take high risks, consult a financial planner who can increase your odds of investment survival by acquainting you with the most reputable high-risk investments available.

CHAPTER SUMMARY

1. Concentrating money in a particular investment can lead to fast profits, but more than likely will result in fast losses.
2. Diversification, or spreading investment funds among several categories, is the safer, and in many cases, a more productive means of achieving a profit.
3. An investor should determine his or her investment goals and strategies before making investments. Then, the investor will be able to select an investment "speed," or appropriate rate of return to generate the capital to realize the goals.
4. The higher the rate of return, the faster the goal can be reached in theory. But higher returns also mean higher investment risk.
5. The lower the rate of return, the safer your investment. But lower returns also mean it will take longer to reach your financial goals.

6. Although most secure financial futures are built slowly, the long-term investor can pursue a goal more aggressively. A longer period of time allows an investor to ride out market fluctuations, which a short-term investor may not be able to do.
7. Determine whether the potential reward is worth the investment risk before charting your financial course. A competent financial planner can offer invaluable assistance in setting realistically high goals and in maximizing the odds of attaining them.

II

THE BASICS OF
FINANCIAL PLANNING

5

GETTING STARTED—IT TAKES MONEY TO MAKE MONEY

Money is a steady worker. It will work for you 24 hours per day. It requires no rest, no reassurance, no motivation, and, once it's put in the right job, little or no supervision. But you've got to put it where it will work for you, not for someone else. You also must put it where it can survive, so it may continue to work for you. If you place it in an unsafe working environment, it can be quickly gobbled up by forces beyond your control.

In short, if you take care of your money, it will take care of you. But many people find it difficult to invest because they feel they don't have any money left over when all of their bills are paid. What they don't realize is that there never will be enough money left over. Most people spend all of their current income, one way or another. If you fall into that category, yet still want to build financial security, then the solution to your problem is simple: You must invest for yourself before paying your bills.

PAY YOURSELF FIRST

Each week, two weeks, or month, you should invest 10 percent of your salary before you allocate any money toward expenses. This is the only way you'll ever achieve financial goals. For example, if you are planning to have your first baby, and want to save to fix up a nursery, you might need $1,000. By saving just $165 compounded at 8 percent over six months, you will have the needed funds in time to greet the new arrival.

If you're living on more than 90 percent of your income, you are maintaining your lifestyle at the expense of attaining future goals. If that practice continues too long, you'll eventually pay a bitter price. For example, a second financial goal to work for (after the baby arrives) might be saving to replace one of your old cars, because a car is a necessity to a successful working career. As you know, automobiles can be very expensive, and you will need to deposit some type of down payment so that monthly expenses can be affordable. If you anticipate spending $10,000 to buy a new car, a down payment of $2,500 will give you a balance of $7,500 to finance over four years. In order to save the $2,500 in just one year, you will need to deposit approximately $200 per month in an account that compounds interest at 8 percent.

Keep paying yourself first. In order to progress toward new goals, you must reinforce this habit. For example, a married couple might decide that, before having a second child, they should save to purchase a new home where the family can grow and expand. As you know, houses are very expensive in today's inflationary economy, so it's important to save and invest to accumulate a down payment. If they plan to spend $250,000 on a new home, in 5 years a working couple would have to save $650 per month compounded at 8 percent interest in order to accumulate a 20 percent down payment of $50,000. Obviously, they might have to cut out a number of other incremental expenses (entertainment, new clothing, etc.) in order to save more every month. By paring your budget, you should be able to come up with extra funds needed to meet your objective.

Never stop paying yourself first. If you don't pay yourself first, the time may come when you won't be able to pay yourself at all. Once you have successfully purchased that new home, begin to save and invest for future educational expenses and eventual retirement. By carefully attaining each goal, you will develop the discipline to meet future objectives as well.

EARN BIG BUCKS BY LETTING YOUR BUCKS EARN BIG

When you take a new job, it's highly unlikely that you'll seek out or even accept a minimum-wage position, unless you're starting out in the work force. You in all probability will set out to get the best-paying position that coincides with your personal career goals. If you won't work for minimum wage, why make your money suffer a similar fate? Your future security depends on how much your money earns today.

Regardless of your income, it's probably a good idea

to avoid depositing large amounts into passbook savings. Of course, with the number of alternative choices available for holding your cash in existence, you won't need to keep excess funds in a savings account for long. For example, various money-market funds offer free checking and higher-than-passbook interest rates. Most require a minimum deposit, some as little as $50.

Or you might park a portion of your reserve funds in a money-market account until you amass an amount sufficient to invest for your future. In the meantime, you will earn more than what a passbook savings or checking account would pay. In fact, a **treasury reserve account** with a portfolio of short-term (one- to two-year) treasury securities usually pays an even higher rate than a money-market account. These accounts typically pay 1 to 1½ percent more in interest, and their value historically has remained relatively stable.

With such choices available, does it make sense to keep money in non-interest bearing accounts any longer than necessary? If you let any excess funds sit idle in such vehicles, you're giving money away to someone else. This is money that could be applied to help you reach future goals. But the money you can save by using these alternatives isn't the entire answer. You'll need to find more investment funds to build for a solid financial future.

FINDING MONEY

At some point in your life, you've undoubtedly looked down at the ground and found a dollar bill, a five, a ten, or a twenty. Wouldn't it be nice if something like that happened every day? Unfortunately, it doesn't. But with a little effort, you can "find" money to invest every day by taking a few simple steps to cut your living expenses without undue pain and hardship.

Pare Budgets

If you operate your household on a budget, you are in a minority. Some figures indicate that fewer than 5 percent of the nation's families operate on budgets. Whether you are just starting out or are trying to match income with expenses, you must have a working budget. If you don't have one, you will need to use the Budget and Cash Flow Worksheet in Figure 5.1.

To make the budget work, your total annual income must exceed total expenses. This surplus is the amount you will save for investment purposes. If you end up with a continuing deficit month after month, you are heading down the road toward financial ruin. Budgeting problems can often be resolved by a close examination of where money is being spent and by taking action to eliminate it.

When you have a household budget, you should find that certain allocated expenses can be reduced to provide extra investment cash. Other than through prepayment, you can't reduce your rent or the amount of your mortgage payment. But some items on the budget can usually be pared.

For example, the grocery section is a target for reduction. Few grocery budgets couldn't be cut by at least

Figure 5.1.
Budget and Cash Flow Work Sheet

	LAST YEAR ACTUAL		THIS YEAR PROJECTED		THIS YEAR ACTUAL	
	Annual Total	Monthly Average	Annual Total	Monthly Average	Annual Total	Monthly Average
INCOME						
Salaries						
Bonuses						
Self-employment						
Dividends						
Interest						
Rentals						
Other						
TOTAL INCOME						
EXPENSES						
Mortgage or rent						
Food and beverages						
Utilities and fuel Gas or oil						
Electricity						
Telephone						
Water						
Insurance premiums Home						
Auto						
Life						
Health						
Installment and credit card payments						
Loan payments						
Household maintenance and repair						
Automobile Gas and oil						
Repair						
Public transportation						
Clothing						
Medical						
Dental						
Personal care (haircuts, etc.)						
Books/magazines						
Furniture						
Entertainment						
Gifts						
Charitable contributions						
Hobbies						
Taxes (not withheld)						
Savings and investments						
Vacation						
Retirement						
Other						
Tuition						
Miscellaneous						
TOTAL EXPENSES						
SURPLUS OR DEFICIT						

5 to 10 percent. Perhaps you can get along without garbage bags, using grocery store bags instead. Perhaps you can stop using paper towels in favor of a washable dishrag. It isn't necessary to eat red meat twice a day, or even once a day for that matter. Vegetarian plates can be just as nutritious and far less fattening. When it comes to items such as candy, cookies, soft drinks, or alcoholic beverages, a little disciplined consumption can eventually add money to your savings (and subtract inches from your waistline as well). You might even save on your entire grocery bill by shopping at a self-service market.

Entertainment budgets can often be cut. If you go out to dinner and a movie every week, you might opt for only one or the other. In fact, you could cut your entertainment pursuits to just every other week. But you need not cut down on your entertainment altogether. Depending on the area where you live, you may find plenty of no-charge activities. Check the entertainment sections of your newspaper.

You can also often reduce your energy costs. You can save a substantial amount of money just by keeping your thermostat several degrees above or below the comfort zone, depending on the season. You can also save money by using appliances wisely. Don't run the dishwasher until it is full. Whenever possible, wash by hand; dishwashers use a great deal of energy, both in operation and in heating the water. Eat cold cuts once or twice per week to keep your oven cool and your energy consumption down. Use energy-saving settings on all appliances that feature them. By taking these and other common sense steps, you can probably save 10 percent or more on your monthly energy bill. This money in turn can be invested to achieve a particular future goal.

Finally, try to cut down on the use of credit cards. For some people, this is the most difficult area to cut back on or eliminate altogether. One client told me that he kept track of all the credit card applications he had received in the mail. Over a one-year span, he had received twenty-four applications, or an average of two per month. He stated that his acceptance and use of just five of these would probably have ruined him financially. Another client told me that he was having so much trouble with credit that the abuser in his family could run as a candidate for the "MasterCard hall of fame." I know of people who have had to destroy their credit cards altogether to break the spending habit. Whatever your situation might be, don't abuse credit, use it affordably.

Avoid Buying Extras

Unless you have a family fortune heading your way, you must delay extravagant purchases. As long as you periodically buy expensive items, it's unlikely you'll ever have any money to invest. Adopt the slogan "If you don't need it, don't buy it!"

If you're like many young Americans, you probably can't wait to buy that new sports car, speedboat, motorcycle, state-of-the-art sound system, or whatever high-ticket item suits your fancy. Suppose you had the money to invest $5,000 in such an item. Twenty years from now, you'll probably have an outdated piece of junk. On the other hand, had you invested that $5,000 at an average of 10 percent interest, and left it and your interest earnings alone for twenty years in a tax-deferred vehicle, you would have accumulated $33,634.

Structure Your Taxes

In the previous example, you would need $18,162 to buy in twenty years (figuring 7 percent inflation annually) what $5,000 will buy today. After your interest earnings have been taxed accordingly, your $15,472 profit (about $4,000 in today's dollars) would be reduced considerably. Therefore, in actual spending power, your gain might be limited to $1,000 or so.

But what if you don't have to pay taxes on your savings? Even with the Tax Reform Act of 1986, there are still various ways the average investor can do just that. Few people build financial security without taking advantage of various tax breaks. To keep more of the dollars that you're accustomed to sending to Washington, study the new tax provisions and find out what breaks you can use to your advantage or consult a specialist.

There are other ways to get the benefit of your tax dollars. If you generally get a refund from the government, you're in effect giving money away. A refund check is positive proof that you paid too much in withholding taxes during the previous year. Assuming your income doesn't jump to excessive levels this year, you should increase the number of your withholding exemptions so you can keep the money and earn the interest for yourself. You'll note that the amount of the check usually coincides to the penny with the amount "to be refunded" on your tax return. This means that the government doesn't pay interest for using your money. If you hang on to the money, you can pay the interest to yourself.

You can also save tax dollars by borrowing money, both for investment and consumer purposes. If you must borrow money for consumer items, borrow against the equity in your home, most popularly known as a **home equity line of credit**. On the first $100,000 you borrow, as of this writing, the entire interest amount is tax-deductible. Consumer interest deductions, on the other hand, are being phased out altogether. The money you borrow, on this type of loan, up to the first $100,000, can be used for any purpose.

Sometimes, if you've saved money to invest, you may suddenly find that you have to use it unexpectedly. In that case you could borrow money to make your planned investment. This has two benefits: first, you don't pay taxes on borrowed money; second, interest on money borrowed for investment purposes is tax-deductible up to the amount of investment income it generates.

Stretch Your Dollars

Some people I know can stretch a dollar until the eagle grins. You can do the same, not so your neighbors can talk about what a tightwad you are, but to help build your financial security. Stretching dollars need not affect your spending habits. Use these investment tactics to put extra dollars in your pockets over the long haul.

1. Open interest-paying checking accounts and money-market accounts. The pennies of interest you'll earn will add up to dollars in no time.
2. Use credit cards only for necessary purchases. Be sure to check cut-off dates and billing cycles. Try to keep cash for yourself as long as possible, where it can draw interest for you. Also, try to pay for multiple purchases with just one check, rather than many over several months. This will save time as well as unnecessary interest charges.
3. Delay paying for as long as possible. If your electric bill isn't due until the fifteenth of the month, don't pay it on the first. If you do, you're giving two weeks' worth of interest to the electric company, instead of earning it for yourself.
4. Step up simple interest payments whenever possible. This won't add money to your investment fund immediately, but it can add to it in the long run. You can save literally thousands of dollars on your mortgage by paying every twenty-five days instead of every thirty. Or you can pay an extra $100 with the regular monthly payment and apply it toward the principal mortgage balance. This can save a bundle later on by paying off your mortgage earlier and saving thousands of dollars in interest payments.
5. Consider refinancing your mortgage when interest rates drop. This is a very popular way to save money

and to build your net worth. Check with your lender to see how you can lower the interest you pay on your home mortgage. For example, if you have a 30-year fixed mortgage, consider converting it to a 15-year fixed loan. You may have to make a slightly higher monthly payment, but you will save thousands of dollars in interest payments which can be used instead to build your retirement security through proper investment strategies.

Keep Idle Money to a Minimum

Everyone must have an emergency fund in a liquid account consisting of enough cash to pay bills for three to six months. Beyond that, there is no need to have extra cash accumulating at low interest rates. Put all of your money to work, except for your emergency fund. The more money you have working for you, the greater your potential for achieving intermediate goals and building financial security.

If you practice these five principles, you will be surprised at the money you will "find." Use this money to prime your investment pump. By continuing to make regular contributions to this fund, you may one day find yourself retired in a style better than you ever knew as a working person.

YOUR NET WORTH

Once you have gotten into the habit of paying yourself first and found places where you can get extra money, you should take a picture of your actual net worth. This is part of the process of getting your financial affairs in order. Even though it takes time and effort, it is essential to know exactly where you stand.

The first step is to assemble and organize all your financial data, including information to calculate your personal net worth. It will clearly show you where you are today, and make it much easier for you to plan where you want to be in the future. In fact, there is no better time than now to organize your financial records and to review your financial status.

After you have all your records together, including your most recent income tax return, you can complete your personal net worth statement (see Figure 5.2). It will show your financial strengths and weaknesses and become the cornerstone of your personal financial plan. By taking a look at your assets, you can determine which ones can be converted into cash in case of emergency, and decide whether or not your investments are sufficiently diversified. Similarly, listing your liabilities will remind you to keep debt under control, or may suggest that you could take on additional debt.

Your ultimate objective in going through this exercise is to determine how to increase your net worth each year as you progress toward financial security. As you take steps to increase your assets and to decrease your liabilities, this goal will become a reality. Your statement of net worth is a jumping-off point for you to begin to take action. We will examine the various asset categories

Figure 5.2.
Where Are You Now?

This worksheet will make it easy to calculate your personal net worth. Just fill in the appropriate blanks, then subtract your total liabilities from your total assets.

		Current Value	*% of Total Assets*
· **What You Own**	**Liquid assets**		
	Checking accounts		
	Savings accounts		
	Money market funds		
	Cash value of life insurance		
	Other		
	Total Liquid Assets		
	Investment assets		
	Stocks		
	Bonds		
	Mutual funds		
	Certificates of deposit		
	Retirement plans:		
	IRA		
	401(k) plan		
	Company pension plan		
	Other retirement plan		
	Other		
	Total Investment Assets		
	Personal Assets		
	Residence		
	Vacation property		
	Jewelry/Art/Antiques		
	Other		
	Total Personal Assets		
	Total Assets		100%
· **What You Owe**	**Liabilities**	*Current Value*	*% of Total Assets*
	Credit card balances		
	Bank overdrafts		
	Car loans		
	Personal installment loans		
	Education loans		
	Mortgage		
	Other		
	Total Liabilities		100%
	Total Assets		
	Minus Total Liabilities	−	
	Your personal net worth	=	

Source: Courtesy of Oppenheimer Fund Management, Inc.

throughout the remainder of this book, and show you
how to strengthen your net worth as you strive to attain
your financial goals.

CHAPTER SUMMARY

1. Pay yourself 10 percent of your income each month
   and apply it to your future. Do this before you pay
   your regular monthly bills. If you're living on more
   than 90 percent of your income, you are maintaining your lifestyle at the expense of your financial
   security.
2. Put your money to work at the highest interest rate
   possible. You work hard for your present income,
   so your money should work hard for your future
   income.
3. You can accumulate extra investment funds by paring
   grocery, entertainment, and energy budgets, delaying
   the purchase of expensive items, and cutting down on
   the usage of credit cards.
4. Structure your taxes to get the benefit of your tax dollars, stretch your dollars through various investment
   tactics, and keep your idle money at a minimum.
5. Your statement of net worth will give you a picture of
   where you stand in relation to where you want to go
   ultimately. Even though collecting the data to accomplish this task is not easy, it is well worth the time and
   effort. This important document is a starting point for
   you to begin to achieve your financial objectives.

CHAPTER APPLICATION

Special Circumstances

Young married working couple, both with excellent career outlooks, and with plenty of extra money to save and invest.

Unexpected Problem

Wife becomes pregnant and will need to temporarily quit work when the baby arrives, cutting their total income in half.

Financial Solution

Pare family budget to save 30 percent of total income in order to make up for wife's temporary loss of earnings and to pay for new expenses after the baby arrives. Calculate a statement of net worth to keep track of assets and liabilities. Then, take steps to strengthen net worth by beginning to save monthly for child's long-term college expenses.

6

RISK MANAGEMENT—THE RIGHT PLAN FOR YOU

When most people hear the word "insurance," they automatically get turned off. They picture in their minds a hard-thumping salesman trying to sell them a policy which they either don't need nor cannot afford. Many people have a similar picture of a broker, a salesman hard-selling stock which eventually falls in value. But not all insurance agents and stock brokers are bad people. In fact, there are many professionals in these two areas who do an excellent job building financial security for their clients. However, you cannot completely rely on their evaluation of your own insurance and investment needs: You must learn enough about the subject to know when you are getting good advice which would be useful in attaining your financial objectives.

You really don't have much need for personal insurance before you enter the work force or become married. The more responsibilities you assume in life and the more people who depend on you for support, the more you will need to purchase various types of insurance. For example, when you get married and begin to raise a family, you need to increase the amount of life insurance you carry to cover your family should some unforeseen event claim your life. When you purchase a car or a home, you need property and casualty insurance to protect your property from damage. As a wage-earner you need disability insurance to help pay your bills if you should experience a crippling accident. Similarly, you need good medical coverage to protect you from rising medical bills.

DISABILITY INSURANCE

The younger you are, the more likely you are to need **disability income insurance**, which is designed to protect you and your family against loss of income due to a prolonged illness or crippling injury. It provides the family with cash income long after other sources of income have dried up. Unfortunately, most American wage-earners do not have sufficient disability coverage.

For example, a $48,000-a-year salesman in his early thirties is disabled in a severe automobile accident. His $4,000 monthly income is suddenly replaced by a $1,500 per month group disability policy, and his benefits end after five years. What income source will make up for the other $2,500 in lost monthly income? If the disability is permanent, what happens to the family after five years?

Likewise, an attorney in her mid-forties and earning $72,000 per year is crippled with multiple sclerosis. Her $4,000-per-month disability policy, purchased 10 years ago, will pay her to age 65. In the meantime, her monthly expenses will continue to increase due to inflation. She will have to endure not only the pain of her disease, but also the growing financial pressures of monthly expenses.

These people were not adequately covered. Unfortunately, many people do not consider the importance of long-term disability coverage, and what financial hardship means until it's too late. If they think Social Security benefits will come to their rescue, they quickly discover how hard it is to actually collect benefits. In most cases, the applicant must be unable to do any work and have little or no chance of recovery to collect.

In order to have adequate disability protection, you can purchase an individual policy or one through a group plan provided by your employer or a trade association. Even though individual policies cost more, they can be custom-designed to fit your specific needs. A group policy will generally cost less than an individual policy, but the former will only replace earnings for a limited period of time. Generally speaking, coverage is less extensive in a group policy and premiums increase with age. Sometimes you can integrate an individual policy with your group coverage in order to get a lower cost plan.

When shopping for a disability policy, consider these features:

¶ *Definition of Disability.* Try to get a policy with an "own occupation" definition of disability. This means that you will be covered for as long as you cannot work in your regular occupation. Under the "any occupation" definition, you cannot collect benefits if you are earning income from another occupation.

¶ *Benefits Period.* The longer your benefits cover you (such as for 5 years, to age 65, or for life), the higher the premium you will pay.

¶ *Length of Waiting Period.* Check the number of days you must wait before you begin to receive payments for your disability. Be sure to consider how much time you can wait before receiving any income. Generally, the longer you can afford to wait, the lower your premium payments will be.

¶ *Cost-of-living Adjustments (COLA).* This is a special feature that must be a part of your policy. A COLA helps to protect you against higher prices in the years to come. For example, if benefits are tied to the Consumer Price Index (CPI), you will have increased benefits after you have been disabled for 12 months.

¶ *Non-cancellable and Guaranteed Renewable.* The best policies offer these essential features. They basically mean that as long as you pay the premiums and keep the policy in force, the insurance company cannot cancel your policy or raise your premiums. However, these special features may not be a part of group policies.

Finally, it's important to also have a separate legal document called the **Durable Power of Attorney**. This will enable you to name someone to handle your affairs in case you are unable to do so as a result of disability. This person could be empowered to handle tax matters, provide income for dependents, continue your business affairs, manage investments, and handle medical matters. In this way, if you become incompetent from your disability, a trusted person would automatically be appointed to work in your best interest.

PROPERTY AND CASUALTY INSURANCE
This type of insurance is most associated with home ownership and with other types of assets (cars, boats, planes, etc.). Here are the most common characteristics which should be included in a policy.

¶ *Replacement Value versus Actual Cash Value.* If you have ever suffered a theft, you will know the difference between replacement and cash value. Under "cash value", for example, if your seven-year-old $300 television set is stolen, its actual cash value today may be no more than $75, and the insurance company would pay you only $75 for the loss. When you go out to buy a new set, it may cost you $600. However, if you had "replacement value" in your policy, the insurance company would pay you $600 to replace your stolen set.

¶ *Deductible Limits.* People sometimes overlook the deductible limits on their policies. By self-insuring for the first $200 to $500, you can often lower the premium cost substantially on both your auto and homeowner's policies.

¶ *Adequate Liability Coverage.* This coverage is also often overlooked, but is vitally important. In our lawsuit-happy society, adequate liability coverage on all personal property is important. It is generally inexpensive, and ought to be equal to your net worth on all personal property.

If you are concerned about having adequate coverage on all personal property, you may want to consider a special **umbrella liability policy**. This will give you very broad personal coverage on all assets, including your home and automobile. Very commonly, a $1 million policy will give you the added coverage you want. Surprisingly, such a policy is very inexpensive and will protect you against large lawsuits. For example, $1 million worth of coverage would cost no more than $100 to $200 per year, and may even be less if added as a rider to your existing homeowner's or automobile insurance policy.

MEDICAL INSURANCE

Most employers offer medical benefits to their employees through a group health plan. This usually includes extensive medical coverage to protect against major surgery, lengthy hospital stays, and large doctor bills. Recently, insurance companies have been receiving more claims due to progress in the field of medical services and more utilization of these advancements. As a result, medical costs have skyrocketed, and insurance companies will continue to be hit with huge claims. Consequently, they will pass their increased costs along to the consumer in the form of higher premiums.

The increasing costs of health care in the 1990s will make medical insurance indispensable. When you buy medical insurance, you first need to examine the maximum benefit allowed over the life of the policy. Even though a maximum benefit of $100,000 may seem like adequate coverage, today's higher costs could exhaust that amount very quickly. For more security, your maximum benefit needs to be at least $500,000 or even higher in order to achieve peace of mind.

You should also consider group coverage, or supplemental insurance, if you are retired. Generally, the more individuals involved in the coverage, the lower the cost of the insurance. A small business employer could join with other groups or a trade association in order to purchase group coverage at a reasonable cost. Also, many senior citizens have turned to supplemental policies in order to offset the rising medical costs that Medicare does not cover.

If you have an individual medical policy, and your premiums seem high, you may be able to lower them by examining your deductible limits and the co-insurance ratio. For example, by increasing a deductible from $200 to $500, you can reduce the premiums substantially. The co-insurance ratio is the percentage the insurance company will pay on covered expenses over and above the deductible limits. If this ratio decreased from 100 percent to 80 percent, the premium would also tend to decline. However, make sure you will be able to handle any expenses before you opt for a lower co-insurance ratio.

Long-term Health Care

While the 1980s have taught us to plan for retirement, the 1990s will stress planning for old age and long-term care expenses. Until recently, long-term care (LTC) for the elderly has been a silent killer of Americans' financial well-being. Retirement planning in the 1980s assumed that living expenses would go down as retirees grew older. This is no longer a sound assumption, especially if you neglect planning for health care expenses when you retire in the 1990s.

LTC must be an integral part of financial planning for anyone older than 50. Presently, 30 million people (12 percent of the U.S. population) are 65 years old or older. By the year 2030, that number is estimated to hit 65 million (21 percent of the population). Mortality (death) rates are declining in the U.S. while morbidity (sickness) rates are increasing. As medicine gets better at postponing death, chronic diseases force more people into nursing homes, increasing the demand for LTC.

The chilling facts are that nursing home care, now $22,000 a year, has historically risen at a 5.8 percent annual clip. That means in 20 years it will climb to $40,000 in 1989 dollars, or $118,000 in 2019 dollars. With these kind of expenses, you could exhaust your life's savings very quickly.

As of this writing, Medicare is designed for short-term coverage and does not provide for LTC. This means that you may not be covered if you need extended custodial care associated with long-term nursing home stays, or if you need prolonged home care on a daily basis. Under the Catastrophic Coverage Act of 1988, Medicare will only cover up to 150 days of skilled nursing care per year, and the individual must cover 20 percent of the costs for the first eight days of care. The cost of LTC beyond the first 150 days is not covered.

What can you do to offset the excess costs not covered by Medicare? There are three options to choose from. The first option is to self-insure. This means relying on private assets such as stocks, bonds, and other investments. Obviously, you would be willing to use the income generated from these investments to pay excess costs. But you should not have to liquidate your principal in order to help pay for LTC care.

The second option is to qualify for Medicaid. This is a joint state and federal program to provide payments for people with incomes at or near the poverty level. You probably do not want to lower your financial position ($1,100 per month of income, along with $12,000 in joint assets) in order to qualify for government relief. So this option can be ruled out.

The third option is to implement an LTC plan through a special insurance policy. With other policy-holders helping to share in the costs, you transfer your risk to an insurance company. One thing to remember is that you must buy insurance before you need it; otherwise you may not qualify for coverage.

At what age do you purchase LTC insurance? Basically, the younger you buy it, the lower the premiums. For example, a policy that pays $100 per day for a maximum of three years (after a 100-day waiting period) costs the 40-year-old $178 per year. At age 55, the annual premium is $341; at 60, it's $519; and at 65, it's $846. Ideally age 55, when you're planning for retirement, is the *latest* time to consider LTC insurance. However, because of the urgency to acquire coverage today, many insurers find that the average age of new policyholders is 70 to 72.

A standard LTC policy needs to include the following:

¶ A fixed amount of each day's cost of care. Factoring in some inflation protection, a good daily rate is $80 to $100.

¶ No prior hospitalization requirement (such as three days) before you can enter a nursing home and get coverage.

¶ A waiting period of only 20 days.

¶ A preexisting conditions clause at a minimum number of days. Preferably, you should eliminate this type of clause altogether.

¶ Homecare at a reduced rate, with the maximum payout equal to about half the amount paid for nursing home care. It is essential for you to also have home care.

¶ A "level premium" based on your age when you purchase the policy. Make sure the rate cannot go up unless the increase applies to every policyholder in your state.

¶ A "guaranteed renewable" clause, which means your policy can only be canceled if you fail to pay the premium.

¶ Coverage for three types of care—skilled, intermediate,

and custodial—so that, no matter what type of care a doctor prescribes, the company will pay for it.

¶ No prior hospitalization requirement for Alzheimer's Disease. Even though most policies say they will cover it, a prior hospitalization requirement could mean you are not covered because the condition doesn't always demand in-patient care.

¶ At least three years of maximum coverage, and four to six years if you can afford it. The average stay in a nursing home is two and one-half years.

Now is probably the ideal time to buy LTC insurance because insurers' premiums are bound to go up when they begin paying an increased number of claims in the 1990s. Also, the level premiums are lower when you are younger. Another reason to buy young is to guarantee insurability. Companies will not accept applicants who already have Alzheimer's or other diseases likely to result in a nursing home stay. For further advice, consult a knowledgeable insurance planner.

LIFE INSURANCE

It's important to have life insurance to protect a growing estate. Life insurance can guarantee that your dependents will be able to maintain their standard of living if you die prematurely. You need to provide this protection for your dependents before you begin an investment program.

How much life insurance you need depends on the

difference between what you have already accumulated in your living estate, and what would be needed to make up the total protection you want for your beneficiaries. For example, if you calculate that your dependents need $4,000 per month (factoring in future inflation) to maintain their standard of living, at a 6 percent return, you would need $800,000 of invested capital; at an 8 percent return you would need $600,000; and at a 10 percent return you would need $480,000. If you have already accumulated a living estate of $100,000 and believe that a rate of return of 8 percent is reasonable, you would only need $500,000 of insurance ($600,000 less $100,000). To determine your actual life insurance needs, complete the worksheet in Table 6.1.

Types of Life Insurance

There are basically two types of life insurance: **term** and **whole life**. Term is protection only; whole life is protection plus a savings program. In general, the premiums are lower for pure protection. But for people who would benefit from an added savings or investment program, a higher affordable premium on whole life insurance will also work well. The general rule is: the younger you are and the better your health is, the lower the premium you will have to pay to own life insurance.

¶ *Term insurance* includes three basic types: level term, decreasing term, and annual renewable term. Level term is a policy where the face value and the premium remain level throughout the time chosen for coverage. Decreasing term is a policy where the premium remains the same for the policy's life, but the amount of coverage decreases. People who determine that their need for insurance will decline as they get older often own this type of policy. With annual renewable term, the annual premium increases each year while the face amount of the policy remains the same. This is because the older you become, the more chances are you will die soon, increasing the risk for the insurer. As people live longer, modification of term policies will make them even more attractive.

¶ *Whole life insurance* is a policy in which the face amount is fixed. Part of the premium is applied to the cost of insurance, and part is applied to a savings program which accumulates funds. The policyholders can now elect to structure vanishing premiums as an option. A portion of the premiums goes toward building up "cash surrender values" in the policy. As cash values go up, the amount of risk for the insurance carrier goes down. In the event of death, the beneficiary receives only the face amount of the policy (less any loans against the cash value). Likewise, when a policy is surrendered or called in, the policyholder will receive the accumulated cash value which is paid according to a schedule listed in the insured policy. Some of the more popular forms of whole life (cash value) policies available today include the following.

¶ *Universal life* is a flexible policy that lets you raise or lower your premiums and the amount of coverage on

Table 6.1
Estimating Your Life Insurance Needs

1. Funeral, estate taxes, etc. _____

2. Home mortgage _____

3. Loans and other debt _____

4. College fund _____

5. Total debts to be eliminated _____
    (add Lines 1 thru 4)

6. Current life insurance:
    a. Company death benefit _____

    b. Personal life insurance _____

    c. Total insurance benefits _____
       (a + b)

7. Insurance needed to eliminate _____
    major debts (Line 5 - Line 6c)

8. Expected living expenses:
    a. Annual living expenses _____
       (excluding 2 & 3 above)

    b. Spouse's annual salary _____
       (after taxes)
    c. Annual Social Security _____

    d. Annual investment income _____

    e. All other income _____

9. Net living expenses to be _____
    covered (a-b-c-d-e)

10. Insurance needed to cover net _____
    annual living expenses on Line 9

11. Insurance needed for full _____
    protection (Line 7 + Line 10)

Table 6.1 (continued)
Explanations

Line 1. If your gross estate (net worth + insurance proceeds) is

Under $20,000   use $2,200
Between 20,000–200,000   use   5,000
Over 200,000   use   10,000

Line 2. Current balance due on home mortgage and/or home equity line of credit.

Line 3. All outstanding loans + credit card debt.

Line 4. Use Table 10.1 from Chapter 10; include estimated expenses for all children.

Line 6. a. Amount your beneficiary would receive upon your death from your current employer.
    b. Face amount of all life insurance you personally own less any loans against those policies.

Line 7. If line 6c is greater than line 5, line 7 will represent excess insurance to be used as new investable cash, which will generate income to help cover annual living expenses.

Line 8. a. All expenses needed to run the household and included as the annual budget.
    b. The average yearly salary of a working spouse—full or part-time.
    c. To estimate yearly social security benefits, use

5,000—2 or more minor children
4,000—one child
3,000—no children

These are average benefits paid to dependent children + guardian
    d. Form 1040—dividends + interest; also add expected income from surplus on line 7, if applicable.

Table 6.1 (continued)
Explanations

e. Form 1040—expected annual income from other assets including the following: business, capital gains, rents or royalties, estates and trusts, farms and partnerships. Also include any expected income from deceased spouse's IRAs and/or company pension.

Line 9. If line 9 is a surplus, it will show excess income over annual living expenses. This money should be saved or invested to protect against future inflation. If line 7 also shows a surplus, you are over-insured by that amount. If line 7 shows needed insurance, that is the amount of coverage you should obtain; skip lines 10 and 11.

Line 10. Divide amount on line 9 by .08; this shows the amount that needs to be invested to generate an annual yield of 8 percent.

Line 11. If line 7 is a surplus, subtract line 10 from line 7 to determine the amount of insurance you actually need.

your life. It is a combination of term insurance and a savings account which the insurer usually invests in fixed-income assets. This choice suits couples with fluctuating income levels or who cannot determine how much coverage to buy. Due to changing economic conditions, the returns paid on this type of policy will fluctuate with the level of interest rates since the funds are usually invested in five- to ten-year corporate bonds, Ginnie Maes, and mortgages.

¶ *Variable life* lets the policyholder choose among a broad range of investments, from zero-coupon treasury bonds to stock and bond mutual funds. The premium and minimum coverage on your life cannot change, but you are allowed to switch your savings among these asset classes. These policies make sense for people who want to combine reasonable risk tolerance and long-term objectives.

¶ *Variable Universal Life is* a hybrid that combines the investment choices of variable life with the flexible premium and death benefit of universal life. In all three types of policies, income, dividends, and capital gains accumulate tax-deferred for as long as the policy remains in force. You can also switch investments without charge and take advantage of the professional management of a mutual fund. These policies are also used for estate planning, retirement planning, and college funding.

¶ *Single premium life* requires the buyer to pay the entire premium, generally from $5,000 on up, at the outset. This option is for people who need some insurance, and who want to park a lot of cash in a safe place. To pay for the protection, these policies offer about 1 percent lower interest than a regular fixed annuity plan. The amount deposited is guaranteed from loss by the insurance carrier, and all income accrues on a tax-deferred basis until withdrawn. These plans are conservative and are therefore popular with retirement accounts, and can also be used to automatically fund an education for children or grandchildren if the owner dies prematurely.

Other needs for life insurance protection include: debt coverage, education funding, liquidity for estate tax liability, business continuation planning, gifts to children and grandchildren, and mortgage protection.

Before purchasing any type of life insurance, make sure you can afford it and that you will receive a competitive rate while owning it. Most importantly, make sure it fits into your overall needs and that it can be used to accomplish your financial objectives. You can obtain financial ratings on insurance companies from your local library in the *A. M. Best's Insurance Reports*. Only consider purchasing policies from companies rated A or A+ by A. M. Best.

CHAPTER SUMMARY

1. Your need for insurance depends on your situation in life. The more responsibilities you have, the more need you have for insurance.
2. The younger you are, the more likely you are to need disability insurance. It is designed to protect you against loss of income due to disability. When shopping for disability insurance, look for the definition of disability, benefits period, length of waiting period, cost-of-living adjustments, and noncancellable, guaranteed renewable.
3. Property and casualty insurance is designed to protect you from loss associated with various types of assets, such as your home, automobile, and personal property. Characteristics to be aware of in this type of policy include replacement value, deductible limits, and proper liability coverage. A $1 million umbrella policy

will give you added protection against an unforeseen lawsuit.

4. Medical insurance is essential to protect against major surgery, lengthy hospital stays, and large doctor bills. Because people are living longer and medical costs are rising, maximum benefits on this type of policy need to be at least $500,000, if not higher.

5. Long-term health care will be a major issue in the 1990s. Costs will be very high, and Medicare is only designed for short-term coverage. Most people will have to purchase LTC insurance to get the protection they need. The younger you buy it, the lower the premium. You must look at daily benefit rates, hospitalization requirements, waiting periods, preexisting condition clauses, homecare rates, level premiums, types of care covered, and length of coverage.

6. Life insurance is designed to protect a growing estate. Protection helps to maintain the standard of living for family members.

7. There are two basic types of life insurance, term and whole life. Before purchasing life insurance, make sure you can afford it and that you will receive a competitive rate while owning it.

CHAPTER APPLICATION

Special Circumstances
Young married couple, first child just arrived, couple plans to have more children, new house required for larger family.

Special Needs
Existing insurance program must be examined and changed in order to meet new needs of the family.

Financial Solution
Increased life insurance and solid disability protection on the family wage earners, updated property and casualty insurance needed for a new home and the family cars, and major medical protection required for all members of this growing family.

7

HOW MONEY CAN GROW FOR YOU THROUGH DEBT AND EQUITY INVESTMENTS

At one time or another, you may have wished for a special tree—one that would grow money! You could go to it at any time and grab as much as you need. Alas, money does not grow on trees, but it will grow for you provided you give it the right start. More realistically speaking, once pushed, money can grow much like a snowball pitched down a steep, snow-covered hill. It will keep growing until finally you will have quite a snowball on your hands. Your money will accumulate into a nest egg through the magic of compounding.

COMPOUNDING

Getting back to our analogy, when a snowball rolls down a hill, it doesn't lose any of its size. On the contrary, it gains until it doubles, then redoubles, then redoubles again. The bigger the snowball becomes, the larger the surface area becomes that attracts more snow, making it even larger still, attracting even more snow. The snowball continues to expand until it reaches the bottom of the hill.

Money works more or less on the same principle. The more interest it accumulates, the more principal you'll have to attract more interest, and so on. Therefore, the real effort in building financial security is getting started, just as the real effort of building a mammoth-sized snowball lies in forming the core. Once that is done, you have only to push it off the hill to produce the desired results. To start, you must get the appropriate amount of money together from your savings account. Once that is done, chances are good that you can build financial security with little or no effort at all, much like pushing that snowball off of a hill. That's the principle of wealth building. To put it another way, wealth is when small efforts produce big results; poverty is when big efforts produce small results. You won't get rich merely by working for a living. Quite the contrary. You'll likely end up in the poorhouse. But if you let your money work for you properly, you can build a strong financial future.

GET TIME ON YOUR SIDE

Let's see how compounding actually works with money. For example, take two people, each of whom invest $1,000 each year at 10 percent interest. The first person invests $1,000 per year for six years, then stops investing altogether. The other waits six years before starting the investment program, then begins investing $1,000 annually, as shown in Table 7.1.

Table 7.1
Amount Invested/Accumulated

Year	By First Person	At Year End	By Second Person	At Year End
1.	$1,000	$1,110	0	0
2.	$1,000	$2,310	0	0
3.	$1,000	$3,641	0	0
4.	$1,000	$5,105	0	0
5.	$1,000	$6,715	0	0
6.	$1,000	$8,486	0	0
7.	0	$9,335	$1,000	$1,110
8.	0	$10,269	$1,000	$2,310
9.	0	$11,296	$1,000	$3,641
10.	0	$12,426	$1,000	$5,105
11.	0	$13,668	$1,000	$6,715
12.	0	$15,035	$1,000	$8,486
13.	0	$16,538	$1,000	$10,435
14.	0	$18,192	$1,000	$12,579
15.	0	$20,011	$1,000	$14,937
16.	0	$22,012	$1,000	$17,531
17.	0	$24,213	$1,000	$20,384
18.	0	$26,634	$1,000	$23,522
19.	0	$29,297	$1,000	$26,974
20.	0	$32,227	$1,000	$30,771
21.	0	$35,449	$1,000	$34,948
22.	0	$38,994	$1,000	$39,543

As you can see, the first person's running fund was greater than the second person's fund, even after twenty-one years. The second person's accumulated funds exceeded the first person's fund in the twenty-second year, but by less than $600.

The first person invested only $6,000 to accumulate about $39,000, while the second person needed $16,000 to catch up because of the initial six-year delay. Time was on the side of the first person. That's an important ingredient of compounding. But it's not the only ingredient.

After $6,000 had been contributed to the fund, the first person could have elected to spend the 10 percent interest earnings each year. If that option had been taken, the fund would have faithfully produced $600 interest each year, as long as the capital was untouched and the interest rate unchanged.

Instead, the investor chose to leave the principal and interest earnings alone. Each year, the interest earnings were similarly pressed into service by virtue of the fact that they were left alone. So, like the snowball, the principal earning interest continued to expand, until a $6,000 investment grew into almost $39,000—about six and one-half times the size of the initial investment.

Of course, this example doesn't take into consideration taxes and inflation. Certainly, the interest earnings will be taxed. And inflation means that $39,000 will buy considerably less in ten years than it will today.

This does not diminish the powerful effect of compounding. To take it one step further, suppose you made a $6,000 investment at 10 percent interest and left it alone for twenty years. You would accumulate $40,870. Although your investment earned only 10 percent annually, the effective annual yield (thanks to the interest accumulations) over the twenty-year period would amount to 29.1 percent. Leave the investment alone for another ten years, and your accumulated funds will amount to $106,006, which makes the effective annual yield about 55.6 percent.

So the longer a financial investment is left undisturbed, the larger it will become. Compounding will only work with time on your side. If you want to acquire financial self-sufficiency by the time you're 65, it's best not to wait until you're 60 to start investing for your future. Five years of compounding probably wouldn't be enough to build a strong financial future, unless you have a large lump sum to invest and your employer has already built up a wonderful retirement plan for you.

The Rule of 72

Wherever you are in terms of years away from retirement, the Rule of 72 will help you determine the interest rate to pursue to coincide with your personal financial goals. If you are considering an investment that earns 10 percent, you can determine how long it will take your money to double by dividing the interest rate (10) into 72. The answer will be the number of years it will take for the money to double, which, in this case, would be 7.2 years.

Using the Rule of 72, you can determine that

invested money at 12 percent interest would double every 6 years. At 15 percent interest, it would double every 4.8 years. At 18 percent interest, a dollar will double in just 4 years. And at 20 percent interest, money will double in 3.6 years.

But remember that higher yields also mean higher risk. Higher-risk investments may turn sour and you could lose part, if not all, of your principal. If you pursue high-risk investments, do your homework. Make certain that you have studied and researched the investment so you'll minimize your chances of making a mistake or mistakes that could cost you plenty in the end.

In fact, if you do pursue high-risk investments, you'll do well to retain the services of a competent financial planner who specializes in this area. Professional guidance can be invaluable to such an investor.

FIXED-INCOME INVESTMENTS

For all practical purposes, there are two types of investments that people can make. A person who invests money is either a lender or an owner, depending on the avenue of investment. Fixed-income, or lender accounts include savings, money-market funds, certificates of deposit, and bonds.

Savings Accounts

Almost everyone has this type of account. These liquid accounts are most often used for cash which is to be transferred to checking accounts, or needs to be with-

drawn for an emergency, or is accumulating for investment purposes.

Some people mistakenly use these accounts to accomplish intermediate or long-term goals. But 5 percent
interest will not keep pace with inflation and taxes in the
1990s. Using the Rule of 72, it would take 14.5 years to
double the money in a savings account (not even taking
into consideration what inflation and taxes will do to the
purchasing power of the account).

Money-market Funds

Money-market funds are popular investments that will
continue to be attractive during the 1990s. They are
made up of short-term government paper (treasury bills)
and higher-paying certificates of deposit that produce
yields which can be very tempting for both institutional
and individual investors. These accounts are highly liquid and are often used for check-writing privileges. They
are offered by all financial institutions and are mostly
used as reserve accounts.

Because their returns are based on short-term interest rates, their yields can fluctuate sharply with changes
in the Federal Reserve's monetary policies. Yields as of
this writing range from 7.75 to 8.25 percent. However,
by the time you read this book, these returns could be
much lower since the Federal Reserve changes its policies on interest rates frequently. But because your principal will not fluctuate in a money market account, you
can be assured of a high degree of safety.

Certificates of Deposit

Certificates of Deposit (CDs) are loans that depositors make to financial institutions with maturities ranging from 30 to 90 days or six months to eight years. Institutions pay higher interest rates for longer maturities (up to 8.75 percent at this writing), but sometimes require a minimum deposit as high as $100,000.

These accounts are useful for some short-term goals, such as the purchase of a large consumer item, where the investor wants to have complete safety of principal and the guarantee of payment on principal and interest by an agency of the federal government (FDIC for banks, FSLIC for savings and loans). Through asset-allocation techniques, which are explained in Chapter 9, you can determine the proper amount of funds which should be invested in CDs for your particular situation.

Tax-deferred Fixed Annuities

These special savings plans are issued by major life insurance companies. They are very similar to CDs because both principal and interest payments are also guaranteed (in this case by the insurance company rather than a government agency). Since their principal values do not fluctuate with the stock or bond markets, fixed annuities are considered to have a high degree of safety. Typically, interest rates can be locked in for from one to six years, depending on the buyers' preference.

Perhaps the best feature of a fixed annuity is its tax advantages. Unlike a CD, interest in this plan will compound tax-deferred (as of this writing) until it is withdrawn. Hopefully, the owner will be in a lower tax bracket when this occurs, so the income tax liability will also be lower. The tax-deferred feature allows the annuity value to grow at a much faster rate for the depositor.

There are two slight disadvantages to these plans. Even though there is typically no sales charge, there is usually a withdrawal fee over a period of years (such as 6 percent the first year, 5 percent the second year, declining to 0 percent after the sixth year). During this time most plans allow the investor to withdraw up to 10 percent of the account balance each year without penalty. But you must keep in mind that the IRS will slap a 10 percent withdrawal penalty on the owner if he or she is under 59½ years of age when withdrawals begin. These plans have become very popular for people who want to save for retirement on an intermediate basis.

Since reforms of the 1986 tax act virtually by-passed most insurance products, now would be a good time to take advantage of one of these plans. The next time around, Congress might close the tax loopholes of more insurance products, including annuities. However, if changes do take place, they are usually "grandfathered" by the IRS, meaning changes will only affect plans purchased after a certain specified date.

Special Insurance Investment for the 1990s
A special hybrid of two investment vehicles, called the "certificate of annuity," is now available. This certificate of annuity is designed to act like a CD with tax-deferred

advantages. The principal and interest are guaranteed for the duration of the contract. Investors view these "no-load" annuity certificates as a win-win situation. Once the contract expires, the holder can surrender the annuity without facing surrender charges and generally has a 30-to 60-day period in which to renew or liquidate the product.

These certificates are actually maturity-driven annuities with a liquidity feature. The duration of the annuity certificate varies from company to company and ranges from one to two, three, four, five, seven, and ten years. It's basically a very simple product. The money you invest is locked in at a certain rate for a specified period of time. Each certificate of annuity carries various stipulations on withdrawals depending on the issuing insurance company.

Certificates allow investors to match their investment choice with their expectations of how future interest rates will perform. For example, an investor whose one-year annuity has just matured may choose a new four-year annuity if he or she feels interest rates are about to fall and will remain low for the next several years.

Bonds

Bonds are IOUs from a government, individual company, or municipality. When you buy a bond, you're making a long-term loan. Of course, the interest rate is higher than what you would get from a passbook savings account, but there are no guarantees of a happy ending.

Interest payments are guaranteed only if the company or municipality remains solvent, and principal will be returned to you only if the company or municipality is solvent at the time the bond matures.

Various rating services for corporate and municipal bonds can help you determine the credit-worthiness of the issuer, and the type of risk you would take in owning these bonds. The most popular services come from Standard & Poor's Corporation and Moody's Investor Services. These publications are available at your local library.

Since there are so many questions about bond ownership today, you need to examine the various types in detail and see how they might fit into your portfolio in the 1990s.

CORPORATE BONDS

A corporate bond is a loan that will bring guaranteed interest and return of principal only if the issuer remains solvent until the bond matures. For example, if you buy a ten-year corporate bond at par (face value, generally $1,000), you are lending $1,000 to the issuer until the bond matures. You may sell your bond prior to maturity if a market exists for it. If the bond is scheduled to pay 8 percent interest, you will receive $80 per year for the next ten years. You must pay income tax on interest generated from corporate bonds. Upon maturity, you will receive back the $1,000 that you loaned.

What type of risks are inherent in bond ownership? If, in 1978, you purchased a ten-year bond that paid 8 percent interest, your bond would have dropped in value when the prime interest rate began its unprecedented climb to the 20 percent level. By the same token, the issuer from which you purchased the bond made quite a profit if they took your $1,000, invested it at an interest rate ranging in the upper teens, and were obliged to pay you only 8 percent.

But had interest rates instead decreased below 8 percent, you would have made a good investment. Sometimes when interest rates drop sharply, corporate bonds are subject to an early call, or redemption, which means the issuer has the right to prematurely return your principal. This prepayment may be accompanied by a slight bonus to compensate you for the early call. The bond issuer could then issue new bonds at a much lower interest rate.

It is important to understand the relationship between interest rates and bond values. The values of bonds fluctuate on the open market because, when interest rates decline below the level of interest your bond pays, there is more demand for the higher interest, so the actual value of your bond increases. Conversely, when interest rates increase above the level of interest your bond pays, the actual value of your bond decreases due to a decline in demand.

Very simply, bonds operate like a see-saw at a children's playground, with the bond values at one end and interest rates on the other end. When one goes up, the other must come down.

Corporate Bonds

Many retired people like to buy corporate bonds today in order to earn higher interest than is paid from their savings accounts or CDs. But changes in interest rates may affect the principal value of your bonds. For a person who is not an expert in bonds the best way to invest is through a professionally managed portfolio run by a mutual fund, which is explained in Chapter 8.

If you have an interest in buying corporate bonds, be sure to check the credit ratings issued by Standard & Poor's and/or Moody's. Generally, bonds rated BBB, A, AA, and AAA are all of good quality. The issuing companies should be financially strong enough to withstand a slowing in business activity due to a downturn in the economy.

Corporate bonds rated BB and below are considered lower quality and are often referred to as "junk" bonds. Even though they pay a higher rate of interest to the purchaser, the issuing companies may default on the payment of principal and interest when there are bad economic times.

Convertible Bonds

Convertible bonds are very special corporate bonds because they can be converted into the underlying common stock of a company. Thus, a certain ratio must be maintained between the stock and the bond. If the common stock moves up in value, for example, the value of the convertible bond would also increase. This type of investment gives you a conservative play on the stock market; you can participate in the growth of the company without actually owning the underlying common stock, where you would tend to experience more volatility. These securities are also popular because their yields are usually higher than the dividends paid by their underlying common stock.

Convertible bonds are best purchased through a professionally managed mutual fund; the leading convertible bond fund averaged a 15 percent yearly compounded rate of return over the last ten years. A rating of these funds, as well as most others, can be obtained from the *Mutual Fund Value Services,* published by Morningstar.

Municipal Bonds

Municipal bonds, which are long-term loans to municipalities, offer a special privilege to their investors. The income is free from all federal income taxes and, in the case of some state municipal bonds, the interest is also exempt from state income taxes. This benefit explains their popularity, particularly among individuals in high tax brackets.

The tax-free status isn't likely to change in the near future because city and state officials need bonds to fund local highways, school districts, and water projects. Without a tax incentive, investors might turn instead to taxable corporate or government bonds paying higher yields.

The investment merits of owning municipal bonds

depends on the investor's financial status. They were very beneficial to the investor who, prior to 1987, was in the currently defunct 50 percent tax bracket, where a 7 percent tax-free yield would equal a 14 percent taxable yield. For people in the 28 percent tax bracket, a 7 percent tax-free yield would be equivalent to only a 9.7 percent yield in a fully taxable investment. For those in a 15 percent tax bracket, the rate of return for an equivalent taxable investment would be only 8.2 percent. During periods of higher interest rates, these returns can be easily attained in government bonds, making them much more viable for lower tax bracket investors.

While after-tax yields of municipals may not be as attractive as they once were, changes in the tax laws during the 1990s could easily reverse this situation. For example, if Congress decides to raise taxes in order to help reduce our federal budget deficit, tax brackets could rise once again and make municipal bonds more appealing. For investors with higher taxable incomes, these vehicles are an excellent way to diversify a portfolio, not only adding more security, but generating tax-free income as well.

U.S. citizens over the age of 65 are currently subject to a relatively new tax called the Medicare Catastrophic Insurance Premium. As of this writing, citizens who pay $150 or more each year in federal income taxes will be subject to a premium surcharge beginning with their 1989 income tax return. The premium begins at 15 percent of tax liability in 1989, jumps to 25 percent in 1990, and increases 1 percent for each of the next three years. For this reason, more senior citizens want to reduce their taxable incomes by buying municipal bonds. Chapter 19 examines this issue in more detail.

If tax-free income suits your investment needs, you may find investing in municipals attractive. But for the purpose of turning a profit in actual spending power of your investment, it might not be the best way to go, because when you redeem the bond, the municipality will repay you with cheaper dollars, courtesy of inflation.

Since good quality municipal bonds are becoming more scarce, unit investment trusts and professionally managed mutual funds are becoming more popular and make it much easier to participate in the ownership of tax-free municipal bonds. An investment planner can explain the benefits of these types of investments, and how they might be advantageous for your portfolio.

Zero Coupon Municipal Bonds

These bonds are very similar in nature to government zero coupon bonds. They are issued at deep discounts from their face value. If held till maturity, although not guaranteed, you will receive $1,000 for each bond.

A key distinction is that with municipal zeros, the difference between the discount price you pay and the face value ($1,000) is exempt from all federal taxes. There is no tax due on a yearly basis as with government zeros, nor is any tax due if held until maturity. Even though you can sell these bonds prior to maturity, it is best to buy and hold them so you won't have to incur a gain or loss for tax purposes.

For example, the Smiths have a newborn child. They purchase well-rated bonds with an interest rate of 8.4 percent and a maturity date of 18 years. The cost would be about $228 for each $1,000 bond. The child will start college about the time the bonds are due to mature. Thus, an investment of $4,560 would mature for $20,000 in 18 years. If the Smiths could invest $9,120, the bonds would mature for $40,000 in 18 years. No matter what the contribution, a portion of the college tuition could automatically be paid for from this type of investment. To add frosting on the cake, no federal taxes will be due on the appreciated value when the bonds mature.

Government Securities

All U.S. issued securities rate high in terms of stability, judging from a historical perspective. The United States has yet to default on an issued security, and virtually all of them are guaranteed by the U.S. government. Therefore, they are popular with investors who are looking for a high degree of safety. For this reason, many older Americans like to include them in their portfolios.

The interest government bonds pay, currently ranging from 7 percent to 9.5 percent, varies depending on the desired maturity date. Some examples include Series EE bonds, Series HH bonds, treasury bills, treasury notes, treasury bonds, and federal obligations issued by agencies such as the Government National Mortgage Association (Ginnie Maes).

More often than not, government bond mutual funds pay higher returns than individual government bonds. Through special investment strategies, they can sometimes pay up to 2 percent higher, with little increase in risk. However, like other bonds, they are subject to market fluctuations when interest rates change.

One way to reduce the interest-rate risk on U.S. government bonds is to invest a portion of your bond portfolio in bonds of foreign governments (such as Canada, United Kingdom, France, and Germany). This can best be accomplished through a well-managed mutual fund that specializes in holding international government bonds. In fact, yields are sometimes higher than with pure U.S. government bond funds. You might want to ask a competent investment planner for specific recommendations.

Government Zero Coupon Bonds

Another popular way to own government securities is with zero coupon bonds. These are treasury securities that are stripped of their interest coupons, so they do not make regular yearly interest payments to the purchaser. Instead, you buy the bond at a deep discount to its $1,000 maturity value (e.g., $250 for a 20-year bond). Since the value of these bonds can be very volatile prior to maturity, it makes sense to hold them until their actual maturity date when they will come due for $1,000 each.

In order to determine taxable interest income, take the difference between what you originally paid for the bond and its $1,000 face value, divide by the number of years till maturity, and this will be the implied annual interest which you would have received. By paying taxes yearly on this imputed annual interest, you will not be taxed on the entire lump sum at maturity.

Zero coupon bonds enable you to pick a maturity date and know exactly how much money you'll be getting on that date. If you know that you will need a specific sum of money at a particular time for retirement, college tuition payments, or a down payment on a home—these types of bonds, if held until maturity, will guarantee that the money you need will be there at the right time.

Some investors like to hold zeros in their retirement plans, such as IRAs, where their money grows tax-deferred until it is withdrawn. Zeros can also be used in a Uniform Gift to Minor's account, since any unearned income of the child, including all investment income of less than $1,000 per year, will be taxed at the child's more favorable rate. For a child under the age of 14 years, any investment income that exceeds $1,000 will be taxed at the parent's highest marginal tax rate.

Special Bond Strategy for the 1990s
Now that you are familiar with various types of bonds, and assuming you have an interest in bond ownership, how can you diversify your portfolio to seek income with maximum stability?

One well-known mutual fund group has produced a variation on the theme of diversification and reduced volatility. Called the "cycle of stability," this method spreads assets across three segments of the fixed-income securities market: U.S. government, corporate, and international bonds. These three sectors seldom move in the same manner at any given time. Therefore, dividing assets across the three sectors can provide the investor with a comfortable degree of stability.

This type of portfolio structure can prepare an income investor for the 1990s. High yield corporate bonds and foreign bonds will help to counterbalance the domestic interest rate sensitivity of U.S. government bonds. High-yielding corporate bonds are responsive not only to sensitive interest rates (as explained earlier), but also to economic growth. Foreign bonds, on the other hand, permit investors to take advantage of currency fluctuations and changes in international interest rates.

While this type of portfolio divides a portion of the investor's money into each sector, the trust manager can adjust it at any time, based on changing economic conditions. For example, some defensive strategies may include reducing maturities, investing in short-term U.S. government securities, or holding cash equivalent investments.

This type of income investment holds merit for the coming decade because its management structure combines expertise within each of the three sectors, along with the guidance of a special asset allocation team to monitor overall diversification. Asset allocation is examined more closely in Chapter 9.

EQUITY INVESTMENTS

Fixed-income investments such as savings accounts, money market accounts, certificates of deposit, bonds (government, corporate, or municipal), and tax-deferred annuities may be good investments, depending on your age, tax bracket, and financial objectives. But these investments will not keep pace with rising inflation over the long term. Since everyone pays varying amounts of taxes, it's possible that a good investment for one person would be a bad one for another.

For the most part, the more you want your net worth to increase, the less that these lending investments suit your financial goals. To build real long-term financial growth, you must become an *asset owner.*

How can you invest your money to become an owner of American business? There are any number of different types of investments you can buy that can generate both capital growth and income that will put you on the path to financial security. Such investments offer higher total returns than lending investments. *Total return* is what the investment yields in dividends or interest plus the potential capital appreciation on the asset itself. But remember, higher returns usually mean higher risks. You'll definitely need to do your homework before putting your money into ownership investments.

Stocks

When buying stock in a corporation, an investor becomes an automatic owner of the company, and receives shares as proof of that ownership. The stockholder shares in the fortunes or misfortunes of the company, and the stock price as quoted on the exchange usually reflects the company's financial condition and future outlook.

Common stock represents ownership of a corporation or company. Common stock shareholders have the right to vote at annual meetings on special issues affecting them as stockholders. This is a very popular form of investment, because people like to own stocks for income, or to participate in the growth of the company, or a combination of both.

Preferred stocks, used primarily by income investors, are issued by corporations to raise money for expansion. Preferred stocks have senior preference over common stocks when it comes to the payment of dividends. One special type, called *convertible preferred stock,* is similar in nature to convertible bonds in that they can fluctuate in value with their underlying common stock's performance.

Many people who own individual common stocks will be participating in the dynamic growth of the 1990s through equity ownership. If you fall into this classification, the 1990s will present an excellent opportunity to make money in the following areas.

1. Consumer Services. As the economy expands, there will be more demand for quality goods and services, including electric usage. Companies to benefit include Walt Disney, McDonald's Corp., Pepsi Co., Wal-

Mart, Sears, Florida Progress Corp., and Pacific Corp.

2. Health Care. As the population ages and medical technology increases our life spans, the demand for drugs, medical supplies, retirement housing, and providers of long term health care will increase. Companies to benefit include Baxter International, New England Critical Care, Bolar Pharmaceutical, Merck, Maylan Laboratories, Pfizer, Community Psychiatric Centers, Bristol-Myers, St. Paul Cos., and American Express.

3. Environmental Services. A tremendous need to clean up our air and water systems along with the proper treatment of waste will dominate the national consciousness in the 1990s. The U.S. will be a pioneer in this area, and the demand for our services will also come from foreign countries. Companies to benefit include Browning-Ferris Industries, Waste Management, JWP Inc., Consolidated Natural Gas, Zurn Industries, and Environmental Systems.

4. Data Processing. The revolution in computers is not over. In fact, it will grow as the demand for newer, innovative services continues. Companies to benefit include Mentor Graphics, International Business Machines, Compaq Computer, Microsoft Corporation, Bolt Beraneh & Newman, Ashton-Tate, Pansophic Systems, and Automatic Data Processing.

As we stated earlier, the stock market is an essential component of our economy, without which we could not function. The Dow Jones Average of 30 blue chip companies is an indicator of the pulse of the American economy. Because it is watched so closely by millions of avid investors worldwide, it can literally rise or fall hundreds of points per day depending on the economic circumstances discussed in Chapter 2.

For those investors who do not have the time or expertise to select individual stocks, a well-managed mutual fund offers long-term capital appreciation. There are many choices from which to select (see Chapter 8).

Real Estate

Real property has built more fortunes than any other investment in the world. Even though the Tax Reform Act of 1986 reduced depreciation benefits and interest payment tax deductions for real estate investors, land can still be classified as a good long-term investment. One thing is for sure: They aren't producing any more of it.

There are two types of investment real estate. Commercial real estate includes shopping centers, office buildings, public storage facilities, and any building used for business. Residential real estate includes single-family homes, duplexes, apartments, condominiums, and senior citizen residential facilities. The latter are becoming increasingly popular investments because, as medical advancements lengthen lifespans, the number of senior citizens living in this country is increasing. Not only will there be an increasing demand for retirement community centers in the future, but the value of these properties should also rise. Investors should take advantage of new trends and attempt to make profits on the viable investments that are developing in the 1990s.

One popular way to own real estate today is through a **real estate investment trust (REIT)**. These special investments issue shares of stock that enable investors to participate in the ownership of specific types of real estate or equity participating mortgages. By law, a REIT must pay out 95 percent of its earnings to shareholders each year, so investors buy them mainly for income. REITs usually pay higher returns than many fixed-income investments. For example, some excellent syndicated offerings guarantee a 12 percent return to the investor for the first two years, after which they guarantee a return of principal if held for the finite life of the investment (usually 10 to 15 years). REITs are traded on major stock exchanges, providing liquidity to the investor. Stick with REITs that have experienced management and higher dividend payouts to have an opportunity for financial success.

Another form of ownership, for those who would like to own real estate, but who do not want the headaches of property management or cannot afford the outright purchase of large pieces of individual property, is called the **limited partnership**. This structure has two partners, the general partner and the limited partner. The general partner is responsible for the day-to-day management of the property and decides when and what type of real estate is to be purchased for the partnership's portfolio.

The general partner has unlimited liability for the overall operations of the portfolio. You should carefully study the general partner's prior performance and track record before making a commitment to enter a limited partnership.

The limited partner(s) is the investor or group of investors who put up the capital to purchase the real estate. They receive certain benefits such as depreciation that shelters part of their income from taxes and equity appreciation, and are liable only for the amount of money they decide to invest. In order to receive the greatest possible return, an investor must wait until the partnership sells its holdings and distributes the proceeds. When the demand for real estate is steady, most partnerships are structured to liquidate in five to eight years. However, for investors who need to sell sooner, certain companies offer to liquidate these partnerships at a substantial discount.

In the late 1970s and early 1980s, these programs did well. The mid 1980s saw an overbuilding of all types of real estate by speculators interested in tax write-offs rather than economic growth. Currently, the real estate industry, other than in residential homebuilding, is suffering a slump from excess capacity (overbuilding). This is expected to last for several more years until excess office and residential space is absorbed. This has caused prices to drop on some properties and has made them excellent buys. Even though this may be a difficult time to commit money to real estate, it could very well be an opportune time to acquire high quality, undervalued properties.

Contrary to what some people think, one of the best features of real estate is its illiquidity, because converting it into cash can be difficult and time-consuming. In 1987 this turned out to be a blessing for investors who otherwise might have invested their money into the stock market before the crash in October. Some fortunes have been built when the investor couldn't get his or her hands on the capital. So a quality investment will continue to grow in value over the years. The 1990s could be an excellent time in which to make money in the now-depressed real estate market.

Equipment Leasing

Equipment leasing is a special equity investment that can provide inflation protection for a portfolio. Through a limited partnership, an investor can own various types of equipment, including computer peripheral, transportation, production, medical, and telephone equipment. When inflation rises, the value of equipment on the secondary market also tends to rise. Because interest rates usually rise with inflation, income from leased equipment also tends to increase.

Experienced sponsors of this type of program lease equipment for as short as three and one-half years to as long as seven years. The objective of the program is to pay the investor a steady stream of income over a five- to seven-year period or longer. The rates of return depend on the sponsor, lease terms, and types of equipment in the portfolio. Recent returns have ranged from 11 percent to 13.5 percent with income paid monthly. A portion of the income is usually sheltered from taxes because the investor can deduct the depreciation on the equipment.

Barring a prolonged recession in the 1990s, the demand for equipment leasing will continue to be strong. When it comes to acquiring the equipment needed to keep industries moving ahead, more and more businesses (8 out of 10 as of 1988) turn to lease financing because it preserves working capital for the company and because lease payments can be taken as tax deductions. This industry has grown dramatically over the last 15 years—currently over $100 billion projected for 1989—and investment in this area should pay handsome dividends while allowing the investor to avoid the fluctuations of more volatile equity markets.

Precious Metals

No doubt about it, you can make a killing in gold and silver. But there's also no doubt about the fact that you can lose a fortune in it too. People who held gold and silver made fortunes during the highly inflated early 1980s. But people who bought gold later, in hopes that its price would rise even more, wound up losing a bundle as prices fell. Inflation won't necessarily increase the price of gold in the 1990s, although it has tended to do so in the past.

Gold is a great deflation hedge. In the event of a depression—when cash is king—gold always retains its value, while the dollar's value is likely to decrease. So precious metals that can be converted into cash offer great protection for your assets in the event of a financial depression. But for building financial security, other methods are more practical and lucrative.

You can invest in precious metals by buying them outright, by buying into a company that manufactures them, or through a mutual fund that specializes in buying their stocks. Generally speaking, people who invest in gold and silver already have a substantial net worth and can afford to take the risk associated with their high volatility.

Commodities

This is a highly speculative field of investment designed for people who really like to shoot craps. Money invested in this field runs a high likelihood of being lost. Of course, a knowledgeable investor who wins can win big, but the chances of winning are relatively slim due to the highly volatile nature of commodities. In any event, both the beginning and conservative investor would be well advised to stay away from this area altogether.

Collectibles

Antiques, works of art, and even popular culture memorabilia can prove valuable assets to an investor. But collecting requires tremendous attention to details pertaining to a particular market. The investor must always be on the lookout for frauds. Furthermore, an investor runs the risk of becoming sentimentally involved with the collection, and refusing to convert the collection to cash at the proper time could defeat the purpose of investing altogether. If you're considering collectables as a form of investing, build your financial future first through other means. Then, if you'd still like to invest in them, use the advice of a specialist.

Other Special Investments

During the 1970s, when oil was scarce and prices were high, investments in oil did very well. But in the 1980s, as oil became more plentiful and prices dropped, so did profit margins, because payment on loans made on these properties absorbed most of the revenues. This type of investment may once again become lucrative during the 1990s, if our oil supplies run short and we continue to depend on foreign oil supplies.

Environmentalists will push for foreign oil during the 1990s in order to avoid such disasters as the recent Alaska oil spill. But the more we rely on foreign oil, the greater the danger that foreign suppliers will increase prices and raise our inflation levels. Investors who want to speculate on rising oil prices during the next decade should look to energy stocks or energy limited partnerships. Make a thorough analysis before investing money with a sponsor of such programs.

Other investments which might fit into your portfolio include historic housing, tax credit partnerships, research and development partnerships, cable television partnerships, agriculture partnerships, and movie partnerships. Since these are very specialized, a financial planner would need a good reason to recommend one of them for your portfolio. They also carry more risks than some of the other investments discussed in this chapter.

A primary source of reliable, unbiased, research information on direct investments such as limited partnerships and mutual funds is Robert A. Stanger & Co., which produces publications to help you evaluate potential investments. For more information on the special investments discussed in this chapter, call them at 800-631-2291, or write them at 1129 Broad Street, Shrewsbury, New Jersey 07702.

CHAPTER SUMMARY

1. The magic of compounding involves the same principle as a snowball rolling down a hill. The more capital an account accumulates, the more interest it will draw, thus further increasing the capital and future potential for interest.

2. A prime ingredient of compounding is time. With an early start, substantial funding can be accumulated with less capital at risk than that used by the investor who postpones making investments. When a procrastinator finally does invest, he or she needs more capital to catch up with the early starter.

3. To determine how many years it will take for your investment to double, use the Rule of 72: divide 72 by the interest rate. For example, if money compounds

continually at 12 percent interest, it will double in six years (72 ÷ 12 = 6).

4. Debt, or lending investments include savings accounts, money market funds, certificates of deposit, and various types of bonds (corporate, municipal, and government). These may or may not be good investments, depending on your age, tax bracket, and financial objective.

5. Fixed-annuities are issued by major insurance companies, and are a very popular replacement for CDs due to their tax-deferred feature. They can be used as long-term savings plans for college education, retirement, or for other purposes. The issuing insurance company should have an "A" or "A+" rating from A. M. Best & Company.

6. Equity, or owned investments include stocks, real estate, precious metals, collectables, and special partnerships. These may give you a chance to build long-term financial security and inflation protection.

CHAPTER APPLICATION

Investor Circumstance

Young married couple, homeowners, two small children, husband's salary $65,000, wife working as homemaker, investable funds $30,000.

Special Objectives

Need to save for two college educations, plus husband's retirement in 25 years.

Financial Solutions
Invest $10,000 for each child in blue chip equities (mutual funds). Invest $10,000 for husband in stocks and real estate ($5,000 in each area).

8

TAKING ADVANTAGE OF MUTUAL FUNDS

The most common form of investment ownership today is through stocks and bonds. People can own them on an individual basis or through professional management.

Since most people must concentrate on their careers, they have little time to devote to learning the complicated techniques of portfolio management. Therefore, most people who want to include stocks and bonds in their portfolios leave the management to professionals who monitor their investments on a day-to-day basis. The best way to do this is through a **mutual fund**.

THE MUTUAL FUND
Mutual funds allow you to make lucrative investments in the stock market on a shoestring budget and obtain professional management at the same time. Surprisingly, this particular avenue is also very popular with experienced investors who want to diversify their portfolios.

Mutual funds are the perfect vehicle for investors who lack the time to devote to proper study of current economic conditions, and who do not want to become experts. For people who lack the ability to apply their findings productively, and the desire to take huge risks, mutual funds fill the bill. Similarly, many investors lack the money to obtain sufficient diversification so they choose to let professional managers do it for them.

If you're like most Americans, you may not have the financial resources to invest up to a quarter of a million dollars in the stock or bond markets. Perhaps you can only afford to invest $1,000 or so, and the mere thought of losing it may bring tears to your eyes. But think of the thousands of other Americans who feel the same. Individually, your investments wouldn't even cause a ripple in the stock market, but collectively you can make a big splash.

The mutual fund is designed to accommodate the masses. If you and 999 other people like you each invested $1,000, you could achieve sound diversification through collective ownership of a million dollars' worth of stocks. By law, no more than 5 percent of any mutual fund portfolio can be invested in any one stock issue. Therefore, mutual funds must consist of at least 20 stocks; some consist of as many as 150 individual securities.

Furthermore, you receive professional management of your money. The stocks and bonds that make up mutual funds are selected by a panel of experts who devote their time and knowledge to apply current trends and economic conditions toward financially sound purchases. By investing in a mutual fund, you automatically solve the problems of time, lack of sufficient knowledge to make investment decisions, and the money to achieve diversification.

For a new or beginning investor, it may be tough to invest even $1,000 without worrying not only about the fate of the investment, but where to put it in the first place. Mutual funds can minimize, if not eliminate, such worries. For example, if you are an intermediate or advanced investor, mutual funds will complement or diversify your existing portfolio and help you to achieve objectives you may not have been able to accomplish in the past. Some investors refuse to buy mutual funds just because they have to pay a small sales charge. Others feel that they have the knowledge to match the performance of professional money managers. Some are right, but more often than not, their results are the same year after year—low returns with the same high risks.

Of course, no one can say for certain that any investment is risk-free. None of us will know what that will be until it happens. But we do know what yesterday has brought, and many mutual funds have enjoyed consistently good track records throughout the years. A good way to check a fund's performance is through the Lipper Analytical Service, available at most local libraries. The measurement of performance depends on the type of fund and what it's trying to accomplish. There are currently more than 950 mutual funds available, and that figure is increasing by about 20 to 30 per month.

THE MUTUAL FUND FAMILY

A mutual fund family consists of many varied types of funds, each investing in securities designed to achieve virtually any and every investor objective. *Mutual Fund Values* (published by Morningstar), shows funds that have had excellent performance records over the last one to ten years. When considering any mutual fund for purchase, read a current prospectus before investing. You might also consult a financial planner to get an opinion on your selection or to get a more specific recommendation to fit your exact temperament and needs. There are several categories of mutual funds you may wish to take advantage of to achieve financial security in the 1990s.

Growth Stock Funds

If you're young with several decades of income-generating ability before you, investing in a **growth stock fund** may appeal to you. These funds, which range from growth to aggressive growth, offer different rates of return and emphasize capital appreciation. This type of investment is specifically designed for the long haul. When growth is the objective, stability and income take a back seat in priority. Therefore, intermittent volatility throughout the investment period can be expected, but should be of little concern to the investor who is primarily interested in long-term growth of capital. Keep in mind that an emphasis on growth, which includes secondary stocks, involves more risk than an investment in more stable, blue-chip stocks. But with greater risk comes greater rewards. For an investor who has time on his or her side, a growth stock fund is an excellent way to diversify a portfolio for the 1990s. One example of a growth fund is the *Phoenix Growth Fund* which has had a 10-year annualized return of 20.1 percent.

Blue-chip Stock Funds

Blue-chip funds offer slower, long-term appreciation potential with some income. They usually appeal not only to the investor in the 40- to 50-year age range, but also to those whose income-generating period is over, such as the retiree or the disabled person. Because the emphasis in a blue-chip fund is placed on gradual growth with income, the investor has the opportunity to receive the best of both worlds. Blue-chip funds are a conservative way to balance a stock portfolio between pure speculation (secondary or start-up companies) and pure income (such as utility companies). An example of a blue-chip stock fund is the *Investment Company of America* which has had a 10-year annualized return of 17.2 percent.

Sector Funds

Sector funds invest in varying sectors of American industry such as airlines, health care, high-tech, consumer goods and services, and energy. An investor who believes that investments into a particular segment of the economy would be potentially lucrative in the 1990s, yet lacks the specific knowledge to pinpoint the best investment, might find this type of fund attractive. Such funds can be designed for growth, income, or a combination of both. Since a sector fund is highly specialized, it involves more risk than a fund that invests in a variety of industry segments. One example of a sector fund is *Criterion Technology* which has had a three-year annualized return of 19.8 percent.

Foreign Funds

Managements of **foreign funds** specialize in buying securities of foreign countries (such as Japan, Australia, Germany, England, and Canada) in the hope that they will rise in value like U.S. stocks. These funds performed well in the late 80s, but this does not guarantee future results. If you believe the entire world economy will expand in the 1990s, use this type of fund to diversify an already existing portfolio of high-quality U.S. common stocks. An example of a foreign fund is the *Templeton Foreign Fund* which has had a five-year annualized return of 20 percent.

Market-timing Funds

Market-timing funds, which are relatively new, attempt to get in and out of the U.S. stock market very quickly. Their objective is to be 100 percent invested in stocks when the market is rising and 100 percent into cash reserves when the market is falling. This type of fund can take the headaches out of when to be in or out of the market for the average investor. Therefore, they will become more and more popular with investors who want peace of mind and preserved capital. Before buying this type of fund, however, be sure to determine whether it actually had its investors out of the market during volatile periods. Also, look at the types of securities currently in the portfolio to determine whether the fund is bullish or bearish. An example of a market-timing fund is the *Lowry Market Timing Fund.*

Corporate Bond Funds

Corporate bond funds are vehicles for investors who prefer to invest in corporate bonds and take advantage of professional management. A panel of experts selects the bonds and decides how much to invest in them depending on economic conditions. The price of the shares fluctuates, depending on the level of interest rates at any given time. When the prime rate dips below the average bond interest value, these funds can be traded at a premium. When the prime rate rises above the average interest value, these funds trade at a discount. Unlike an investor who tends to hold bonds until their maturity, professional money managers trade bonds when economic conditions warrant it, or when they think their values will start to decline. One corporate bond fund, the Kemper High Yield Fund, has had a five-year annualized return of 15 percent.

Convertible Bond Funds

Convertible bond funds invest primarily in a special type of corporate bond which can be converted into a specific number of shares of its underlying common stock. But the fund manager will usually not convert to stock because the bond pays more interest. This type of fund gives the owner an opportunity to participate in the growth of the stock market without actually owning stocks. For more conservative investors, this approach can offer more rewards with less risk than investing in common stocks. These balanced funds are popular because they offer a combination of income and growth in a diversified portfolio. If left untouched over a period of time, the results can be excellent. One example of a convertible bond fund is *Dreyfus Convertible Securities,* which has had a five-year annualized return of 15.6 percent.

Municipal Bond Funds

Investments in **municipal bond funds** are very popular as a result of the Tax Reform Act of 1986 because they can yield tax-free income for investors. An investor getting a tax-free return from such a fund would have to receive a higher return from a taxable investment to fare as well financially. For example, a 7 percent tax-free yield for someone in the 28 percent tax bracket would be equal to a taxable yield of 9.72 percent. If a taxable government bond fund was yielding only 9 percent, the tax-free bond fund would be a more lucrative investment because it would net more return after tax. Ordinarily, you should consider only tax-free bond funds that contain the highest quality bonds (A or better). You also may want to consider a fund that has insurance backing up the individual bonds in the portfolio. An example of a municipal bond fund is the *Putnam Tax Exempt Income Fund,* which has had a five-year annualized return of 11.6 percent.

Government Bond Funds

Government bond funds invest strictly in direct obligations of the U.S. government (treasury bills, bonds, and notes). These bondholders have peace of mind because their investments have the full faith and credit of the U.S. government backing them up. The government has not defaulted on any of its bonds since it began issuing them during the Revolutionary War. Investors enjoy a high degree of security with such an investment. Ordinarily, you can receive a higher return on these funds than you can with regular money market accounts and CDs. The investor also has the convenience of receiving monthly distributions, which can be reinvested or paid out in check form. One government bond fund, the *Transamerica (Criterion) Government Securities Fund* had a four-year average yield of 11.4 percent.

Government National Mortgage Association Bond Funds

Government National Mortgage Association (GNMA) funds have become very popular over the past several years. The Government National Mortgage Association is a U.S. government agency that lends money for home ownership. They guarantee the principal and interest on these bonds to maturity. It's much better to own GNMAs through a mutual fund rather than individually because the monthly income distribution usually comprises interest only and does not include a portion of your principal. The *AARP GNMA & Treasury Fund* had a three-year annualized return of 6.35 percent.

International Government Bond Funds

International government bond funds are comprised of government bonds from foreign countries such as Canada, France, England, and Australia. During periods of unstable interest rates, each country will be different with respect to whether they raise or lower their own interest rates. This helps to stabilize overall market values and allows the fund to continue to pay an excellent return. This is yet another example of how to diversify a government bond portfolio in an attempt to add more stability. One international government bond fund, *Putnam Global Government Income Fund,* had a two-year annualized return of 15 percent.

Asset Allocation Funds

An **asset allocation fund** divides its assets among cash equivalents, stocks, bonds, foreign investments, precious metals, and, sometimes, real estate. Several portfolio managers usually run the fund, and each has expertise in one specific area. Because these funds are relatively new, they do not have an established track record. Although they tend not to perform well in bull markets, they hold up better in stock market declines, because their losses are cushioned by the combination of cash, bonds, and even gold in the portfolios. This was proven in the 1987 stock market crash, when these funds did better as a whole than other types of mutual funds. One asset allocation fund is the *Oppenheimer Asset Allocation Fund,* which has shown a one-year return of 14 percent.

Precious Metal Funds
Precious metal funds are used by investors that like to own gold and silver through a managed stock portfolio. Because it is so hard to predict what the prices of precious metals will do in the open market, certain portfolio managers devote all their time and effort attempting to do so. A study of the fund's track record is essential in this area before investing. One precious metal fund, *Colonial Advanced Strategic Gold,* has had a three-year annualized return of 19 percent.

FLEXIBILITY
Suppose you have invested money in a growth mutual fund for many years, but are now retiring and would like to transfer your investments to the income fund under the same management. This can be done for a nominal $5 transfer fee. Compare this advantage to the situation of the investor who invests in a variety of growth stocks. To change to income-oriented stocks or bonds, the investor would have to pay commissions on each buy-and-sell transaction. This usually adds up to be a lot more in total transaction costs.

There may be times other than retirement when investment transferral would be beneficial. In a faltering economy, growth investments would not be to your advantage. Therefore, money market funds may be the most lucrative route to take. Most mutual fund families offer money market funds, which have lured many investors away from non-interest paying checking accounts and low-interest paying passbook savings. These funds, which invest in high-yielding certificates of deposit and short-term government obligations, pay higher-than-passbook rates for deposits and offer free check-writing privileges. Even in sound economic times, money market funds are more flexible than certificates of deposit because they can be liquidated without penalty. In tight economic times, when interest rates spiral, money market fund interest rates react accordingly and, thus, can become a far better investment than fixed-rate investments.

MULTIFUND INVESTING

With all the different types of mutual funds that are available today, owning more than one type gives your portfolio more safety. This strategy gives you broader diversification and a balanced portfolio. For example, you can mix income funds with growth funds to generate both income and inflation protection. By purchasing these funds under the same management, you can often save substantially on commission costs.

But selecting mutual funds for a portfolio is not a simple task. Even though research services make the selection process easier, the real work is in narrowing the field. Is the manager who compiled a fund's successful track record still directing it? How is the fund performing compared to funds of a similar size and with similar objectives? How has the fund performed in both good and bad times?

One of the chief benefits of mutual fund ownership is ease of recordkeeping. When opening an account, you usually have four choices.

1. Reinvesting all distributions (capital gains and dividends) to purchase more shares.
2. Reinvesting capital gains and receiving dividends in cash.
3. Receiving both capital gains and dividends in cash.
4. Reinvesting all regular distributions, but receiving a specified check each month from the account.

You will receive a new statement every time there is activity generated on your account. Also, a 1099 form, showing all distributions paid during the year, will be mailed to you for income tax purposes at the beginning of each new tax year.

The concept of dollar-cost-averaging also can be used with mutual funds. By putting the same amount of money into the same fund at the same time each month, you always purchase more shares at a lower cost. This will give you an average lower cost for the whole investment. Also, this means that when the market eventually rises, you make money. During uncertain investment climates, this strategy is particularly effective, especially when larger sums of money are involved.

A good financial planner should keep you informed

about the status of your funds through special mailings or investment reviews. You should also receive monthly or quarterly statements directly from the funds showing the number of shares you currently own and the amount of distributions that have been paid. You may also want to know the value of your investment, and should learn how to keep track of it in the daily newspaper. The quarterly or annual report, which is sent to all registered shareholders, will also give you information on specific investments in the fund's portfolio.

PROFESSIONAL HELP

The stock market can be rewarding for the informed, but, by the same token, it can be cruel to the ill-informed. Beginning investors who learn by trial-and-error can almost count on having problems. Even seasoned investors occasionally feel the sting of financial loss. The prospect of financial loss doesn't appeal to anyone expect speculators. Therefore, most people seek advice before making investments.

Suppose you experience severe chest pains. You can elect one of two options. You can either diagnose your pains as indigestion, treat them accordingly, and pray that you aren't, in fact, suffering from a serious heart ailment. In so doing, you have saved a physician's fee. But if you are wrong in your diagnosis and a heart attack permanently puts you out of commission, the doctor's fee you saved would go straight to your heirs. Had you paid the fee in the beginning, your life may have been saved, and a paltry physician's fee wouldn't even begin to compare with a saving of such magnitude.

The same analogy can be made for seeking professional financial assistance. True, it may cost you a fee or commission, but what you make by receiving and following professional advice can recoup this fee many times over. On the other hand, if you decide to go it alone you could eventually lose an amount far greater than a planner's fee or commission.

FEE STRUCTURES

There are several types of mutual fund fee structures with which you should be familiar.

1. Load funds charge an up-front commission which is included in the purchase or asking price. These range from 1 percent up to 8.5 percent, depending on the fund family. In the 1990s load funds will continue to lower their sales charges in order to stay competitive.
2. No-load funds do not charge a commission to either buy or sell their shares. Instead, as with any fund, they charge a yearly management fee and sometimes other expenses to run the fund.
3. 12(b)-1 funds do not charge an up-front commission, but incorporate a small yearly fee and a declining sales charge on the back-end when the investor wants to liquidate in the first five to six years after purchase. You can generally avoid back-end charges by switching money within that particular fund family over the penalty period.

LOAD AND NO-LOAD FUNDS

Which type of investment will give you the best performance for your money, load or no-load funds? There seems to be an ongoing debate on how to answer this question. Certainly, when considering the purchase of any mutual fund, you should take into consideration its fee structure. Fees come in several forms: general annual expenses, 12(b)-1 fees, front-end loads, and back-end loads. Most important is the impact these expenses have on an investment's total performance.

Recent studies have shown that load funds are able to compete with, and surpass, no-load funds in total return. Aegan USA Investment Management, Inc., recently compared the performance of a 5.75 percent load fund, a 5.5 percent load fund, a 12(b)-1 fund, and a no-load fund over 20 years. The initial investment was $10,000 in each type of fund with an assumed 10 percent annual yield. The study showed that, after four years, the load funds began to out-perform the 12(b)-1 and no-load fund because, after the initial sales charges were taken out, the load funds had lower expense ratios than the 12(b)-1 or no-load fund. These lower annual expenses improved their total performance.

The study also showed that the load funds continued to dominate after the fourth year. For example, the 5.5 percent load fund had the highest account value at the end of the 20-year period, or $14,000 more than the no-load fund. Interestingly enough, the 5.75 percent load fund finished $9,000 higher, and the 12(b)-1 fund accumulated $3,500 more than the no-load fund. Ultimately when making the final decision, choose the fund(s) which you feel will bring you the best results.

Rather than worrying about the type of charge you will pay, select your fund based on its track record and performance. Many financial planners subscribe to the "Mutual Fund Valuation Service," published by Morningstar, which independently ranks most major funds according to their overall performance and risk under various market conditions. Such a third-party opinion can help you make a better decision about whether or not you should invest in a particular mutual fund. Remember, better decisions mean better investment results for you.

CHAPTER SUMMARY

1. Successful investing in the stock or bond market requires keeping abreast of business trends and market conditions that can affect investments. It also requires significant investment funds, generally more than the average citizen has, in order to achieve adequate diversification.
2. Mutual funds offer professional management in a diversified vehicle from which many investors can achieve substantial returns with minimal risk in both the stock and bond markets.
3. There are many mutual fund families available in today's market. Most offer particular funds designed to provide capital growth, income, or a combination of the two, such as sector funds.
4. Mutual funds allow transferal of funds from one area

to another within the same family for a very small fee. This allows the investor to take advantage of economic trends by changing investments without paying commissions.

5. Timing services offered by some mutual funds can benefit an investor during uncertain economic times by moving his or her holdings out of the market and into more lucrative money market funds. These funds generally offer higher yields during periods of rising short-term interest rates.

6. Multifund investing can simplify the selection process and help you keep better track of your mutual fund performance.

7. A professional financial planner can be of great assistance to beginning and seasoned mutual fund investors. The amount of the planner's fee can be recouped many times over with the lucrative returns that are likely to result from competent advice and counsel.

CHAPTER APPLICATION

Investor Circumstance
Middle-aged couple, no children, homeowners, husband earning $70,000, wife earning $45,000.

Special Objectives
Need to support elderly parents, begin investing for supplemental retirement program, and reduce income taxes.

Financial Solutions

Invest $50,000 of savings in a family of mutual funds, with $5,000 in a money market fund for liquidity, $15,000 in a municipal bond fund for tax savings, $20,000 in stock mutual funds for retirement program, and $10,000 in a government bond income fund for parents' support. The $50,000 breakpoint will qualify for lower commission charges.

9

HOW YOU CAN BENEFIT FROM ASSET ALLOCATION

As a result of recent volatility in both the stock and bond markets, many people are now utilizing a special technique to improve the performance of their portfolios.

Asset allocation is a formalized method to insure that portfolios do not become overly concentrated in a single security or asset type. In other words, as grandma used to say, "Don't put all your eggs in one basket." You simply decide which asset classes you wish to have in your portfolio, in what proportions, and then adjust the portfolio periodically to maintain the allocation that's right for you.

For example, a financial planner may first determine your risk tolerance (high, medium, or low), then the type of investor you are, and finally your outlook for the economy. This data then guides the planner in determining how much money you need to have in the following asset categories: cash, fixed income (bonds), equities, real estate, equipment leasing, and precious metals.

Figure 9.1 shows a sample allocation strategy from one of my investment newsletters for a moderate

Figure 9.1.
Model of Asset Allocation

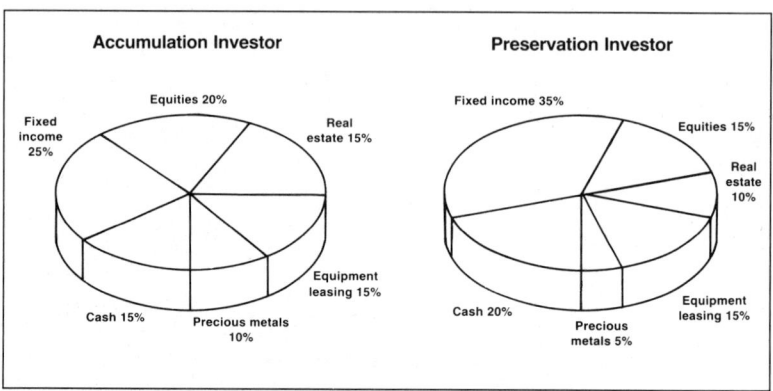

inflation scenario. As you can see, the accumulation (pre-retirement) investor tends to be more aggressive, with the following allocations: 15 percent in cash, 25 percent in fixed income, 20 percent in equities, 15 percent in real estate, 15 percent in equipment leasing, and 10 percent in precious metals. The preservation (post-retirement) investor tends to be more conservative, with the following allocations: 20 percent in cash, 35 percent in fixed income, 15 percent in equities, 10 percent in real estate, 15 percent in equipment leasing, and 5 percent in precious metals. If a client feels uncomfortable owning one or several of these asset classes, they can be eliminated, and the percentages readjusted over the remaining classes.

Moderate inflation is one scenario I have developed for clients. The others take into consideration the effects of deflation, slow growth, high inflation, and hyper inflation. Allocation percentages also vary for the high-, medium-, or low-risk tolerances of clients. During the 1990s, I expect our economy to remain strong with controlled growth and inflation ranging between 4 and 8 percent. If we were to experience a recession during the first part of the decade, I would use a model emphasizing deflation.

PREPARING TO INVEST

When people ask me how to invest the cash that they currently have in money markets and maturing CD accounts, I cannot give them a direct answer until I know more about their financial situations. Sometimes, as with a visit to a doctor's office, I will ask them to fill out a confidential questionnaire which will give a complete picture of their past history. Instead of questions about medical-related matters, they answer questions regarding important financial matters. This includes listing various assets, their investment objectives, sources of income and expenses, and income tax situation.

Important questions to ask yourself before you invest include the following: What are your financial objectives? How many dependents do you have? What type of insurance coverage do you have? Will your family be fully protected if you were to die unexpectedly? What is your investment philosophy? What is your past investment experience? How are you preparing for eventual retirement? What is your age and projected tax bracket? (Sometimes it's helpful to examine a copy of your latest income tax return.) Where are your assets invested now and what is your risk tolerance? The answers to these and other questions are important if you are to invest money properly.

RISK TOLERANCE

It is important for investors to understand certain types of risk. People often fail to recognize the various dangers that face a portfolio. Consequently, even conservative investors overlook serious threats to their financial well-being. Be on guard against the five major risks so that you can strive for excellent long-term returns in your portfolio.

Economic Risk

When the economy turns sluggish or is threatened by a recession, equity investments tend to fall in price. Especially vulnerable are shares of small, emerging growth companies, since they need a booming economy to sustain operations and to survive. An economic downturn can also be a threat to junk bonds which are issued by financially weak firms that might file for bankruptcy.

Interest-rate Risk

As explained in Chapter 7, bonds will drop in price when interest rates rise, because higher rates make yields on existing bonds less attractive, causing a decline in their market value. Likewise, rising rates also threaten dividend-paying stocks, since their yields will look less attractive. For investors who borrow money to buy securities, rising interest rates will increase their borrowing costs and work to reduce their net profits.

Inflation Risk

Since rising prices reduce the purchasing power of your dollars, they will also lower the value of your investments. Using the Rule of 72, an annual inflation rate of only 6 percent over 12 years will cut the value of $1,000 to only $500. The danger for over-conservative investors who place all their assets in fixed income investments is that they may not earn enough to keep pace with the cost of living. Likewise, rising inflation depletes the future value of income from a portfolio of fixed income investments.

Market Risk

Stock market volatility is attributed to many factors, which include program trading by institutions, changing investor psychology, new tax laws, sudden political developments, and Wall Street scandals. Economic and interest-rate risks also have a direct bearing on market risk.

Specific Risk

This applies to a particular industry or company which could be vulnerable to the unexpected. For example, if a company's founder dies or if some key executives are indicted for fraud, the outlook for future growth could be clouded, and investors could sell their shares in panic. Likewise, government regulatory bodies could negatively affect an industry as a whole, e.g., the coal industry will be forced to spend more money on environmental clean-up.

Temperament Is Important

The investment program you choose must fit your temperament, or it will not be the right program for you because you will not have peace of mind. Only after you balance the risks and feel comfortable with the structure of your entire program should you implement it. Then you should look at how you might best allocate your funds among alternative investments.

Insurance

First, you must have the right insurance coverage. Not until you have begun to accumulate an estate to take care of your family should you invest one penny. Estate preservation will make sure your heirs are provided for if you were to die unexpectedly. As explained in Chapter 6, proper insurance planning involves analyzing the type of coverage you now have, whether it be through your employer or through personal policies, and determining whether you need more coverage to make up for any shortfall.

For example, let's assume you are 40, have several children, and that your family would need $5,000 per month to live on if you were to die. Let's also assume that Social Security would provide about $1,200 per month and that your pension would pay your survivors $800 per month, for a total of $2,000. This means they will need an additional $3,000 ($5,000 less $2,000). You must now determine the amount of capital you need to provide this amount. If your heirs could earn an 8 percent return on the principal, multiply $3,000 by $150 (12 months at .08), or $450,000. If your present living estate totals $100,000, subtract that from $450,000 to arrive at your final answer, $350,000. This is the amount of life insurance you will need if your spouse averages 8 percent on the investments he or she makes with the money. At age 40, assuming you are a non-smoker and in good health, $350,000 of annual renewable term life insurance would cost you $392 the first year, with gradual increases thereafter.

Cash

When it comes to the cash portion of your account, keep only the amount which will give you peace of mind. This is the guaranteed portion of your portfolio. If you have a definite purpose for money within the next one to two years, keep that amount in the cash portion of your account. This includes checking and savings, money market accounts, and CDs. If you want to invest for a longer period (a minimum of five to seven years) and defer the taxes on your earnings to a later date, consider a guaranteed fixed-annuity savings plan issued by a major life insurance company.

Fixed-Income

The fixed-income portion of a portfolio includes the debt instruments or various types of bonds discussed in Chapter 7. Maturities also can be arranged to fit your life expectancy. These include government, corporate, and municipal (tax-free) bonds which produce higher income than the cash portion of your portfolio and provide relative preservation of capital. An investor, for example, seeking a high level of income would allocate more money to bonds and cash than to stocks and real estate. A fixed-income portfolio can be structured so that assets are divided among various classes of bonds to achieve diversification and more security.

Invest for Growth of Capital

Equities and real estate comprise the capital growth portion of our asset allocation model. Accumulation investors put more money in this area than preservation investors. A good way to invest in American industry is to invest in stock mutual funds (described in Chapter 8). A systematic investment program lets you establish a bank draft so the fund can draft your checking account each month. In this way, the same amount of money is invested each month in the same security. We described this as "dollar cost averaging," which lets you purchase more shares at a lower cost over time so that you will receive a lower average price for your securities. If the market eventually rises, as it has in the past, you'll make money. Equities also will give you liquidity if you need to use your funds for a specific purpose.

Once you have established liquidity in your portfolio, you can examine special investments such as real estate. The most popular way to own income-producing properties is to use the registered limited partnership structure. Choose a partnership based on the type of properties you feel will be in the greatest demand in the 1990s. That way, when the properties are sold, you stand a better chance of maximizing your profits. Also, because this type of investment is not liquid, you only invest funds you can afford to part with for five to eight years. An "all-cash" program, where the general partner purchases properties without the use of leverage, usually begins distributions at between 6 and 8 percent, and are partially sheltered from taxes in the early years of the program due to depreciation.

If you are a more aggressive investor looking for intermediate growth of principal (in 6 to 10 years), you may also want to include a cable television limited partnership in your portfolio. Based on the expected high demand for cable television systems in the future, this type of investment may grow tremendously in the 1990s. It will also not be subject to stock market volatility. Look for a general partner with a good track record who has expanded and enhanced the cable systems purchased. Generally, these programs pay very little in cash distributions, so they are not for investors who need income.

Equipment leasing also fits in asset allocation model. The Tax Reform Act of 1986 made it more feasible for companies to lease rather than buy their equipment.

Through a limited partnership, you are able to buy the equipment, lease it, and receive a cash flow which is partially tax sheltered. Yields as of this writing generally begin in the 11 percent range, and sometimes increase every year. Since this type of investment is not traded on an exchange, it is not liquid, and will not be subject to stock or bond market fluctuations.

Finally, you might consider investing a small portion of your assets in precious metals or "hard assets" in case we encounter hyper-inflation. Gold and silver are examples of hard assets. Even though they won't pay you a dividend, you can hold them for eventual appreciation. The prices of precious metals fluctuate depending on various economic conditions and are more speculative in nature than other investments in our asset allocation model.

CHAPTER SUMMARY

1. The purpose of asset allocation is to improve the safety characteristics of your portfolio.
2. Asset allocation enhances portfolio performance by dampening volatility and reducing risks.
3. Various types of risks you should consider when structuring a portfolio include economics, interest rates, inflation, market, and specific.
4. Diversification is extremely important for reducing risks, while the right temperament will give you peace of mind.
5. By positioning your assets in various classes to fit the

investment climate and your comfort level, you will be able to reach your predetermined financial goals.

CHAPTER APPLICATION

Investor Circumstance

Middle-aged female professional, single parent, just divorced, has custody of one child, last year's income $90,000. Can invest $30,000 now and will be able to invest more as funds accumulate.

Special Objectives

To purchase a condominium in two years and to provide for child's educational expenses, beginning with high school in four years.

Financial Solutions

Invest $30,000 based on temperament and needs, set up an asset allocation program as an accumulation investor under the moderate inflation scenario. As funds accumulate, they will be divided as follows: 15 percent in cash, to provide liquidity and safety; 20 percent in fixed income, to provide supplemental tax-free income; 55 percent in various equities, to build funds for educational expenses and to purchase the condominium; 10 percent in real estate and equipment leasing, for partial tax-free income and inflation protection.

III

HELPING YOURSELF PREPARE FOR THE 1990S

10

HOW YOU CAN PREPARE FOR EDUCATIONAL EXPENSES

A college president once told me that, during the course of his administration, he had talked with dozens of parents of college students who were forced to seek financial assistance. Sometimes the students had to withdraw from school altogether because they didn't have the necessary funds to pay tuition and related expenses. This is a sad fact of life for some people. It's not that they didn't know their children would some day become young adults in need of education. It's just that they never got around to putting money aside for this purpose. They procrastinated.

In some cases, the lack of planning could be understood. Bad fortune had befallen the family's finances, or the parents held jobs that produced minimal income. But other cases weren't so understandable. This same president told me that many parents had arrived at his office in Cadillacs and Mercedes to report that they didn't have any money budgeted for educational purposes.

Whatever the reason, the result is the same: The child misses out on a college education, which is virtually a necessity in today's world. More importantly, a quality education's impact in terms of human fulfillment is an invaluable and life-long gift.

As Table 10.1 shows, the younger your child is now, the more you'll have to fork out for tuition and other related expenses in the years ahead. In order to determine what your costs will be, find your child's age and go across that line to the dollar figures for either a public college or private institution, whichever you prefer. Don't let the answer discourage you. If you save and plan for college expenses, now you can have the money to pay these higher tuition bills later on.

There are four ways to pay for a child's education.

The Student Works His or Her Way Through College
This has worked for many college students. Unfortunately, this method often limits the student's choices of schools and can place a great burden on the student, whose grades may suffer in the process.

As a parent, you would rather have your child spend more time studying than washing dishes in the college cafeteria or working in a department store. After all, his or her primary job is to receive a well-rounded education in order to become successful in a life-long career. This option ranks at the bottom of the totem pole.

Scholarships or Loans
This method works for some, but it doesn't work for all. First, not every student qualifies for a scholarship or a loan. And, in the case of loans, payback can be a

Table 10.1
Future College Costs with Inflation at 6 Percent

Child's Age	Year Child Will Enter College	Four-Year Costs: Public College Resident Student	Four-Year Costs: Private College Resident Student
18	1990	$22,532	$ 40,956
17	1991	23,884	43,413
16	1992	25,317	46,018
15	1993	26,836	48,779
14	1994	28,446	51,706
13	1995	30,152	54,808
12	1996	31,962	58,096
11	1997	33,879	61,582
10	1998	35,912	65,277
9	1999	38,067	69,194
8	2000	40,351	73,345
7	2001	42,772	77,746
6	2002	45,338	82,411
5	2003	48,059	87,356
4	2004	50,942	92,597
3	2005	53,999	98,153
2	2006	57,239	104,042
1	2007	60,673	110,285

tremendous burden, no matter who may be responsible for the debt. For the graduate, starting out a new career with a big educational debt to repay is getting started on the wrong foot.

Some financial aid is provided on a no-need basis to talented students, but most is provided to students based on need. In this case, a school or trust determines what a family can afford to pay based on a formula that includes the total value of their assets (home, business, and so forth). This amount is subtracted from the total cost and the difference is the amount a college may loan out.

There are several things to consider in applying for financial assistance. First, the cost of attending a particular college is not the sole factor determining whether or not a student applies. Second, if you feel you need assistance, that's reason enough to apply. Keep in mind that, at higher-cost institutions, the average family income of a need-based aid recipient is about $45,000. However, it is not uncommon for families with higher incomes, large families, and those with more than one child in college to qualify for assistance. Don't disqualify yourself by not applying, and don't let costs alone dictate your decisions.

The Parents Pay

You can pay your child's college expenses out of your current income and assets assuming you can provide for such expenses. But you won't know whether your income will be sufficient until it's time to pay the bills. If you have not set up a plan previously, it could become very difficult to pay these bills. Sometimes, one or more grandparents of the student may chip in or pay for part of the tuition expenses. Under current gift tax laws, grandparents can make a gift of up to $10,000 per child per year, or $20,000 jointly, and not be required to file a gift tax return.

During the 1980s, college costs exploded. Tuition costs on average have risen 10 percent a year, almost twice as fast as inflation. Currently, yearly costs at a private school average around $11,500 compared to $6,200 for a state school. If your youngster makes the grades and gets accepted into a good school, you don't want to have to look that child in the eye and say, "You did your part, but I can't afford to send you."

Planning Pays

When a person establishes a systematic plan to accumulate money in high quality investments over a period of years, a child's education is more likely to be assured.

By placing small amounts of money in mutual funds on a regular basis, you can accumulate large sums to help pay future college expenses. For example, a fund designed to provide income and growth (balanced) may have limited upside potential, but it will protect investors on the downside because it's more conservatively structured. In the same way dollar-cost averaging, or investing the same dollar amount into an investment each month, can accumulate large sums of money over time for educational purposes.

Whatever method you choose to provide for your child's education is up to you. But if you want to spare your child the burden of working through college, the only method that you can really count on is prior planning. There are a number of different investments, like the mutual funds discussed in Chapter 8, that can help parents accumulate capital for educational purposes.

INCOME SHIFTING

Unfortunately, the Tax Reform Act of 1986 eliminated the tax advantages of the Clifford Trust, which served as an income-shifting vehicle for wage earners who wanted to accumulate money for any purpose, including a child's college education. A Clifford Trust (named after George Clifford, the man who first used the trust and successfully defended it in court) permitted a parent in a high marginal tax bracket to shift income into a trust fund opened in the name of a child who was in either a low or zero tax bracket. The income was not included on the parent's return, but taxed at the rate of the beneficiary or the trust itself (in either case, the tax rate was considerably lower than that of the contributor). After ten years and a day, or the life of the beneficiary, whichever was shorter, the trust could be dissolved and its funds dispersed by the parent. At that point, the parent could do with the funds as he or she saw fit, whether that included a college education, investing, or playing roulette in Las Vegas.

Of course, the fund was most popular with people who wanted to use pre-tax dollars to send their children through college. In effect, many children went to college with the U.S. government subsidizing the expenses. However, the Tax Reform Act of 1986 put a stop to these tax benefits. Most people today no longer use the Clifford Trust because it is constantly being attacked by the IRS. This also means that the favorable tax benefits are gone. Starting in 1987, contributions made to a Clifford Trust are taxable at the higher contributing parent's marginal tax rate. So before using this vehicle for education funding, you should consult your attorney or tax advisor regarding the possible consequences.

CROWN LOANS

Another popular technique that has worked in the past, much to the consternation of the IRS, is the Crown Loan. Under this plan, which like the Clifford Trusts costs several hundred dollars to establish, the parent may make an interest-free loan to the child. The money then is invested and the earnings are taxed at the child's lower tax rate.

Unfortunately, when Congress eliminated the tax benefits of short-term trusts, they effectively rendered this method impractical also. Interest earnings that the minor child accrues must be placed in a trust, and these earnings now must be taxed at the grantor's tax rate.

GIFTS

Congress, not being without empathy for the poor soul who struggles to pay his or her children's tuition, still allows a parent or grandparent to make a child a gift of up to $10,000 ($20,000 per couple) annually without suffering any gift tax consequences. The money can then be invested, and the interest income is taxed at the child's lower tax rate, provided the child is 14 years of age or older. Congressional members realized that parents who actually put money aside for these older children were likely to use the money for college. But money invested for children under the age of 14 earns interest that is taxable in the parent's higher bracket. Don't let this tax law change discourage you from making the investment. Just review Table 10.1 to remind yourself that the longer it is before your child enters college, the more it will cost to fund the education.

As stated previously, grandparents who want to help fund tuition costs can make investments for their grandchildren. This accomplishes two things: the gift transfers capital out of an estate with pending tax problems, and it sometimes shifts taxable income from the grandparents' higher bracket into the child's lower bracket.

Uniform Gifts to Minors Act
This is a very popular way to save for college. A Uniform Gifts to Minors Act account is available in most states, and must have a custodian, who can be anyone but is usually one of the child's parents or grandparents. As with income-shifting, any property contributed to a child in a custodial account becomes the actual property of the child, who is free to dispose of it in any way he or she sees fit upon reaching the age of majority, age 18 in

most states. However, since most children understand that their parents are saving to pay for their education, they will not abuse this privelege.

When children are under the age of 14, parents should give them non-income-producing investments, such as EE savings bonds, low-dividend paying growth stocks, zero-coupon municipal bonds, or any investment that can appreciate in value without generating much taxable income. Investments that produce income, such as government or corporate bonds, money-market funds, or CD accounts, are best made to a UGMA account when a child reaches 14 years of age because income over $1,000 will be taxed in the child's lower bracket.

PRIVATE AND PUBLIC PROGRAMS

Just recently, private and public programs have begun to appear in the college funding arena. These programs fall into two categories: guaranteed prepayment plans and savings incentive plans.

Guaranteed prepayment plans already instituted in states such as Michigan, Wyoming, Tennessee, Maine, Florida, and Indiana enable parents to prepay their child's tuition for a designated school or group of schools at today's prices. By reinvesting the proceeds, the states claim they are able to meet rising college costs. But parents in the program also run the risk of their child failing admissions requirements or choosing another school. At this writing, most of the states with such plans are waiting for a favorable IRS ruling on how earnings would be taxed before going ahead with them.

The other type of plan gaining favor with states is the *savings incentive plan*. These are college-funding programs that give parents a subsidy or tax break. These plans circumvent the problem of having to designate a specific school, but are not without problems of their own. For example, the College Savings Plan, which sells CDs at interest rates guaranteed to cover rising college costs, requires that parents pay a larger premium. For a private school that costs $17,000 today, these premiums can be as high as $22,000.

By carefully estimating future costs and using a blend of investments, you can provide for greater flexibility in funding. For example, using a mixture of growth mutual funds, zero-coupon bonds or bond funds, and CDs could help provide the needed funds. The actual mix should depend on your child's age and income and on your own tax bracket. A tailor-made program can be set up for any family that takes into account these variables.

PRACTICAL SOLUTIONS

Without question, the Tax Reform Act of 1986 makes it tougher to accumulate funds for a college education. But it's still not impossible. There are some ways you can build an educational fund for your children. Bear in mind, however, that any property placed in a child's name will legally become the child's property when he or she reaches majority.

EE U.S. Savings Bonds

EE bonds can be bought at a discount and will mature in 12 years for a higher face value. For example, you can purchase a $50 face bond for only $25 today. These bonds are guaranteed to earn 6 percent during the first five years. Thereafter the interest rate fluctuates based on 85 percent of what U.S. Treasury notes are paying.

These bonds generate no taxable earnings until they are cashed, which can be any time after the first six months. Although they are not ideal investment vehicles for adults, they're not bad for children, provided they pay competitive interest rates. However, 6 percent is not considered a very competitive yield in today's interest rate market. Suppose you buy them when the child is two years old. When they mature, the child will be 14 years old and the earnings will be taxed at the child's lower tax rate. You must be sure the child is not under 2 years old when you purchase these bonds, because there could be higher tax consequences if they mature before the child turns 14. Remember, for any child under 14 years old, all income over $1,000 will be taxed in the parents' higher bracket.

Hire Your Child

If you operate a small business, you can hire your child on a part-time basis to stock shelves, sweep floors, carry out the garbage, or whatever tasks that may be within his or her abilities. The income you pay the child will not be subject to taxation, provided it falls under the single person's minimum income for taxation ($3,000 in 1988). In the meantime, you get to write off the salary you paid your child as a business expense, which means you can subtract it from your taxable income. Also, a child under age 18 working for a parent is not subject to FICA (social security withholding) which means an additional tax savings. Just make sure you pay your child a fair wage for the job and don't abuse child labor laws (child must be at least age 14), or the IRS may request an audience with you.

Salary Reduction Plans

Salary reduction plans, detailed in Chapter 16, allow employee contributions, along with employer matching contributions, to accrue tax-deferred interest. With such a plan, not only is Uncle Sam contributing to your child's college fund, so is your employer. The 403(b) plan permits withdrawals of funds at any time for any reason without penalty. The 401(k) fund permits early withdrawals without penalty only under certain circumstances, and college tuition for a child is one of them. If you work for a company that offers such a plan and you have a child you would like to send to college, this is a good opportunity to accumulate tuition and expense funds.

Mutual Funds

History has shown that if you start early enough in a good aggressive growth fund, you can build capital for college much faster than you could by merely depositing money in a savings account. But remember that, as the time draws near for the child to attend college, the investments need to be switched to a more conservative, income-producing fund, especially after the child turns 14. Don't put your capital at unnecessary risk when the time draws near to use the money.

Investment Real Estate

Parents who own rental property situated on land owned by their child or children can split the rental income with their children. For a tax break, the parents get all the depreciation deductions.

Equipment Rental Income

Parents who operate businesses that use equipment can form a carefully structured trust that owns the equipment, and the rental income can be routed to the children. However, be aware that this method comes under close IRS scrutiny.

Single Premium Whole Life Insurance Policies (SPWL)

Parents in good health who have substantial liquid assets can make a single payment and obtain an insurance policy that will guarantee their young child's college education in the event of their deaths. While the money is in the plan, during the accumulation period, all compounded interest is tax deferred. If the parents live to see the child reach college age, they can use money for tuition by borrowing against the accumulated cash value of the policy, although they must pay taxes on the drawn earnings at that time. Furthermore, the loan does not have to be repaid because it is subtracted from the actual death benefit of the policy.

Universal Life Insurance Policies

Families without ready cash to purchase SPWLs may consider universal life policies. The key feature of ULs is flexible funding: The policyholder can make regular monthly or quarterly payments, skip payments, make large lump-sum payments or otherwise tailor the payment schedule to changing needs, without penalty. "Variable" universal policies allow the policyholder to allocate the cash value portion within a family of mutual funds. Assuming tax laws do not change, all accumulated earnings will compound tax deferred.

Municipal Bond Funds

Municipal bond funds generate no taxable income and are highly liquid. Once a child reaches the age of 14, the funds can be moved to a taxable vehicle with a higher yield, such as a corporate bond fund. Any income over $1,000 would then be taxed at the child's lower rate.

Zero-coupon Municipal Bonds

Zero-coupon bonds that are set up to mature after your child's 14th birthday are fine for people who are certain the funds won't be needed until maturity. These can be bought at a discount from face value and all income accrues free from federal income taxes. These bonds will also lock in the interest rate and the ultimate accumulated value.

Borrow Money from Your Child

Under current gift tax laws, you could give your child up to $10,000 per year, put the money in a bank account, and appoint a trusted friend (not a spouse or relative) as trustee. Then borrow the money and invest it. Each year, pay a fair interest or more to the child. The money goes to the child, and you can deduct the interest from your taxes up to the amount of your investment income. The Tax Reform Act of 1986 states that a parent can pay up to $1,000 of interest to children under 14 at the child's lower tax bracket. In this case, the child can use the money as he or she sees fit, so you must have a trustworthy child or forget this method.

Financial Aid and Scholarships

Even if you're not sure whether your child will qualify, it can't hurt to apply for financial aid. The worst thing that could happen is that the application will be refused, which means you'll be no worse off than you were before. On the other hand, you may be pleasantly surprised. Many scholarships are awarded on the basis of academic standing, rather than financial need. If your child has the potential, qualifying for a scholarship might give him or her the incentive to excel in the classroom. This method must not be used exclusively, because, if all applications are refused, the child may not be able to attend college. If you plan ahead, you'll be in good shape if a scholarship or financial assistance isn't forthcoming. But if you plan ahead and financial assistance does materialize, you'll have a substantial nest egg to help other children or to use for your own financial objectives.

Except for the previous suggestion, all of these points involve prior planning, well in advance of the time that your child reaches college age. The earlier you start contributing to your child's education in a quality investment program, the less money you'll have to beg, borrow, or steal when the time comes to begin college. The amount of money you invest in a program will depend upon your child's age and what type of college (public or private) he or she will attend. The program can be tailor-made to determine the amount to be invested each month in order to achieve your goal.

GO MILITARY

The armed forces are making a comeback on campus for both financial and political reasons. For example, scholarships are sponsored by the U.S. Army, Navy, and Air Force at more than 2,300 colleges for the Reserve Officers Training Corps. These deals can pay for tuition for two to four years plus other benefits such as books and lab fees, and a $100 monthly stipend. In exchange, the student who qualifies must serve for eight years after graduation on active duty or in the Reserves, or a combination of both. To date, there have been 30,000 applicants for only 5,700 available four-year scholarships.

ADULT STUDENTS

Many schools offer tuition breaks to students over age 25. If you are an adult considering going back to school to earn a college degree, check with the institution in your area to see if a discount would apply for you.

Likewise, you can sometimes save when you cross state lines. For example, Morningside College in Sioux City, Iowa, offers free room and board to top students from neighboring states outside Iowa. In other instances, public colleges will charge out-of-state students more in tuition than for in-state residents. Be sure to check for the best tuition breaks in your area.

Being a veteran can sometimes also help to qualify a student for additional aid. For example, when a veteran applies to a college, the aid process goes into effect, classifying him or her as an independent student. The amount of aid granted is based on the student's income and assets, which are assumed to be more limited.

Oftentimes your employer will offer assistance with tuition fees. A self-motivated employee can only become a better asset to the company and will contribute to its profitability. Many companies will pay either a portion or all tuition fees outright or offer to reimburse the employee after each course is completed.

EDUCATE YOUR CHILD ABOUT MONEY

It would be an excellent idea to start your child early on a program of systematic savings. Usually such programs are connected to an allowance or to gifts received from parents or grandparents. My own children are encouraged to put away a portion of their allowance in a savings account.

Going to the bank to make deposits and withdrawals can be fun for a younger child. Having an account at the local bank can teach your child the basics of savings. This is also an excellent way to explain that the bank pays interest on the money that's deposited.

Preteens or teenagers often begin tracking the performance of individual stocks after receiving shares as a gift. To make this a more interesting experience, use categories of companies whose products are naturally more appealing to youngsters, such as fast-food companies (McDonald's), toy-makers (Toys-Я-Us), entertainment companies (Disney), and sports-related firms (Brunswick).

Needless to say, paying for college can challenge your money-management skills. Because meeting college bills usually involves some sacrifice on the part of the entire family, it is a good idea to have your college-bound child take on some of the responsibility. College-age students should definitely make a contribution toward meeting expenses. And remember, the way you solve money issues now will affect your child's attitudes about managing money in the future.

SELECTING A COLLEGE

One way to make an education more affordable for your child is to select a college that doesn't cost an arm and a leg to attend. Although a private college may be more prestigious as well as academically sound, many state-supported schools can be just as good, if not better. Depending on what your child prefers to study, a public college may be the most cost-effective school to attend. Technical or trade school could also be a consideration.

To further cut college costs, consider the possibility of sending your child to an accredited community or state college for the first two years. Tuition expenses are significantly lower than for most four-year institutions, and virtually every area in the United States is within driving distance of such an institution. This can eliminate the need for housing expenses, since the student may continue to live at home. Even though travel expenses may increase because of the commute, such expenses pale beside the costs of room and board at a four-year college.

Because community colleges usually do not grant four-year degrees, your child may transfer to a four-year college, providing his or her grades and course study are acceptable. The degree obtained from the new college will be the same as if the student had attended the new college for the full four years.

Again, some careful forethought is required when selecting a college as well as planning for accumulating sufficient capital to fund your child's education. If this task seems overburdening, you might want to contact a financial planner who will be able to assist you in this area. After analyzing your unique situation, the planner should be able to recommend the best approach which will help to fund your child's education.

CHAPTER SUMMARY

1. There are only four ways for a child to attend college: through the child paying his or her own way, through financial assistance and/or scholarships, when the parent pays tuition out of his or her current income, and through prior financial planning. If you would spare your child the burden of the first option, the only sure way to pay for a child's education is through prior financial planning.

2. Clifford Trusts are still available, although they are not frequently used because their favorable tax rates are gone, courtesy of the Tax Reform Act of 1986.

3. Income may be shifted to a child who is 14 years of age or older at the child's lower tax rate. Below that age, the income's earnings are taxed according to the parent's higher tax bracket. Money or assets shifted to the child become the property of the child, who may liquidate them and spend them as he or she pleases upon reaching the age of majority.

4. A parent or a grandparent may give each child up to $10,000 per year ($20,000 from a couple) as a gift, tax-free. This is usually set up under the Uniform Gift to Minors Act, with one of the child's parents or grandparents as custodian. The child may spend the money as he or she wishes upon reaching majority.

5. There are still several ways to prepare for a child's education other than by depositing funds into a savings account. Such methods include investing in U.S. Savings Bonds, hiring your child and writing off the

salary from your income, joining a company employee-employer contribution plan, investing early in growth mutual funds, and applying for financial aid. The latter should be used along with another plan to ensure that the child will receive an education.

6. It's never too late to earn a degree. Many adult students are now enrolling in colleges across the country to earn a degree and become more competitive. There are numerous forms of financial assistance available for veterans, active military personnel, and civilian employees as well.

7. You can cut college costs by sending your child to a state-supported school instead of an expensive private college. Also, you can reduce costs even further by sending your child to a community college for two years, after which the child may transfer to a four-year college to complete a degree.

CHAPTER APPLICATION

Investor Circumstance

Middle-aged couple; three children aged 16, 13, and 8; little saved for college; grandparents have contributed $10,000 for each child; parents will contribute $5,000 per child from their own savings.

Special Objectives

To invest $15,000 for each child based on age, minimization of taxes, and quality of investment.

Financial Solutions

Child (age 16) is scheduled to begin college in two years. Investments must be conservative in nature. Divide $15,000 equally among three vehicles: two-year CD, U.S. government bond fund, and convertible bond fund. Any income over $1,000 is taxable in child's lower bracket.

Child (age 13) is due to begin college in five years so investments can be more aggressive. Divide $15,000 equally between three vehicles: CD annuity, high-yield corporate bond fund, blue-chip common stock fund. There will not be enough income generated to cause tax problems.

Child (age 8) will begin college in 10 years. Investments must be very aggressive because tuition costs will skyrocket. Divide $15,000 equally between three vehicles: growth-stock fund, asset-allocation fund, zero-coupon municipal or government bonds. This program is designed for growth of principal with minimal taxes.

Parents need to pare their budget to make additional monthly deposits for each child, at an amount to be based on projected future college costs.

11

PREPARING FOR RETIREMENT— WHAT YOU NEED TO DO NOW

You need to do a number of things to prepare for retirement. You already know the importance of savings—the earlier you start, the more you will have to invest so that you can build an estate during your working years. Although not always easy to do, a systematic savings plan (monthly contributions) will go a long way toward building retirement security. You must establish a budget to determine how much you can afford to save each month.

To reach retirement security, you also need to know how long it will be before you retire and the various types of assets you have working for you to help build your estate. An analysis of your investment program should reveal any flaws which need correction, and will also show you how to allocate your funds amongst the assets suited to your needs and comfort level.

THE FUTURE OF RETIREMENT

It used to be much easier to plan for retirement. You worked for 30 or 40 years, accepted a gold watch, and then lived off your pension and Social Security benefits.

But that formula no longer applies. Because more people are retiring earlier and living longer, their golden years may be much longer than their parents or grandparents enjoyed. So they're going to have to give more thought to their financial strategies and determine how to make their money last longer. More and more people would like to retire at age 55, but without a good financial plan, they will probably not be able to do so.

An unprecedented number of people will be affected as the post-World War II baby-boom generation heads toward retirement. Future Ballot, a California research group, estimates that 75 million Americans will be retired by the year 2010. That's more than double the roughly 30 million retirees today.

This problem is complicated by improved health care. As we move into the 1990s, it won't be unusual for a 55-year-old retiree to have both parents still living. And the cost of improved health care continues to mount. The Employment Benefit Research Institute in Washington states that, if medical bills keep rising at the rate experienced for the last 15 years, eventually 100 percent of the gross national product would be needed to fund both private and public health care programs.

HOW TO AVOID SURPRISES IN THE 1990S
1. Before changing jobs during your working years, consider pension vesting schedules. In other words, if you will be fully vested in your current employer's retirement plan within a year or two, you might wait so that you can take the full balance of your retire-

ment account with you. Also consider whether you will have time to qualify for full-vesting at the new employer before you plan to retire.

2. If your company has a good qualified retirement account (see Chapter 16), be sure to set aside the maximum amount allowed by the plan. The power of compounding will take effect because the interest income is allowed to accumulate tax-deferred until you begin to withdraw it at retirement.

3. If you leave your current job and your pension plan offers a lump-sum distribution of cash and/or securities, put those funds into an IRA rollover account. That way, the money or securities will remain sheltered from taxes until your retirement. You can also direct how the money is to be invested and will be able to begin withdrawals at age 59½.

4. Make sure you have adequate health insurance before you get close to retirement. Chances are you will face additional medical expenses after retirement.

SOCIAL SECURITY

The Social Security Administration, in an attempt to help Americans plan for retirement, will publish your own "Personal Earnings and Benefit Estimate Statement," which spells out all the benefits you are entitled to receive. To order one, call their toll-free number (800-937-2000) and request Form SSA-7004. This is a questionnaire which will ask you to list your name, Social Security number, date of birth, previous year's earnings, current year's estimated earnings, the age you plan to retire, and your projected earnings from now to retirement.

After you send in Form SSA-7004, you can expect to receive a list of estimated benefits in about four to six weeks, which includes the following:

1. The monthly retirement check you would receive from Social Security in today's dollars at your stated retirement age. If you decide to collect your money at age 62 (the earliest allowable), you will have to settle for 80 percent of the regular benefit you would receive at age 65.
2. The full benefit you would receive by waiting until age 65 to begin collecting. After 1999, the age for collecting a full benefit will start to rise until it gets to age 67 in the year 2027. There it will remain unless changed by Congress.
3. The 33 percent larger benefit you may receive if you continue working until age 70.
4. What your survivors will collect in monthly benefits if you were to die during the current calendar year. Your children are likely to be eligible for these benefits until they finish high school. So long as your spouse stays home with the children and doesn't take an outside job, he or she can collect survivors' benefits until the youngest child is 16.
5. Your disability benefits if you are unable to work for at least a year or if you become terminally ill. These benefits include income for dependent children.

6. A year-by-year listing of your earnings that have been subject to Social Security taxes and the actual taxes you paid into the system. Be sure to check these numbers against your own records for accuracy. If you find any errors, contact your nearest Social Security office to receive instructions for correcting your records.

   With these figures, you can more accurately estimate what your benefits will be at retirement from Social Security. The next step is to obtain an estimate of retirement benefits from your employer. Then you must estimate what you will need from your own investment program to complete your retirement income picture. If you estimate an overall shortage, take action as soon as possible to make up the difference between now and retirement.

INDIVIDUAL RETIREMENT ACCOUNTS

In 1981, the U.S. Government offered American wage earners a deal they couldn't refuse. In fact, so many people took advantage of this opportunity that the goverment five years later had to revise their offer.

The deal was the **Individual Retirement Account** (IRA), a tax-deferred means of accumulating money for retirement—compounding with interest—that caught on like wildfire with taxpayers all across America. Although the IRA had been created in the mid-1970s for people who were not covered by company retirement plans, it didn't become a household word until the Reagan administration offered IRAs to all wage earners.

With an IRA, a wage earner was able to contribute a maximum of $2,000 per year (or all of his or her earned income, whichever was less) into the account ($2,250 for married couples with only one earned income). The contribution was fully tax-deductible, and the subsequent interest that accumulated was tax-deferred until the money was withdrawn at retirement.

These funds could only be used for retirement. When a contribution was made to the fund, the contributor had to be virtually certain that he or she wouldn't need the money until after age 59½, or the account holder would have to pay a 10 percent IRS penalty and suffer the tax consequence of early withdrawal. On the other hand, withdrawal of the funds was required to begin when the account holder reached age 70½.

Funneling pre-tax dollars into a personalized retirement fund was favored by people in all tax brackets. For example, a person in a 30 percent tax bracket who made the maximum IRA contribution of $2,000 could count on getting a $600 tax refund for that particular year. In short, the contributor could have $2,000 working for him or her, accumulating tax-deferred interest over the years, for an actual cost of just $1,400. For the contributor in a 50 percent bracket, a $2,000 contribution amounted to a whopping $1,000 in tax savings.

People throughout the country decided to divert their IRS dollars into an IRA. The government knew the program would be popular, but they had no idea that it would meet with such success. By June 1985, deposits had skyrocketed: banks claimed $54.8 billion; savings and loans, $51.6 billion; mutual funds, $24.9 billion; stock brokerage self-directed accounts, $30.6 billion; life insurance, $14.7 billion; and credit unions, $12.7 billion. All totaled, $189.3 billion were invested in IRAs.

Out of all that earned income, the IRS wasn't getting one red cent. However, with the country trying to catch up on a burdening budget deficit, government officials decided that allowing almost $200 billion of earned income to be socked away tax-deferred was not the most prudent course of action.

Therefore, with the passage of the Tax Reform Act of 1986, and beginning in 1987, the IRS was able to get its hand into the IRA cookie jar. As a result, many people lost the contribution deduction they were able to take from their federal taxes. But not everyone. If you and your spouse are not covered by a company-sponsored pension or tax-deferred savings plan (see Chapter 16), you may both continue to invest in IRAs and continue to deduct your investment from your taxable income.

Likewise, you may continue to make tax-deductible IRA contributions even if you are covered by a pension plan at work, provided that your adjusted gross income ranges below certain ceilings. Single people with adjusted gross incomes below $25,000 and married couples with adjusted gross incomes under $40,000 may continue to make fully deductible contributions regardless of what corporate retirement plan, if any, is available to them. Above these amounts, the deductions gradually decrease and disappear altogether when the adjusted gross income reaches $35,000 for a single person and $50,000 for a married couple.

With these new stipulations, some married couples may find themselves at a disadvantage. Suppose a couple earns more than $50,000, and one spouse is covered by a company pension while the other isn't. No IRA contribution deductions would be allowed for that couple, even for the spouse without the pension. In such a case, the spouse covered by the pension may choose to opt out of the plan, provided the lost benefit is relatively small in comparison with the gain that could be made by making two tax-deductible contributions to IRAs. Check with your company's personnel office if you are a pension-covered spouse.

But even if you lose the tax deductions for contributions, IRAs are still an excellent investment, because interest earnings are still allowed to accrue tax-deferred. For example, if you are in a 33 percent marginal tax bracket and you make annual investments of $2,000 at 10 percent in a taxable vehicle, your earnings after tax will accumulate to only $79,900 in twenty years. However, if you make that same investment in a tax-deferred IRA that also paid 10 percent interest, your fund will accumulate to $114,500 in twenty years! This summarizes the power of compounding on a tax-deferred basis.

Even though IRA income is fully taxable when it is withdrawn after age 59½, you probably will not withdraw all your funds at once. Instead, you can limit with-drawals to the amount of money you need in any given year. If you have not begun withdrawals by age 70½, the IRS will require you to withdraw a minimum amount each year based on your remaining life expectancy, or joint life expectancy if your spouse is still living. You can withdraw more if you so desire.

For example, a 70-year-old woman has (according to present actuarial tables) a 15-year life expectancy. Therefore, she could withdraw one fifteenth of her total IRA account balances. The next year, she could with-draw one fourteenth, then one thirteenth, and so on each year until she reached 85, when the account would be depleted. If the woman lives longer than 85, she may experience financial trouble.

However, it is possible to withdraw smaller amounts based on new life expectancy tables calculated each year. In actuality, life expectancy doesn't decrease a full year for every year of life. For that reason, the account probably never would be depleted, and the amount that remains after the account holder's death may be passed on to heirs. Through proper financial planning, all retire-ment assets should not be in IRA accounts subject to forced liquidations.

Withdrawals for married couples may be based on joint life expectancies—the number of years remaining until both spouses are dead. Also, withdrawals may be based on a joint life expectancy of a spouse and a ben-eficiary, such as a son or daughter. If this is done, the technique of calculating the beneficiary's life expectancy each year is prohibited.

Switching IRA Accounts

Although you cannot withdraw IRA funds without a 10 percent government penalty before age 59½, you may transfer these funds to different IRA investments without penalty. But the withdrawn funds must be redeposited in another IRA within 60 days to avoid taxation. IRA funds may be invested in any vehicle you'd like, with the exception of life insurance, collectables such as stamps or antiques, and precious metals. The Tax Reform Act of 1986 does allow IRA funds to be invested in gold and silver coins minted by the U.S. government.

It may be advantageous to switch your IRA investments periodically, depending on how the interest rate you're currently earning compares with what you could be earning on a new investment. A percentage point or two can make a lot of difference over the course of several years. For example, $2,000 invested in an IRA every year for ten years compounded at just 6 percent interest will grow to $27,942. At 8 percent the fund would accumulate to $31,290; at 10 percent it would equal $35,062; and at 12 percent it would grow to $39,308.

If you're younger and starting an IRA program, time also becomes a powerful asset for you. Let's take an example of a 25-year-old who starts investing $2,000 per year in an IRA. In 40 years, assuming the account compounds at a rate of 10 percent per year, the fund total will be $973,702. Compounded at 12 percent the total would be an astonishing $1,718,284. The 2 percent additional interest over a 40-year period amounts to an increase of more than $740,000 in retirement funds, or an additional 76 percent.

No matter what the inflation rate is in the 1990s, this kind of money, if invested properly, will help you retire in more dignity and give you more retirement capital than if you did not take advantage of it during your working years. Not only is it important to make a contribution to the IRA, but one which is tax-deductible is like icing on the cake.

Selecting an IRA

Many people who invested in IRA CDs are quickly becoming dissatisfied with their unstable returns and lack of growth potential to offset inflation. In order to remain conservative, many people have transferred their old bank and savings and loan IRAs into government bond mutual funds, which usually pay 2 percent more in interest. Younger, more aggressive people favor stock mutual funds.

Custodial fees for mutual fund IRAs generally run only about $10 per year, and you receive professional management of your money. Depending on your objectives, you can also invest an IRA into any number of mutual funds, such as those described in Chapter 8. If you're at all confused about where to transfer your money, get professional counseling before attempting to make the move.

WHEN TO START

With time on your side, you can build quite an impressive IRA account. Who do you think would accumulate more money for retirement between the following hypothetical cases? A person who contributes $2,000 into an IRA account each year for eight years ($16,000) from age 19 to 26 and then stops contributing? Or a person who starts contributing $2,000 at age 27 and continues making contributions until he or she turns 65 ($78,000)?

Surprisingly, the person who contributes only $16,000 for 8 years would accumulate $1,019,160 by retirement at age 65, assuming 10 percent annual compounded interest. The person who contributes $78,000—nearly five times as much as the first person—would accumulate only $805,185. In either case, the retirement income that can be generated from these amounts would be considerable. If you have stopped making IRA contributions because of changes in the tax laws, you should again start making those contributions as soon as possible.

If you have yet to open an IRA account, you cannot afford to wait much longer. If you are still able to make a contribution, even if it is not tax-deductible, don't pass up the opportunity. Ideally, you need to make your contributions as early in the year as possible in order to maximize your tax savings and can earn more tax-deferred.

CHAPTER SUMMARY

1. To prepare for retirement, you should begin an early savings program, set up a budget, and allocate your funds among various investments.
2. Since people are living longer and retiring earlier, planning for retirement is one of their most important jobs.
3. To avoid unwanted surprises at retirement, take advantage of vesting schedules, use IRA rollovers (if applicable), enroll in a qualified pension plan, and maintain adequate health insurance.
4. To estimate your Social Security benefits at retirement, request a "Personal Earnings and Benefit Estimate Statement" from the Social Security Administration. This is a key tool in planning your personal retirement income program.
5. Individual retirement accounts (IRAs) were initially offered in the mid-1970s to wage earners not covered by company retirement plans. The Reagan administration offered IRA eligibility to wage earners in 1981, regardless of whether or not they were covered by a company retirement plan.
6. The Tax Reform Act of 1986 eliminated tax-deductible IRA contributions for wage earners covered by pension plans and whose adjusted gross incomes are at or above certain levels. People with adjusted gross incomes below certain levels are eligible for tax-deductible contributions of no more than $2,000 annually, regardless of whether they're covered by

company retirement plans. The ceilings are $25,000 for singles and $40,000 for married people. Above those amounts, the deductions gradually decrease and disappear altogether when the adjusted gross income reaches $35,000 for a single person and $50,000 for a married couple.

7. Even if you lose tax deductions for contributions, an IRA is still an excellent investment, because interest is allowed to accrue tax-deferred. Everyone who has earned income from wages, salaries, or commissions should use an IRA, even if it is non-deductible.

8. Withdrawals from IRAs may not begin without penalty until the account holder reaches the age of 59½. Distribution of funds is required when the account holder reaches the age of 70½. Not only can withdrawals be made as needed, but ordinary income tax laws will apply to them. The account holder generally will be retired and, hopefully, in a considerably lower tax bracket when distribution begins and taxes have to be paid.

9. Withdrawals from IRAs may be made on the basis of either standard life expectancies or life expectancies revised each year of the account holder's life.

10. Switching your IRA investments may be a good idea, depending on the rate of return available. A percentage point or two can make a big difference over the long haul.

CHAPTER APPLICATION

Investor Circumstance

Single, male blue-collar worker, age 50; living in apartment; engaged to be married; portfolio value $100,000.

Special Objectives

He would like to retire at age 60 so he and his new wife can travel and enjoy their retirement years together.

Financial Solutions

Obtain a current history and projection of social security earnings; request an updated projection of company retirement benefits; reevaluate and make changes in personal portfolio, including any existing IRA accounts, to reflect any deficit or shortfall projected in his retirement income stream beginning at age 60.

12

SELF-EDUCATION—YOUR KEY TO FINANCIAL SUCCESS

There are a number of ways to learn about financial planning. You can take adult education classes, read books, magazines, and newspapers published by various financial organizations, experiment through trial and error, talk with successful investors, attend seminars and workshops, purchase cassette tapes, or meet with a financial planner. The more areas you tap into, the better decisions you will be able to make when it comes to your financial success.

Another method that will gain popularity in the 1990s will be through organizational education. For example, if you're a member of a trade association, professional group, or organization, you can contact a financial planner who is a member of the National Speaker's Association (NSA) to give a speech or conduct a workshop on some financial topic that is especially designed to address the problems of your group. Experience shows that people want answers to questions that relate to their financial problems. For example, I will prepare a presentation around those needs, and allow plenty of time for questions and answers. In this way, participants always learn more than they ever anticipated, and are able to apply common sense approaches to solve their own financial problems.

Of course, there are other ways to learn in addition to soliciting professional advice. Even though you plan to retain the services of an experienced financial planner, you should still learn about investments on your own. The more knowledge you have, the better you will be able to analyze the financial advice given you, and determine whether your chosen advisor is serving you as well as you would like. Such knowledge can help maximize your peace of mind when it comes to making investments recommended by professionals.

SELF-EDUCATION

There are many ways to learn about investing. Depending on your personal situation, some may be more practical and less costly than others.

College Courses

If you live near a college (either a community college or a four-year institution) that offers financial courses at an adult education level, it will pay you to enroll. Such courses often range from very basic approaches to more in-depth instruction, depending on the educational needs of the student. If you are a full-time college student already, you're in an excellent position to take advantage of such an opportunity, regardless of your major. You may never have an opportunity like this again to prepare for your future. In addition, you'll be able to enter the working world with the knowledge to succeed financially, unlike others who graduate with you.

Books

Your public library is likely to have a fine collection of material for your review. This would certainly be a good method for learning, and one that you could pursue in your own spare time. Some people say that they tend to doze when reading financial material, because the subject is not the most stimulating in the world. One way to judge such a book is to study its table of contents. Look for subjects that will hold your interest.

When it comes to the ever-changing world of investing, books can become outdated within a couple of years. Try to find books with the most current information and a recent copyright date. Also, make sure the information pertains to problems you're trying to solve.

Trial and Error

Trial and error may work eventually, but the disadvantages tend to outweigh the advantages. First, the penalty for investment error is great. Second, it takes more than one or two errors to learn from experience. Some people make a lifetime of investment mistakes and still never learn. Finally, it's possible that, by the time you obtain sufficient investment knowledge on a first-hand basis, you may have already spent a fortune on bad investments. Trial and error may work eventually, but it is not cost-effective.

Consult Successful Investors

If you know people who have a habit of making good investments, talk with them. It's possible that they'll share their information and techniques with you. After all, many investors are like proud grandparents; they'll jump at the chance to talk about what interests them the most. But be careful: They may be investing to accomplish goals that are entirely different than yours. Listen selectively.

Seminars

Many people are discovering that attending seminars is a fine way to learn about investing. They get the benefit of the best information that books have to offer in a condensed form. A competent seminar leader makes it his or her business to keep abreast of changing factors that influence investments, and to present this information in a lively fashion. Generally, good seminar leaders also provide handouts to reduce if not eliminate the need for note-taking. They may also permit you to make a cassette recording so you can concentrate more fully on what is being said. And the pressures of making a good grade won't weigh on you, making the atmosphere for learning more relaxing.

A good seminar typically includes a mix of visual aids (color slides or overheads) with handout materials so that audience participants not only remain attentive, but tend to remember what they learn for a long time to come. A good seminar is more like a workshop where attendees can learn about their own financial situations.

For example, a handout might illustrate a new tax-rate table, so you can determine your own tax bracket and whether taxable or non-taxable investments are more suitable for your particular situation. I've found that an explanation of different financial strategies or practical applications an investment strategy can offer make the whole presentation much more meaningful to the group.

A good seminar leader will usually get requests to conduct the same meeting for another organization. Typically, the leader should ask for general comments and suggestions on new topics and ways to improve the seminar content, thus learning first-hand what each participant thinks of the entire presentation and how it can be improved for the next group. In summary, a seminar should address your problems and your questions, inspire you to succeed, and motivate you to take action.

Sometimes you may be interested in learning about an investment opportunity, that could help your specific financial situation. These sessions should not only explain the advantage of a particular investment opportunity, but also should examine the risk involved in making a monetary commitment. Preferably you want to concentrate on generic, educational seminars or workshops that address your specific financial needs and answer your most important questions.

Some seminars will charge a small fee to attend. If the education is converted into action, you'll be repaid many times over. Whenever you enroll in a seminar, make up your mind to walk out with several ideas that will recoup your costs and then some. If you do that, you won't mind enrolling in future seminars so you can get more ideas and make even more money.

If you live in a major metropolitan area, chances are you'll have access to all the informative seminars on financial planning you'll ever need. If you do not, you may have to travel to another area to get the information you need.

Under the Tax Reform Act of 1986, travel and lodging expenses are no longer deductible from your income taxes. However, the attendance fee of the seminar itself is deductible, provided that the expense, when combined with other deductions, exceeds 2 percent of your adjusted gross income. These deductions are available only to people who itemize on Schedule A of Form 1040.

You may want to combine attending a seminar with a vacation. A seminar in New York could give you just the excuse you've been waiting for to take the family to the Big Apple to see the sights. Just be sure that you bring home ideas that will not only pay for the seminar, but for the cost of the entire trip.

Tapes

Some seminar leaders market their educational investment material through cassette tape packages. People who invest in these educational programs are buying a patient instructor, because a tape can be replayed as many times as necessary for the benefit of the student.

There are advantages to cassette tape programs. They can be played virtually anywhere—at home on a stereo cassette player, on the road via an automobile cassette player, or on an airplane with a pocket-sized tape player and an earphone jack. With such a system, an investor may convert down time into productive learning time and reap the rewards.

CHOOSING A FINANCIAL PLANNER

The field of financial planning has exploded in the 1980s. Unfortunately, almost anyone can call him or herself a financial planner. This abuse is leading individual states to regulate the industry, and we may see legislation on a national level. This will ultimately serve to protect you, the consumer.

There are a number of ways to determine whether you are dealing with a proficient person who is qualified to really help you toward financial success. Unless you already know the reputation of a person, you must ask some or all of the following questions.

1. What is your educational background and experience?
2. How long have you been working in this field?
3. What experience do you have in helping people with financial problems similar to mine?
4. Can you give me two or three references and/or letters of recommendation from clients?
5. May I see a sample of your work?
6. What professional organizations are you affiliated with and how do they help you maintain your educational standards?

7. Are you certified or do you plan to become certified through the College for Financial Planning in Denver, Colorado?
8. What are your areas of expertise? What other professionals do you work with?
9. What is your general philosophy on investing (aggressive, conservative, etc.)? What types of investments do you usually recommend?
10. What form of compensation do you receive? Fees, commissions, or both?
11. How do you plan to keep the costs of my program to a minimum?
12. How will you keep me informed of new financial information?

The answers to these simple questions will give you a good idea as to the overall qualifications of the individual. Most importantly, you must be able to feel comfortable talking with the planner and develop a sense of confidence in that person. If not, take your business to someone who can earn your trust and respect.

USING THE FINANCIAL PLANNING PROCESS
Comprehensive financial planning focuses on psychological and financial factors that may have an impact on your financial goals and objectives. Financial planning provides a long-term strategy for your financial future, taking into consideration every aspect of your financial situation. It also shows how those aspects relate to achieving your goals and objectives. A financial plan will

help you construct the foundation on which to build your financial future.

The following six logical steps are known as the *comprehensive financial planning process*.

1. Clarify your present situation by collecting and assessing all relevant personal and financial data, such as lists of assets and liabilities, tax returns, records of securities transactions, insurance policies, wills, trusts, and pension plans.
2. Decide where you want to be by identifying both financial and personal goals and objectives. The financial planning practitioner helps you clarify financial and personal values and attitudes. These may include providing for your children's college education, supporting elderly parents, or relieving immediate financial pressures to help maintain your current lifestyle and provide for retirement.
3. Identify the financial problems that create barriers to your financial independence. Problem areas can include too little or too much insurance coverage or a high tax burden. Your cash flow may be inadequate, or your current investments may not be winning the battle with inflation.
4. Create a written financial plan. The length of the plan will vary with the complexity of your individual situation, but it should always be structured to meet your needs, goals, and objectives.
5. Implement your financial plan. A financial plan is only helpful if the recommendations are put into

action. The decision to implement, modify, or reject the recommendations presented in the plan remains your responsibility. A financial planner can only assist in the implementation of the agreed-upon recommendations with your permission.
6. Periodically review and revise your plan. A financial plan is no better than the data on which it is based. Periodic reviews with a financial planner and subsequent revisions of the plan are therefore essential to accommodate changes in personal and economic conditions.

For a clearer picture of this process, review the financial planning sequence shown in Figure 12.1.

Partial Plans

Sometimes, people do not want a complete, comprehensive plan. Often retirement planning, investment planning, tax planning, or a plan for another specific purpose is all they want. For example, clients have come to me close to the end of their 60-day grace period to roll over a lump sum distribution from their employer's retirement plan. We had to concentrate on a specific plan for investing these funds before the expiration of the 60-day period or the IRS would have taxed them on the full amount of their distribution.

Although these plans may satisfy your current needs, they are not a comprehensive financial plan. This does not mean that a partial plan is not excellent in content or appropriate in the areas covered, or that you were not

Figure 12.1
The Financial Planning Sequence

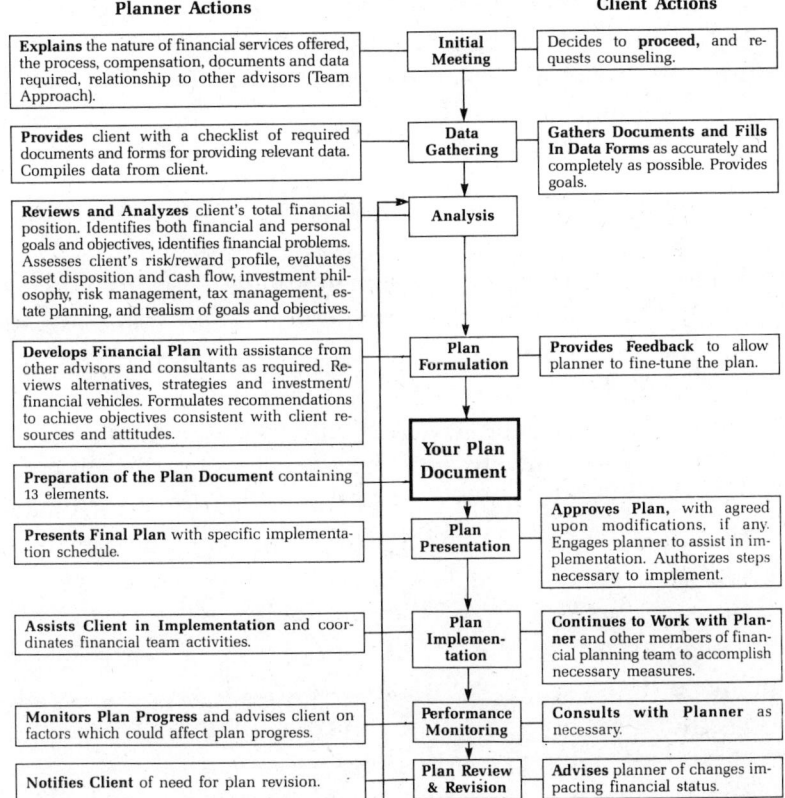

Planner Actions		Client Actions
Explains the nature of financial services offered, the process, compensation, documents and data required, relationship to other advisors (Team Approach).	Initial Meeting	Decides to **proceed**, and requests counseling.
Provides client with a checklist of required documents and forms for providing relevant data. Compiles data from client.	Data Gathering	**Gathers Documents and Fills In Data Forms** as accurately and completely as possible. Provides goals.
Reviews and Analyzes client's total financial position. Identifies both financial and personal goals and objectives, identifies financial problems. Assesses client's risk/reward profile, evaluates asset disposition and cash flow, investment philosophy, risk management, tax management, estate planning, and realism of goals and objectives.	Analysis	
Develops Financial Plan with assistance from other advisors and consultants as required. Reviews alternatives, strategies and investment/ financial vehicles. Formulates recommendations to achieve objectives consistent with client resources and attitudes.	Plan Formulation	**Provides Feedback** to allow planner to fine-tune the plan.
Preparation of the Plan Document containing 13 elements.	Your Plan Document	
Presents Final Plan with specific implementation schedule.	Plan Presentation	**Approves Plan,** with agreed upon modifications, if any. Engages planner to assist in implementation. Authorizes steps necessary to implement.
Assists Client in Implementation and coordinates financial team activities.	Plan Implementation	**Continues to Work with Planner** and other members of financial planning team to accomplish necessary measures.
Monitors Plan Progress and advises client on factors which could affect plan progress.	Performance Monitoring	**Consults with Planner** as necessary.
Notifies Client of need for plan revision.	Plan Review & Revision	**Advises** planner of changes impacting financial status.

Source: Reprinted from the IAFP's Registry of Financial Planning Practitioners' A Consumer Guide to Comprehensive Financial Planning.

served professionally or ethically. It only means that you must be aware that a *comprehensive* plan, which is the preferred process, was not developed for your particular situation. If desirable, you may go back later to have a more comprehensive plan developed for your overall financial needs.

CHAPTER SUMMARY

1. Investing is the cure for financial distress. To avoid the distress, learn and practice the cure.
2. There are five ways to learn about investing: take adult education courses, read books and magazines, practice trial and error, talk with successful investors, and attend seminars.
3. Education isn't nearly as expensive as ignorance. What you learn can help you to make good investments and recoup the cost of the education. But what you don't know about investing can cost you plenty.
4. Out-of-town seminars can be combined with vacations, and the cost of the seminar can be deducted from the itemizers' taxes.
5. Cassette tape instructional programs can be good methods for learning. They may be played repeatedly on cassette players anywhere.
6. By asking a prospective financial planner the right questions, you can decide whether he or she is the person to help you achieve your financial objectives.
7. The financial planning process includes preparing a comprehensive financial plan. However it's also acceptable to seek planning advice in only a specific area.

13

BRINGING IT ALL TOGETHER—
FINANCIAL PLANNING OVERVIEW

Obviously, there is no way I could include in this book a financial plan that would accommodate your every need. A financial planner charged with that responsibility would need to know many things very personal to you, such as how much money you earn annually, how much your monthly expenses are, how many children you have and whether college is part of their future, and when you'd like to retire and what income you want to have then.

Still, looking at an average financial plan geared to make an investor comfortable now and financially self-sufficient in his or her later years of life can be helpful. Critical to the success of any financial plan is being prepared for your future, both short-term and long-term.

As you know, you must determine what you want out of life for yourself and your family, and then map a sufficient strategy to attain it. Formulating and following a viable action plan that can achieve your goals is the only sure way of getting what you want out of life. Yet, most people don't set investment goals. They feel that such a task requires a great deal of technical investment skills and large amounts of investable cash. But these are not out of your reach. You can reach your goals if you are capable of earning a reasonable income, disciplining yourself to save regular portions of it, and have the knowledge to make lucrative investments.

When it comes to investments, even professional investors can't call them right all the time. After all, it isn't easy to pick out individual investments that won't fluctuate in value. That's why stock mutual funds are often best for the investor who wants to accumulate serious capital for the 1990s. Again, no investment is risk-free. But mutual funds historically have offered good solid returns simply because the funds are collections of solid, diversified stock holdings. When you add to this the planning tool of asset allocation, your chances of achieving financial success during the next decade become even greater.

But for different phases of your life, you will have different needs. A retired couple depending on investment income couldn't afford to take the same financial chances that a younger working couple could take. By the same token, a couple with small children won't have the same needs as a couple with children in college. While a young person may be interested in investing for growth, a retired or disabled person might be primarily interested in income.

Still, it might be a mistake to invest in one area or the other if greater financial strength could be obtained by investing in several funds. In fact, such an investment strategy offers true diversification for the average investor. Not only does each mutual fund consist of diversified stocks, but the investor can achieve even greater diversification by investing in several different mutual fund families.

Let's track a hypothetical couple through the various stages of their lives in terms of seeing how they would best be served by various financial plans.

THE SMITHS
John and Susan Smith (in their late twenties) have been married for six years and live in an apartment. Together, they earn $48,000 a year. They have no children and don't plan to have any in the near future. Therefore, they have been able to save about $4,000 per year, which they have done for each of the six years they have been married, while living quite comfortably off of what was left. They have accumulated about $24,000 in cash, which they want to invest. Considering that they are young, without children, and in good health, with at least four decades of income-generating ability ahead of them, they have decided to invest 50 percent of their holdings in growth stock mutual funds, which gives primary attention to capital appreciation and secondary attention to income. They will also continue to invest, using dollar-cost averaging to lower their overall costs and increase their opportunity for capital appreciation.

Because they are in sound financial shape with no

long-term obligations ahead of them, the Smiths have decided to invest the other 50 percent in convertible and government bond funds for a combination of growth and income. Their ultimate goal is to purchase a home in 4 to 5 years. A combination of these three investments will provide the down payment necessary to take that important step.

But four years later the Smiths experience an unplanned pregnancy that adds two new members to their household. Consequently, life as the Smiths have known it has suddenly changed. Susan, who was advancing in her career and making up to $18,000, must stop working for a while, which means that John's salary of $30,000 is the family's main source of income. That provides for their higher expenses, but it leaves absolutely nothing for investments.

Through their mutual fund investments made four years earlier, plus four additional years of saving $4,000 per year, John and Susan have accumulated over $50,000, of which $30,000 will now be used as a down payment on a new three-bedroom home. The monthly payments have been worked into their budget which pares back funds for entertainment, vacations, and credit card use.

John and Susan will remain on a tight budget until Susan returns to work. After all, feeding and clothing two more people requires a lot of money in itself. But then there will be college to consider later, and the Smiths will also have to come up with tuition and expense payments too. Although John has a good job with a bright future, he knows that his salary won't be enough to pay their monthly expenses and college tuition at the same time. He also knows that at the time college begins, he probably will be making too much money for his children to qualify for federal education loans.

Six years later the twins are in school full-time, and Susan returns to the work force. But even though their annual income has increased to $60,000 (John's is $42,000 and Susan's is $18,000), the Smiths are only able to save $6,000 per year, or 10 percent of their income. If they are to realize their financial goals, their investments will have to work hard to make the money for them. So their financial planner advises them to shift their investments to reflect the change in their family status and, as a result, their long-term needs and wants.

John and Susan decide to invest $200 per month into a growth stock mutual fund to build an educational account for each twin. It will be 12 years before the twins start college, and the Smiths' objective is to build capital of around $80,000 for each child ($2,400 per year for 12 years compounded at 15 percent) by the time they begin college. This will give them the option to attend either a public or private university.

As the years roll on, John and Susan come to a startling realization: While they are far from being old, they certainly aren't young anymore (now in their late 40s). Neither are their two children, who are now about to enter college. Up until now, the Smiths have been successfully able to invest for college and have progressed in their jobs as well. In fact, John has recently changed positions and is now earning $68,000 while Susie is earning $32,000. They have been able to use extra funds to buy a new car and to meet rising expenses in their budget. Out of their $100,000 per year income, $10,000 is being funneled into their investment program.

John received a distribution of $26,000 from his previous employer's pension plan, which he rolled over into an IRA to postpone the payment of taxes. These funds have been divided between growth stocks, corporate bonds, and zero-coupon government bonds in an attempt to maximize growth and build income for retirement.

Coupled with this, the Smiths have decided to review their entire financial program, which will now place emphasis on saving for retirement in fifteen years. Because their home has appreciated in value, they will also use a home equity line of credit to do some major repairs and purchase another new car. As they progress into their 50s, John and Susan are able to increase their savings and investments, even though funds are needed to help the twins after graduation (one needed financial help to attend medical school, the other wanted to make a down payment on a sports car).

Retirement

If you're prepared, you can look forward to retirement with great expectation. But if you're not financially prepared for it, you may not look forward to it at all. You may feel impoverished without any source of income other than Social Security and a company pension plan.

Fortunately the Smiths are prepared. With their children grown and working to support families of their own, John bade farewell to the working world at age 62. Susan had opted for early retirement at age 55 in order to pursue other interests and enjoy the grandchildren. She stopped working and had also taken advantage of an IRA rollover from her employer at that time. John began to collect Social Security, and both of them withdrew income from their company pension plans. However, this total was not enough to cover their monthly expenses, which had risen with inflation over the years. So the Smiths were able to make up this deficit with income from their retirement savings program started twenty years earlier. With a combination of income from their IRA rollover accounts and personal retirement fund, they will be able to continue to enjoy life well into their elderly years.

Of course, they have reached a point in their lives when aggressive growth offers more risk than reward. Because their income-generating years are now behind them, they cannot replace money lost in more risky investments. But there is still room for solid, sane growth, and even that area of investment is pared a bit to reflect their change of status from employed workers to retired citizens.

So the Smiths reallocate their assets to decrease growth from 30 percent to 20 percent. But some growth is necessary after retirement, to keep pace with inflation, and, with medical advancements, they might very well live another twenty-five years or more. Their income funds have increased to 50 percent of their holdings because now they need to generate income more than ever. Also their investment plan needs stability, so the remaining 30 percent of assets was added to their money market account.

That's not a bad way to end up, is it? If you make the proper investments and begin as early as possible, you could end up the same way as the Smiths did—financially independent at retirement.

Multiple Strategies

As you can see, one financial plan wasn't enough for the Smiths. Even if they hadn't been blessed with children, their needs and wants still would have been changed by, if nothing else, the fact that older people cannot afford to take the financial risks that younger people can.

Having children, of course, alters a family's financial situation from the start. A person's wants and needs, along with those of the individuals who depend on that person, are always changing. Therefore, a person's portfolio needs to be adjusted periodically to accommodate for his or her current circumstances and preparations for future needs. If a sound financial plan is started early enough, returns on investments can be maximized while the risks of losing money can be minimized through proper planning. This is essential for the 1990s.

No matter how old an investor may be, his or her best chance to succeed with a solid financial plan is to stick with it. The market's frequent ups and downs can be enough to scare anyone. The stock market is known for its volatility, but patient investors in well-managed mutual funds have survived it.

If you still have doubts about the benefits of mutual-fund investing as compared to a guaranteed fixed-rate investment, consider the next scenario.

THE THOMPSONS AND THE TAYLORS

In 1958, Martin and Kate Thompson inherited $100,000 from Martin's father, who died the year before. That same year, Sam and Harriet Taylor also inherited $100,000 from Harriet's mother. Although they both could have gone out on a spending spree ($100,000 was indeed an impressive bankroll in 1958), both couples invested their funds as a nest egg for retirement and to provide income to help with current expenses.

The Thompsons checked around and found a fixed-income investment that offered them an extremely generous income of 8 percent. By investing their $100,000, they received an average income of $8,000 per year, which, in 1958, was more than enough to pay a year's worth of bills. Martin and Kate Thompson were happy with their investment. For the time being, they thought they were safe. "With an investment paying 8 percent per year," they concluded, "we have no worries about inflation; we're set for life."

However, their thinking changed as the years rolled by. Now they are retired and still drawing $8,000 per year from their investment. By the 1990s, $8,000 will equal only about two or three months' salary at the most. Fortunately, the Thompsons are drawing Social

Security and a pension, so they have just enough money to pay their bills, although they have to maintain a tight hold on their monthly budget.

If the Thompsons live for another twenty to thirty years, and medical advancements have made this prospect very likely, they will have major problems. Unless inflation makes a dramatic turnabout, the purchasing power of the Thompson's annual $8,000 per year will shrink even more. All things considered, the Thompsons just may live long enough to experience extreme financial difficulty. That would have been difficult to believe when they invested their $100,000 at 8 percent interest 30 years ago.

Even though they still have their original $100,000, inflation has hurt it. In 1958, a person could have purchased several homes with $100,000. If inflation continues in the 1990s, it won't be long before that sum won't even buy one home. The taxes they paid over the years on their annual income of $8,000 have also hurt. Their "safe" investment has turned out to be not so safe after all.

Sam and Harriet Taylor also invested their $100,000 in 1958. But they selected a different investment altogether. The Taylors realized that the only inflation-proof investment was one that would protect their purchasing power. Because the couple undoubtedly would need more income in the future to accommodate increasing prices, they needed an investment that would increase in value accordingly. So they decided to invest in a high-quality stock mutual fund (with a 6 percent sales charge to boot) containing blue chip common stocks. Like the Thompsons, they took their income in cash. But they reinvested all capital gains generated by the profits of the fund.

The Taylors knew that the value of their investment and the size of their income dividends would fluctuate. But they also recognized that a rising income is the best hedge against rising inflation. Even though they were assuming some risk, they believed that a mutual fund investment and the income it was capable of producing would continue to grow over the long term, because it would reflect the increasing earnings and dividends of the companies in which the fund invested.

So while the Thompsons received $8,000 per year, every year, the Taylors' annual dividends varied greatly. In 1958, they received $3,215, an average worker's salary for about three months. In 1962, they received $4,070; in 1967, $7,297; in 1972, $10,355; in 1977, $14,104, which at that time wasn't a bad annual salary at all; in 1982, $33,552; and in 1987, while the Thompsons drew their annual interest of $8,000, the Taylors drew an income of $50,400 from their mutual fund investment.

If, for any reason, the Taylors decided to liquidate their original $100,000 investment, they would find that it had grown substantially and was worth, in 1987, $1,296,795. They could have bought several houses with their original $100,000 investment in 1958, and their recouped investment in 1987 could still buy several houses.

Chances are, the Taylors will leave their investment where it is and continue to reap favorable returns. Thus, while the Thompsons struggle to make ends meet in the 1990s, the Taylors are likely to be cruising the world on an ocean liner. Think of the peace of mind the Taylors must have, as well as the flexibility to enjoy the extra luxuries of life.

The moral of this story is simple: No fixed rate of return investment you can find will provide for you sufficiently over the long run. If you would provide for your future, not to mention the futures of your children, you must invest in something that will increase the value of your actual investment. History has shown that well-managed mutual funds represent such vehicles for the individual investor.

Needless to say, back in 1958, there were not many investment choices available. But today there are many different kinds of investments available for the 1990s. An investment in a quality blue chip stock fund will hopefully attain similar results for you over the next 30 years. However, there is no guarantee that past performance will be repeated. In structuring a portfolio for the 1990s, it will be wise to diversify, using asset-allocation techniques, to achieve your financial objectives.

CHAPTER SUMMARY AND APPLICABLE ALLOCATION

1. A young married working couple without children, while tempted to spend money as fast as they make it, should have a financial objective of accumulating

capital. As inflation rises and their financial needs increase, they should build a portfolio with 50 percent growth stocks, 20 percent investment real estate, 20 percent income through bonds, and 10 percent in cash reserves.

2. However, a young married couple with two children will have more expenses and will probably save less money. Since their chief financial goal is still capital appreciation, 60 percent of their assets should remain invested for growth (stocks and real estate), while 40 percent should consist of more stable investments (bonds and money market funds).

3. A middle-aged couple with college-bound children become more conservative because half of their income-generating years are behind them. At this point, 50 percent of their portfolio should be invested in bond and money market funds, while the other 50 percent can remain in growth funds and real estate.

4. A preretirement couple will typically have fewer financial demands. With children leaving college, a major financial burden will begin to decrease, and more money will be available to invest for their retirement. Therefore, 60 percent of their portfolio should be concentrated in conservative investments (bonds and cash equivalents), while 40 percent can remain in blue chip growth funds.

5. A retirement-aged couple have fewer financial demands than ever. They don't want to lose what they have, so their objective will be to conserve the capital they've built up during their lives. Only 25 percent of

their portfolio should be in growth assets as a hedge against future inflation, while income assets should comprise the other 75 percent of the portfolio.

6. Well-managed stock mutual fund investments historically have performed far better than fixed-income investments because history has shown that the best hedge against rising inflation is rising income.

IV

SPECIAL FINANCIAL SITUATIONS

14

INVESTING THE WINDFALL

Wouldn't winning a state lottery be great? Just think about how it could change your life. In addition to buying all the expensive items you've ever wanted and going to all the faraway places you've ever dreamed about, you could walk into work tomorrow and hand in your notice, if that suited you.

Of course, the odds of winning a state lottery are very much against you. You actually have a greater chance of being killed in an automobile accident on any given day. But even if you did win an enormous amount of money, quitting your job might be a big mistake. If you don't know how to properly invest and handle the money, you are doomed to lose it. This has happened time and time again, even to people who thought they were too smart to have it happen to them.

First, winners must pay taxes on their winnings, which can amount to quite a piece of the change itself. Then they reward themselves for having won by making several expensive purchases. They put the remainder into fixed income accounts where it steadily loses its value to inflation. On top of that, any interest which is earned on the balance is subject to both federal and state income taxes.

Sometimes, the winners might decide to try their hands at investing, because they have so much money at their disposal. So they play the market, only to realize that the market plays rough with investors who have insufficient financial education. Or they invest in risky ventures, only to discover first-hand that such investments have a high failure rate. Then again, a taste of the good life sometimes only whets a person's appetite for more. As a result, some windfall recipients get spending fever and can't stop until the money is gone entirely.

A person who receives a windfall had better know how to properly manage the money. And the odds are very good that at some point in your life, you'll receive a windfall of some sort. Windfalls generally come from five sources. Let's examine the various sources and study some examples of how practical investments work to achieve financial solutions.

TYPES OF WINDFALLS

Insurance

If you're the beneficiary of someone's life insurance policy, you may be destined to receive a windfall. It may not please you to think of getting a substantial amount of money on the condition of a loved one's death, but the fact remains that you'll benefit financially from the event. That's exactly the way the insured wanted it to be, or they wouldn't have selected you as the beneficiary. You might receive as little as $5,000 or as much as $200,000 or even more. Either sum would be worth collecting, especially when it comes to you tax-free.

You may also become the beneficiary of your own insurance, if, for example, you are injured in an automobile accident. With the increasing number of cars on the nation's highways in the 1990s, there will be more serious accidents, and your chances of being involved are greater. If the other driver was the cause of the accident, you could receive an insurance settlement for mental anguish, pain, and suffering. In the course of your life, a substantial insurance settlement of some type could very well come your way. If and when it happens, it would be better to invest it, rather than spend it.

For example, an older widow came to me with a settlement from her husband's life insurance company of approximately $125,000. She wanted to invest for income and inflation protection. We divided the proceeds accordingly: 80 percent, or $100,000, went into income securities (CDs, money markets, government and corporate bond mutual funds) and 20 percent, or $25,000, went into two growth investments (a blue chip stock fund and an equipment-leasing income partnership). This diversification provided her with security, monthly income checks, and some inflation protection.

Inheritance

You may not get great pleasure in thinking about this method of obtaining investment fodder, but if your

ents or other close relatives accumulated more than they could spend in a lifetime, you are likely to get a piece of it. Other than from life insurance, you could inherit an estate worth many thousands of dollars. This could be made up of various assets such as stocks, bonds, real estate, cars, and personal possessions.

Some people inherit large investment portfolios that were not designed to accomplish their objectives. They need to determine how the structure fits their needs, and what changes can be made to benefit them with minimal costs. A growth portfolio that has been designed for the donor can be modified to include some income investments for the recipient.

For example, a gentleman contacted me about an inheritance from his mother's estate of over $200,000 worth of stock. According to her will, it was to be divided between her four children (of which he was the oldest) so that each would receive $50,000 worth of securities. After the securities were transferred to the new owners, this man decided to have his portion of the portfolio evaluated based on his own special needs for income and tax savings. Several speculative stocks with poor performance records were sold and the money was repositioned into a combination of government securities and tax-free municipal bonds in order to provide him with more safety and tax-free income. When he told his three sisters of what we had accomplished, two of them also contacted me for evaluations and subsequent changes to achieve their own objectives.

Buy-outs

Perhaps you'll one day sell an asset you own, such as a highly appreciated security, a business, your residence, or second home. After holding back enough money to pay income taxes, the balance of the funds should be reinvested very carefully.

A widow came to me with $150,000 from the sale of her house. She had decided to move into a retirement center for independent adults and leave behind the heavy responsibilities of home ownership. We, in turn, developed a plan together with a combination of cash equivalent and debt investments to not only help pay for her monthly living fees at the retirement center, but to give her some extra income to enjoy other recreational activities. She recently reported that she had accumulated enough extra income to take a Caribbean cruise.

Also included in this category, and which will probably continue to be prevalent in the 1990s, are large sums received by stockholders from leveraged buy-outs of their company's shares. Although Congress has threatened to control this type of activity, many larger American corporations, as well as foreign firms, continue to buy up smaller, profitable ones. The windfalls derived from these transactions need to be carefully reinvested to achieve financial security.

Jackpots

Although you may have never won anything before, you could very easily win a substantial sum of money in the future. It could happen during a lucky streak in Vegas, during a good day at the races, or on a nationally televised game show.

Lotteries are currently the most thought-of form of winning jackpots. A recent jackpot in Pennsylvania got up to $100 million, which at that time was the highest in U.S. lotto history. But winners have to pay taxes, and sometimes these monies are withheld even before a check is sent to the recipient. No matter what the circumstances, these funds, if invested carefully, can be used to build financial security for the recipients.

A young couple who recently won a small jackpot from a state lottery were referred to me for counseling. They had been tempted to spend their winnings with the use of credit cards, but had decided to also check out various investment opportunities. After they completed a confidential questionnaire, I discovered they had not planned for the education of their four-year-old daughter. We immediately set aside a sufficient sum into several investments which were designed to grow with inflation and to also give some security (blue chip stocks and zero coupon municipal bonds). Likewise, since the husband did not have a retirement plan at work, other winnings were invested to help provide for his future retirement (growth stocks, special equity investments, IRA). Through a careful analysis, this couple still had funds available to celebrate their winnings, while the other money was set aside to meet their future financial objectives.

Early Retirement Incentives

Early retirement incentives may come to anyone who has worked for a company for more than twenty years. Today's modern business world is focusing more on early retirement as a means to save money and replace senior workers with lower-paid subordinates. Early retirement incentives often are described by corporate officials as humane and sensible ways to reduce the work force, so such incentives are becoming more and more common throughout corporate America. Most plans give the individual from four to six weeks to accept the offer and may include an up-front cash incentive. Some incentives even offer health benefits until the employee qualifies for Medicare.

Experts say that downsizing and restructuring American corporations will continue into the 1990s. The early retirement trend could pick up steam if the economy goes into a recession. If you are lucky enough to receive an attractive incentive package, you may want to take advantage of it. But your earning power more than likely has to be replaced with income from a successful investment program in order to maintain your current standard of living.

MAKING UP FOR LOST TIME

A 25-year-old can build a $300,000 retirement fund simply by investing $30 per month at a 12 percent average annual return for the next 40 years. Who couldn't afford $30 per month for a potential retirement income of

$36,000 per year? Yet, how many people at age twenty-five start investing for their retirement? Definitely less than 5 percent of the population, since 95 percent wind up flat broke at retirement, and, more than likely, less than 1 percent, since most twenty-five-year-olds are either struggling with new families or chasing dreams that don't include retirement planning.

Therefore, a person may be 35 years old before he or she even thinks about starting to invest for retirement. When this person decides to start investing, the monthly financial contribution that would yield $300,000 over the next thirty years is $90 per month. If this person waits 10 more years, when he or she is 45, the monthly sum necessary for a $300,000 retirement fund becomes $300 per month. By age 55, the monthly sum increases to a staggering $1,275 per month.

Waiting can cost you money. But a windfall can make up for lost time. If you're 35 years old and haven't invested one red cent toward your retirement, a lump sum investment of just $10,020 at a 12 percent average annual return could be all that you need to make to achieve a $300,000 retirement fund by age 65. At age 45, a $31,101 lump sum contribution would provide for your $300,000 future, and at 55, a single contribution of $96,501 would do the trick. With this in mind, a windfall contribution that comes your way could not only make up for lost time in your retirement plan, but it also can eliminate the need to make future investments.

Of course, if you're a young person with several decades between now and retirement, you will want a retirement fund of considerably more than $300,000 to keep up with inflation and a longer life span. But a single substantial contribution toward your retirement fund can put you well on your way. You also can continue to make investments to increase the fund's value even more.

Suppose you're 40 years old and you receive a $50,000 inheritance from the death of a parent. It probably wouldn't take you long to spend it. But properly invested at a 12 percent average annual return, your retirement fund in 25 years would be equal to $850,002. Granted, after 25 years of 7 percent annual inflation, an annual income of $195,387 will match the spending power of today's annual income of $36,000. But if you also start making monthly contributions to the investment fund, the total in a quarter of a century might very well yield such an amount. If you don't have to make house payments when you retire or send your children to college, you may be able to get by on considerably less. In any event, when you receive a substantial lump sum of cash for any reason, you can make a solid contribution to your financial future by investing it right away.

But sometimes successful investing is easier said than done. If you inherited a windfall, would you know how to invest it so you could derive the maximum financial benefit from your money? If you don't think you have sufficient investment expertise, start getting it now.

Also, if you would not feel comfortable in selecting all the individual investments, your knowledge will go a long way in working with an experienced financial planner to accomplish this objective.

CHAPTER SUMMARY

1. Chances are that sometime during your lifetime, you will inherit a windfall of some sort. But this should not give you an excuse to procrastinate in developing your own investment program.
2. Windfalls may come from various sources, including insurance settlements, inheritance monies, lump sums from buy-outs, jackpot winnings, and early retirement incentives.
3. Even if you haven't begun a retirement program, a windfall invested properly can help you make up for lost time.
4. The burden of investing money from a large windfall can sometimes be stressful. Your knowledge, along with that of an investment planner, can help relieve your anxiety and point you in the right direction toward success.

15

HOW YOU CAN MAKE THE BEST OF BAD INVESTMENTS

If there were no such thing as a bad investment, you could simply lay down your money and win, much like a lucky gambler at the roulette table in Las Vegas. But because bad investments are sad realities of life, uninformed investors (and, occasionally, even savvy ones) often lay down their money and lose. More often than not, they didn't identify the bad investment early enough to spare themselves the financial consequences. They didn't take action to move out of the bad investment before it lost money.

Of course, hope springs eternal. There is always the possibility that the stock that takes a nose dive may suddenly regroup and soar to a level higher than its original purchase price. But when a stock falls in price, it usually falls again before the price rises. By the time it returns to its original purchase price (if ever), time will have passed, and the value of money deflates with the passage of time. The investor takes a loss in actual spending power, if not in actual dollar value.

A bad investment eats money, your money, and it

will continue to do so for as long as you keep it in your portfolio. Although it sounds silly to keep money in a known bad investment, some people do just that. It's not that these people enjoy financial losses. But selling and taking their losses after the initial price plunge is a conscious admission that they had made a horrible mistake. Because some investors' egos won't allow them to make such admissions, they will keep a useless investment forever.

Such investors had better have pocketbooks bigger than their egos if they want to continue investing. Successful investors don't have money to lose. If their invested money isn't earning interest or making money for them, they take their money out of the failing investments and look for more lucrative ones. This should only be done, however, if the outlook for that particular investment is extremely poor and if there is probably no chance of recovery.

PROFIT FROM YOUR LOSS

A loss can't be turned into a gain any more than oil can be turned into water. But a stockholder can avoid a bigger loss by selling the stock when its price starts to fall. If you own individual stocks, you must always set a limit on the amount of loss you are willing to tolerate. When a market correction causes a quality stock to fall in value, you might want to buy more shares at a lower price if the outlook for the company is still good.

You can't profit from a bad investment financially. But you can make your losses minimal, then re-invest your capital into a more lucrative opportunity. You could then gain in a new investment enough to break even. In the meantime, your investment could earn interest or dividends while you're waiting for it to appreciate in value.

LOSING PROPOSITIONS

Insurance

People lose money every day with old cash-value life insurance policies. For example, suppose you own a fully paid-up policy that will pay your next-of-kin $10,000 upon your death. The actual cash surrender value of the policy generally averages about two-thirds of the death benefit, which, in this case, would amount to about $6,600. If you've invested that $6,600 at 10 percent, you'd receive interest earnings of $660 per year.

Now, suppose you are 50 years old and in good health. Based on current life expectancy tables, you can look forward to about 24 more years of life. If you keep that old life insurance policy, your next-of-kin can expect to receive $10,000 upon your death, whether you die tomorrow, next year, in 10 years, or a quarter of a century later. The longer the wait, the less valuable your death benefit will be to your beneficiary. The policy isn't costing you anything because it's already paid up, but it may be costing you plenty in terms of what you could be making with another investment during your lifetime.

Since you're 50 and in good health with nearly 2 dozen years of life expectancy ahead of you, it might make better sense to cash in your old life insurance policy for its approximate $6,600 cash surrender value, assuming you don't need the protection for your family. You would gamble on losing $3,400 on the deal if you died suddenly (or rather, your beneficiary would lose it), but consider taking that $6,600, invest it at an average of 10 percent interest, and let the earnings compound over the years. In five years, when you are 55 years old, your fund will total $10,629 (not counting taxes, of course, which you might pay from another source). In another five years, when you are 60, the fund will total $17,118. At the age of 65, you will have $27,569. At 70, your account will total $40,365. And at 75, the year that your next-of-kin would stand to receive a $10,000 death benefit had you held onto your old policy and lived out your life expectancy, your account will total $65,008.

Which amount would you rather leave to your next-of-kin? If they had a choice, I'm sure your beneficiary would rather gamble on accumulating $65,000 than wait for a $10,000 insurance benefit. You can't profit from a bad investment, but you can certainly stop losing money and start profiting by liquidating the bad investment in favor of a better one. People do it every day. If you still hold some bad investments that you've made in your lifetime, take action to improve your financial situation as soon as possible.

Bonds

Are you holding bonds that haven't yet reached their maturity and won't for some time? Are they paying you decent interest rates in today's competitive market? If they don't, holding these bonds may be the worst thing you could do.

If you're a young investor with a portfolio of individual bonds, you can evaluate them or contact a financial planner for assistance. Depending on your cost basis, keep only those issues that pay good returns and will work to achieve your long-range financial objectives. Sell the issues with lower rates and longer maturities (over 10 years) and reinvest the money in more lucrative vehicles that will keep pace with inflation.

If you are an older, more experienced investor and your investment objectives are income and security, you will want to hold only quality issues (BBB- up to AAA-rated) with competitive interest rates and shorter maturities (under 10 years).

If you were fortunate enough to have bought bonds when interest rates were high in 1982 and have held them until now, you may very well profit from selling because falling interest rates probably increased the value of those bonds. Since the economic outlook is for interest rates to fall in the early 1990s, you could hold the bonds for further appreciation.

But if you need to change your strategy or raise cash, you can always sell your bonds before they mature. If you sell your bonds early, take a profit, and use the money for a more lucrative investment (for example, paying 12 percent rather than 8 percent), you're literally costing yourself money if you procrastinate in doing so.

Stock

If you bought bonds prior to a rise in interest rates, you can trade for a discount. But if you are patient, you can at least regain the loss on the date the bond matures. This is true provided you can wait patiently and don't need the money working in the meantime to achieve other financial goals.

But stocks are different animals. A stockholder has no idea what he or she will be worth tomorrow. Stock investors know only what they're worth today. When a particular stock takes a nose dive, an investor whose ego is under control can guess what tomorrow will bring. If a stock purchased for $15 per share suddenly plunges to $10, the investor has lost $5 for every share owned. If the investor holds 100 shares, he or she has just suffered a $500 paper loss.

At this point, the investor has three options: hold steady, sell, or buy more. With the first option, the investor regains the $500 if the stock price rises back to $15 per share or loses another $200 if the stock price drops further to $8. Generally, when a stock price drops substantially, excluding market corrections, there is a reason, such as lower earnings or a cut in dividends, and the odds are against it rising anytime soon. For example, a utility that does not get a rate increase to cover higher operating costs on a new nuclear plant could lose substantial sums of money. When the dividend payment is threatened, share prices fall and may not recover for quite some time.

The second option, selling, means the investor takes a $500 loss. Under the Tax Reform Act of 1986, losses can be deducted up to $3,000 per year against ordinary income to reduce taxes. For an investor in the 28 percent tax bracket, a $500 loss would save $140 in taxes. Meanwhile, that person could recoup $1,000 (100 shares at $10 each) to funnel into a more lucrative investment that might partially, if not completely, recoup the loss.

The third option is to buy more shares. You might wonder why anyone would purchase additional shares of stock that was losing money. If the stock represented a good, solid company that was experiencing a temporary setback, the stock itself may be good although its earnings are temporarily down. Such is the case with major oil stocks during oil gluts. When supply of a manufactured product is greater than demand, prices of the company's stock fall. But when another oil shortage rolls around sometime during the next decade (and it seems that oil shortages are periodic), then the demand becomes greater than the supply, and the company's stock price could rise again.

Suppose you were the investor in the previous scenario: You purchased 100 shares of a stock for $15 per share. Total cost of your holdings is $1,500. Then the stock price drops to $10 per share. Total value of your holdings is now $1,000, and you would lose $500 if you sold. So you decide instead to buy another 100 shares at $10 per share, for a cost of $1,000. Now you own 200 shares, for which you've paid a total of $2,500. This means that your average price per share is now $12.50, much lower than the original $15 per share cost. Now suppose that next month, the price of the stock recovers to $13.50 per share, giving you a profit of $1 per share. Since you own 200 shares, your profit is $200, which amounts to a 10 percent return on your investment.

This practice of making regular purchases of the same stock using the same amount of money for each purchase is called *dollar-cost averaging*. While it's not infallible (even dollar-cost averaging won't turn a profit if the company goes belly up), it can certainly help you turn a loss into a profit eventually. After all, had you made your first purchase of 100 shares of $15 per share and stopped there, you would have to wait until the price topped $15 per share to turn a profit. When you buy the same dollar value of stock at regular intervals, the average price per share decreases along with the value of the stock. The level the stock price would have to rise for you to realize a profit is similarly lowered, giving you better odds of eventually making a capital gain.

This concept is basic to most mutual funds. When dividends and capital gains distributions, which are paid either monthly or quarterly, are reinvested dollar-cost averaging is automatically achieved. That is how investors who own shares of high quality mutual funds for a long period of time can show huge profits.

So, as strange as it may seem, investing deeper into a declining stock can be one way of profiting from a bad investment. But be careful. Stay informed on the state of the company. If it goes bankrupt, dollar-cost averaging can greatly increase your losses. However, dollar-cost averaging is not a bad strategy, even with stock that is increasing in value.

AVOIDING BAD INVESTMENTS

The best way to profit from bad investments is to recognize and avoid them. There are a number of things you can do to stay away from losing propositions.

1. Stay away from "hot tips." Investors often buy stocks because a friend literally guaranteed them that it would rise in value. More often than not, a hot tip ends up a cold dud. So be careful from whom you take advice. If you decide to buy on such advice, be prepared to lose the entire amount—it's gambling money!

2. Unless you are highly experienced and know what you're doing in the commodities markets, stay away from them. Index futures are considered to be one of the most volatile investments in the United States. It's like shooting craps in Las Vegas: You could win big or, more likely than not, lose everything you throw on the table very quickly.

3. Be leery of advice from brokers who are out to sell you anything just to earn a commission. Professionals sometimes get several calls a day from these kind of people. These peddlers don't even know, or care for that matter, what the client's investment objective is. So it's generally a good idea to avoid their recommendations altogether.

4. Before putting money into any type of investment, be

257

sure it has a chance of achieving your objectives. Before you add an investment to your portfolio, define your objectives and stick to them. If you have doubts, you can work with one professional, or two or three advisors to get different opinions. These people should know your situation and recommend the right investments for your account.

CHAPTER SUMMARY

1. You can't profit from an investment you've lost money on, but, if its outlook is bleak, you can get rid of the investment, charge off your losses, and reinvest in a more lucrative one.
2. If you have old cash value–life insurance policies, you can cash them in and re-invest the money in a vehicle that can provide you with greater returns than your death benefit.
3. Long-term bonds have traditionally been bad investments because inflation has been greater than their rates of return. Inflation also greatly erodes the value of the principal. If you've recently purchased a long-term bond that has fallen in value, you can sell it at a discount and re-invest the money elsewhere to achieve your financial goals.
4. When a stock plunges in value due to company misfortunes, you can sell immediately and charge off the loss to reduce income taxes.
5. When a quality stock drops in value temporarily, use dollar-cost averaging to maximize long-term profit potential.

6. The best way to profit from bad investments is to avoid making them. Stay away from losing propositions such as hot tips, commodities, and inexpert advice.
7. If you make a bad investment, don't hesitate to liquidate it and re-invest. Learn from your past mistakes so that you won't repeat them in the future.

16

WHAT YOU NEED TO KNOW ABOUT COMPANY RETIREMENT PLANS

If you can no longer deduct contributions to an IRA fund, it's likely because you're covered by a company pension plan, which may be more advantageous than an IRA anyway. If you've yet to take advantage of such a program, you may be missing out on a great opportunity to build for your retirement.

Likewise, several different corporate retirement plans are available. With some of them, employees are automatically covered, unless they opt not to be included and the company permits their withdrawal. Such is the case of the individual who decides he or she can fare better by contributing tax-deductible dollars to a personal IRA. The exception is a participant who elects not to participate under a "defined benefit plan" but who is still considered a participant of the plan for purposes of IRA deductions. As a result, that person is not eligible to make a deductible IRA contribution.

If you're satisfied with your employer and your career situation, it's doubtful you would seek out another job simply to get the benefit of a corporate retirement plan. After all, you can build financial security without such a vehicle working for you.

But there's no question that a corporate retirement plan working on your behalf can simplify the process of building financial security for your retirement years. With such a plan, an employee, a corporation, or both can funnel pre-tax dollars into a tax-sheltered account in the employee's name, where interest is allowed to compound tax-deferred over the years. If you're considering looking for a new position for any reason, keep in mind the types of corporate retirement plans available. All other factors being equal, the retirement plan may be the deciding factor in selecting a new employer.

Don't pass up a favored job situation for a less palatable one solely on the basis of the retirement program offered by the company. But you may favor a particular plan over some others, depending on many factors, not the least of which is your personal tastes and the status of the company itself.

Let's detail several of the more popular retirement plans offered by many companies operating in the United States today.

PROFIT-SHARING PLANS

Under a profit-sharing plan, an employer allocates a certain percentage of company profits to the plan for a given year. For the employer's protection, the contribution formula can be changed whenever necessary. Funding is discretionary, not mandatory, even if the company has

massive profits. The board of directors can decide to retain the profits for distribution to shareholders, or to pay
bonuses to officers. This type of plan can be determined
by the IRS to be terminated if the board of directors fails
to fund it for several years.

Once the profit percentage is determined, the contribution is credited to the account of each participating
member of the plan. Although any one of many formulas
may be used for individual allocation, the one most commonly used distributes the profits to each employee on
the basis of his or her salary in comparison with the sum
of all employees' salaries.

Generally, a participant must remain with a company
for a stated number of years before he or she becomes
vested, or eligible to receive all of their profit-sharing
benefits. For example, if the vesting period is ten years
of continuous service, an employee who terminates service (or is terminated by the company) after being employed more than ten years is entitled to all of his or her
portion of the profit-sharing account. However, an employee who resigns or is terminated with less than five
years' service may be ineligible to receive any profit-
sharing benefits contributed to his or her account.

When an employee leaves a company prior to being
vested, any forfeited amount in the profit-sharing account is redistributed to the remaining members of the
profit-sharing plan. These contributions can be applied
to reduce the employer's total contribution for that year.

A profit-sharing plan is also classified a "defined
contribution" plan. Under this structure, an employer is

allowed to put either 25 percent or $30,000, whichever is lesser, of each participant's salary into the plan. However, since only 15 percent is allowed as a deduction, many employers usually fund only up to 15 percent of compensation into the plan.

Self-employed people can also establish their own retirement plans, often referred to as "Keogh - HR 10 Plans." This means that you don't have to run off and work for someone else just to be eligible for pension benefits.

Profit-sharing plans favor younger employees. The longer an employee participates in the plan, the greater his or her retirement benefit will generally be. If your company is a member of the Fortune 500, a profit-sharing plan might be a lucrative vehicle for your financial future. On the other hand, if your employer corporation is struggling to survive, a profit-sharing plan may be of little consequence, especially if the company itself is having a hard time making any profits.

PENSION PLANS

Money-purchase Pension Plans

Money-purchase pension plans generally require employers to contribute a specified percentage of each participating employee's compensation (up to 25 percent) to an account set up for that employee, regardless of company profits.

The employee's account balance at retirement determines the amount of his or her retirement benefit. As with a profit-sharing plan, the account balance depends on the employee's years of service, the amount of contributions the company has made over the years, and the plan's investment performance.

Sometimes, a money-purchase pension plan may be used in conjunction with a profit-sharing plan. The advantages of sponsoring two plans are two-fold. One, the employer may be able to make higher deductible contributions than with a profit-sharing plan alone. Two, the employer is not locked into a high contribution when company profits are low.

Vesting rules also apply to pension funds and there are no guarantees with a pension fund. If the company that offers such a fund is solvent at the time you retire, you'll receive your pension. But if the company goes bankrupt, the pension funds can be liquidated to satisfy creditor claims, thus leaving little or nothing for the employees. However, a pension trust can be set up to separate the plan from the employer so it is not subject to attack by an employer's creditors.

Defined-benefit Pension Plans

Defined-benefit pension plans pay employees fixed retirement benefits. These benefits are based on a formula written in the employer's plan. The employer has to contribute whatever amount is necessary each year to fund the employees' defined benefit when they retire. Because the contributions depend on several variables—employees' ages, compensation and life expectancy, plan turnover rates, and projected plan earnings—

pension law requires employers to consult an actuary to determine their yearly contributions.

The actuary calculates the minimum amount the employer must contribute to provide the plan with sufficient funds to pay the benefits promised by the plan. When the employer wants to contribute more than the minimum amount, the actuary determines how much more is permitted. People eligible to participate in pension and profit-sharing plans include self-employed individuals, members of partnerships, and employees of small- to medium-sized companies.

EMPLOYEE-EMPLOYER CONTRIBUTION PLANS

As a result of recent congressional legislation (TRA, OBRA '86, OBRA '87), many employers are liquidating their pension plans. They are making lump-sum distributions to vested employees in favor of one of three long-term savings plans that allow for both employee and employer contributions. These plans also allow the contribution of pre-tax dollars from employee and employer to be deposited in the name of participating employees. Three popular funds are available.

403(b) Plan

This plan was designed for employees of qualified non-profit organizations such as hospitals or clinics, and the faculty and staff of local school districts, colleges, and universities. A contributor to the plan benefits in two ways. First, money contributed to the plan is deducted from the employee's salary for income tax purposes, thus reducing the employee's subsequent tax bill. Second, the employee builds capital for retirement by contributing money to a tax-sheltered account.

Under this plan, an employee may contribute any amount of salary he or she prefers, up to a ceiling set by the company. This ceiling usually ranges between one-sixth (16.66 percent) to one-fifth (20 percent) of the employee's salary, or $9,500 per year, whichever is less. Contributions are made by the employer at an amount not to exceed this ceiling. For that reason, a company may set a lower employee contribution ceiling to ensure that employer contributions don't push total contributions over the prescribed limit.

Any employee may participate in the plan with the consent of the employer. There is neither a minimum age nor minimum service requirement that determines eligibility. When the employer makes no contributions to the plan, all employees must be allowed to make salary reduction contributions.

Starting in 1987, a 10 percent penalty is imposed for withdrawals taken before the age of 59½, unless the participant is at least 55 years old and retired. Nor is a penalty imposed if the participant dies or becomes disabled, elects annuity payments for life, receives distribution for payment of deductible medical expenses, or is required to make payment in accordance with a qualified domestic relations order. As with an IRA account, distributions must begin by age 70½. A participant also may borrow funds from his or her account under certain circumstances. Generally, repayment must be made with interest.

Investments in a 403(b) plan may be made to a tax-sheltered annuity or a mutual fund. An annuity can guarantee a lifetime income. However, a mutual fund offers no such guarantee because share values and income paid will fluctuate. If you are a participant in a TIAA-CREF plan, Chapter 17 will give you direction on new retirement options.

401(k) Plan

An employee participating in a 401(k) plan may contribute a certain portion of his or her gross income in accordance with a company-established ceiling. That ceiling must be no higher than 15 percent of the employee's salary or $7,313, whichever is less.

As with the 403(b) plan, contributions from the employer must not surpass an amount that would exceed the prescribed limit when combined with the employee's contributions. The average deferred percentage of the lower two-thirds of eligible employees determines the maximum average percentage contribution for the top one-third of eligible employees. Total contributions for any year from employee and employer cannot exceed current or accumulated excess revenues of the employer.

Generally speaking, participating employees must be at least 21 years of age and must have completed at least two years (one thousand hours each) of continuous service. Some employers have more liberal requirements in allowing employee participation.

Early withdrawals are not allowed, except under certain circumstances, including retirement, death, voluntary or involuntary termination of service, attainment of age 59½, financial hardship resulting from disability, and other circumstances approved by the plan administrator, such as the purchase of a principal residence or paying for a child's college education. Lump-sum distributions may qualify for special five-year tax-forwarding rates. Partial withdrawals do not qualify.

Distributions must begin the year after the participant reaches the age of 70½. Participants who own at least 5 percent of the company also must start withdrawing funds at age 70½. When loans are permitted under certain circumstances, interest must be paid on the borrowed funds.

IRA-SEP Plan

IRA-SEP plans are also known as simplified employee plans, individual retirement accounts, into which an employer may contribute up to $30,000 or 15 percent of the employee's salary, whichever is less.

A participating employee must be at least 21 years old, receive compensation of at least $200 annually, and have served the employer during three of the preceding five calendar years. An employer may be more liberal, but requirements must apply to all plan participants on an equal basis.

Since SEPs are a form of IRAs, withdrawals can be made at anytime after age 59½, subject to income taxes. Early withdrawals are permitted only in the event of death or disability. A 10 percent penalty applies to all other early withdrawals. Distribution of funds is required when the employee reaches age 70½. Loans are not permitted under this plan, nor is five-year averaging allowed on withdrawals.

The Tax Reform Act of 1986 might make this plan more popular by default. A SEP plan is easy to establish, requiring less paper work and no special IRS plan approval. It also has low administration costs when compared with 401(k) plans. As a result, the SEP has become a favorite with small business operators who want to provide for their employees' retirement while sheltering a portion of their own income from taxes.

Combination Plans

In rare cases, employees may participate in several plans offered by their company concurrently. Total contributions for non-incorporated businesses cannot exceed 20 percent of an employee's annual salary. Contributions for corporations cannot exceed 25 percent of an employee's salary.

Sometimes, the employee may have his or her own IRA, in addition to these plans. Under the Tax Reform Act of 1986, IRA contributions are not tax-deductible unless the contributor's adjusted gross income falls below previously stated levels. Only people who are not covered by a corporate retirement plan may deduct IRA contributions, regardless of their incomes.

EMPLOYEE STOCK OWNERSHIP PLANS (ESOPS)
Employee stock ownership plans invest plan assets in the company's stock for employees. Upon reaching age 55, employees must also be given a choice of other investments for a portion of their retirement account. When an employee retires, the ESOP pays retirement benefits either in cash or in company stock, whichever the retiree desires. When the company stock is not readily marketable, the plan must give employees the option to sell their stock back to the plan or to their company for a fair price. You may want to examine the specific features of this type of plan if your employer offers one.

WHAT IS YOUR RESPONSIBILITY?
Over the past decade, employees have taken over more of the responsibilities in managing capital accumulation plans such as profit-sharing, 401(k)s, and IRA-SEPs. This means that the risk traditionally borne by the employer is now being passed on to the employee. Thus employees are making more of the decisions on where their retirement funds should be invested in these types of plans. But in traditional pension plans, such as defined-benefit or money-purchase plans, where you have no control over how funds are invested, your responsibility is to understand how and what your benefits will build to at retirement.

Table 16.1
The Lord Abbett Guide to Tax-Sheltered Retirement Plans under the Tax Reform Act of 1986 and the Tax and Miscellaneous Revenue Act of 1988 (This table is a generalized summary of tax-sheltered retirement plans. Reference should be made to plan documents prior to establishment of a retirement plan. Defined benefit plans, nonqualified deferred compensation plans, and Code section 457 deferred compensation plans for all nonprofit organizations are also available.)

Type of Taxpayer	Type of Plan	Eligibility Requirements
Individual	IRA (Individual Retirement Account)	Individual must have earned income and be under age 70½.
Individual with nonworking spouse	Marital IRA	Married couple must file joint return, and only one person may have earned income (subject to special "de minimus rule").

Maximum Annual Contributions	Financial Benefits for Planholder	Setup Deadline	Contribution Deadline	Distributions Start at:
100% of earned income, but not more than $2,000 100% of earned income, but not more than $2,250; separate account for each spouse with maximum of $2,000 to any account (If nonworking spouse is not 70½ by close of taxable year, an IRA for that spouse is permissible (maximum $2,000), even though working spouse has attained age 70½).	1. In certain cases the contribution is tax deductible. 2. Growth and income generated by funds in plan are not subject to current taxes. 3. Benefits are 100% vested at all times.	Due date for filing federal tax return—regardless of extensions[1]		Earliest (without penalty): 59½ years; disability; death; or a series of similar periodic payments over life expectancy (starting at any age). (Note: To avoid 10% penalty tax, the periodic payment method must be in force for at least 5 years or age 59½, whichever takes longer.) Latest: 70½ years

Table 16.1 (continued)

Type of Taxpayer	Type of Plan	Eligibility Requirements
Recipient of a qualifying rollover distribution from a tax-deferred retirement plan on account of: a. retirement or termination of employment at any age, or b. termination of plan while still employed, or c. death of employee (spouse)	Rollover IRA	Recipient must receive at least 50% of entire balance within 1 taxable year.
Employee of nonprofit organization (educational, medical, religious, plus others)	403(b)	Generally, participation by employee is voluntary.

Maximum Annual Contributions	Financial Benefits for Planholder	Setup Deadline	Contribution Deadline	Distributions Start at:
No limit. Entire distribution may be rolled over except for nondeductible employee contributions. Partial rollovers of the amount distributed are permitted; however, the amount not rolled over is taxed as ordinary income.	In addition to Benefits 2 and 3, *no taxes are paid on distribution— full amount is available for investment.* Without rollover, distribution is immediately taxable and may, in limited cases, be eligible for special income averaging or partial capital gains treatment.[2]	No later than 60 days after receipt of distribution		
Employee voluntary contributions may be made up to 20% of compensation, not to exceed $9,500. ("Catch up" provisions are permitted.)	1. The contribution is subtracted from the total taxable income of the planholder. 2. Growth and income generated by funds in plan are not subject to current taxes. 3. Benefits are 100% vested at all times.	Anytime, but salary reduction applies only after salary reduction agreement is entered into.		Earliest (without penalty)[3]: age 59½; death; disability; retirement at age 55; certain medical expenses; after termination of service, at any age, distributions taken in a series of similar period payments over life expectancy; or on account of a qualified domestic relations order Latest: 70½ years

Table 16.1 (continued)

Type of Taxpayer	Type of Plan	Eligibility Requirements
Corporations, Subchapter S Corporations, Partnerships, and Self-Employed Persons (sole proprietors) (Note: State and local governments and nonprofit organizations may not sponsor 401(k) plans.)	401(a) Plans Defined Contribution Plans: Profit Sharing (Employer contributions made at employer's discretion) a. Thrift Savings (Employee contributions based upon percentage of compensation made in after-tax dollars; employer matches these contributions at a designated percentage) b. 401(k) (Employee contributions based upon percentage of compensation made in pre-tax dollars; employer may, but need not, match these contributions) Money Purchase Pension (employer contributions required, based on salary)	Employees meeting specified age (21) and service requirements (1 year) must be eligible. (Note: A service requirement of up to 3 years may be imposed if plan provides for 100% vesting.) (Note: 401(k) plans are subject to additional nondiscrimination tests.) (Note: A 401(k) plan cannot impose a service requirement of more than 1 year.)

Maximum Annual Contributions	Financial Benefits for Planholder	Setup Deadline	Contribution Deadline	Distributions Start at:
For Defined Contribution Plans: 15% or $30,000 (Profit Sharing, Thrift Savings, and 401(k))[4] 25% or $30,000 (Money Purchase Pension Plan) Nondeductible voluntary contributions of up to 10% of compensation permitted in limited cases	1. Employer contribution to plan is not included in employee's taxable income until distributed. 2. Employer contribution to plan is tax deductible for the employer. 3. Employee contribution to plan is not included in employee's taxable income until distributed (401(k) only). 4. Growth and income generated by funds in plan are not subject to current taxes. 5. Generally, plan loans are permitted. 6. "Hardship" distributions are permitted in limited cases. (Profit sharing only)	End of fiscal year	Due date for filing federal tax return (including extensions)[1]	

Table 16.1 (continued)

Type of Taxpayer	Type of Plan	Eligibility Requirements
Employers and their employees, whether Corporation, Partnership, or Self-Employed Person	Simplified Employee Pension (SEP), a form of IRA with higher maximum contribution For Salary Reduction SEP, see footnote 5.	Generally, all employees over age 21 who have worked for employer for any part of 3 of last 5 calendar years and have compensation of at least $300 are eligible (subject to cost-of-living adjustment).

Maximum Annual Contributions	Financial Benefits for Planholder	Setup Deadline	Contribution Deadline	Distributions Start at:
15% or $30,000, whichever is less[5]	1. The contribution is tax deductible for the employer. 2. Employer contribution does not result in additional taxable income to employee until distributed. 3. Growth and income generated by funds in plan are not subject to current taxes. 4. Benefits are 100% vested at all times.	Due date for filing federal tax return—regardless of extensions[1]		Earliest (without penalty): 59½ years; disability; death; or a series of similar periodic payments over life expectancy (starting at any age) Latest: 70½ years

1. *For contribution based on previous year's compensation.*
2. *Those who reached age 50 by 1/1/86, had at least 5 years of participation prior to the year of the distribution, and receive a lump-sum distribution from a tax-qualified plan may elect 5-year income averaging under the tax rates that are in effect when the distribution is received, or 10-year averaging under 1986 rates. They can also elect to use full capital gains treatment on the pre-1974 portion of the lump-sum distribution.*
3. *The penalty tax is 10%. In most cases, this tax can be avoided by rolling over the distribution into a rollover IRA.*
4. *The maximum annual employee 401(k) pre-tax contribution is $7,000 (subject to cost-of-living adjustment).*
5. *Small companies (other than nonprofit organizations) with 25 eligible employees or less throughout the preceding year can have a special Salary Reduction SEP where the employee can elect to contribute up to 13.04% of compensation in pre-tax dollars (maximum $7,000, subject to cost-of-living adjustment). Requirements: At least 50% of all eligible employees must elect to have the contribution made to the plan; and the plan must meet the special 401(k) discrimination test requirements. Additionally, employer contributions on behalf of all eligible employees may be required.*
Source: From Retirement Planning News, *1988 Edition.*

If you have a traditional retirement plan controlled by your employer, you may be hampered in changing jobs. Most pensions entitle you to a certain retirement payment after you become vested. Beginning in 1989, employees must become vested after their fifth year or gradually between their third and seventh year of service. Thus, even though shorter vesting schedules help job hoppers, they may not help to boost their retirement incomes because benefits can be frozen when they leave a pension plan. When you begin to collect checks from the old pension at age 55, inflation may have seriously eroded its value. Therefore, if you plan to retire sometime in the 1990s, don't change jobs or accept an early retirement incentive without evaluating the pension benefits you stand to forfeit.

Typically, the value of your pension quadruples between ages 55 and 65 because the payment is based on an ever-larger percentage of your higher salary. So you might stand to get a large retirement benefit if you have worked for your current employer for a long time. Before accepting an early retirement offer, determine whether the lump sum payout will be more than what you would receive in regular monthly retirement checks over your life expectancy. If it will not, you may want to refuse the offer and continue to work until retirement at age 65.

Capital accumulation plans will not guarantee your retirement income. They are established by your employer on your behalf. But the responsibility for managing the account may largely fall on you because you decide where the money is to be invested and thus take responsibility. On the other hand, you will be able to change jobs without affecting your payment, because your accumulated account balance will simply go with you and can be rolled over into an IRA or into a capital accumulation plan offered by your new employer. Whichever you decide to do, the money continues to grow tax-deferred. Finally, you must weigh the advantages and disadvantages of each option to determine which choice will support your overall retirement plan.

CHAPTER SUMMARY

1. Company retirement plans often are good ways to build financial security. Through employee and/or employer contributions, earnings may accumulate on a tax-deferred basis.
2. Profit-sharing plans are built through contributions of certain percentages of profit by the employer. If the company doesn't turn a profit in a particular year, it need not make a contribution to the plan. Contributions are divided among employees, and forfeitures resulting from terminations of employment are redistributed among remaining recipients.
3. Traditional pension plans consist of contributions made by an employer on the basis of total salaries paid. Contributions are made to each employee's account on the basis of his or her salary and what percentage of total salaries the individual salary comprises. Vesting rules apply, and forfeitures adversely affect future employer contributions.

4. Employee-employer contribution plans are fine investments for tax-deferred income. The employee contributes a certain percentage of salary and the employer pitches in a set percentage of each employee-contributed dollar. The total contributions and resulting interest accrue on a tax-deferred basis, and withdrawals are permitted on varying conditions, depending on the plan. Examples of these plans include the 403(b), 401(k), and IRA-SEP. Although most companies only offer one plan, some offer two or three.

5. A summary of these plans is depicted in Table 16.1. It gives an excellent guide to: eligibility requirements, yearly contributions, benefits, when a plan must be established and funded, and when distributions must begin.

6. Not only is it a good idea to know what type of retirement plan your employer offers, but also whether you will receive a yearly summary of plan benefits and the accumulative value, for retirement planning purposes.

7. If you have a traditional retirement plan (pension or profit-sharing), be sure to evaluate an early retirement incentive and choose the option that will provide you with the most retirement benefits.

8. If you participate in a capital accumulation plan, you not only take full responsibility for the successful management of your account, but you also have the flexibility to change jobs later on.

17

SPECIAL OPPORTUNITIES FOR TIAA-CREF PARTICIPANTS

In December of 1988 the Investment Company Institute, the Teachers Insurance and Annuity Association (TIAA), and the College Retirement Equity Fund (CREF) filed a settlement agreement with the Securities and Exchange Commission (SEC) that will end the "lock-up" of billions of dollars in retirement savings. Employees of certain nonprofit organizations such as public schools, colleges, and universities will be able to transfer their retirement accumulations in TIAA (fixed annuity contracts) and in CREF (variable annuity contracts) to other mutual funds under the 403(b)(7) plan. The actual implementation of the new agreement is expected to occur in early 1990. If you have funds in this retirement system, this chapter will be of special interest to you and will explain the various options available to you for transfer or retirement.

BACKGROUND

In 1918, TIAA was installed to provide a fixed-dollar retirement annuity and remained the chief funding vehicle for college and investment retirement plans until 1952. At that time, its companion organization, CREF, began to offer a variable annuity, the CREF Stock Account and (in 1988) the CREF Money Market Account. As of this writing, TIAA-CREF is the nation's largest pension fund with about $70 billion in assets. Its 1.1 million policyholders include the faculty and staff of more than 4,000 American educational institutions, including colleges, universities, independent schools, nonprofit research organizations, and educational associations.

Until now, TIAA-CREF did not permit its participants to withdraw funds. Nor could they take lump-sum distributions at retirement or on leaving or changing employment. Limitations only permitted transferring funds from CREF into the annuity of TIAA, but switching was not permitted back from TIAA into CREF.

SETTLEMENT

Once the new plan is approved by individual institutions, retirement accumulations will be eligible for transfer from CREF to other funding vehicles under these conditions: (a) if permitted by the terms of the employer's retirement plan; or (b) if the plan does not mention such transfers, and the employer makes other funding options available; or (c) if the employer consents to a particular transfer.

There will be a separate agreement to provide for the gradual transfer of funds from TIAA that is expected to take place over a 10-year period. Also, a special permission will state that CREF may not allow a transfer of funds to any new CREF funds, except into its own money-market fund until switching is allowed out of any TIAA-CREF funds as a whole. This will be allowed only after SEC approval, notification by applicable state agencies, and notification of TIAA-CREF policyholders.

Who May Participate
The following may participate in the new plan:

1. Colleges, universities, and other tax-exempt organizations that currently participate in TIAA-CREF.
2. Retiring employees who want to withdraw lump-sum distributions from CREF.
3. Terminating employees who wish to roll CREF accumulations into IRA rollovers.
4. Those individuals no longer associated with the retirement plan who wish to roll CREF funds into new IRA rollovers.

CAUSE FOR CONCERN
TIAA-CREF is not taking this situation lightly. This giant tax-exempt organization will introduce new investment products for those existing policyholders who want more flexibility within their TIAA-CREF accounts. This will benefit participants who have accumulated 15, 25, or 30 years' worth of retirement savings and who have been satisfied with their current plan. Despite the availability of new outside choices, some participants will not

want to change. But for those who want the flexibility of directing their pension plan assets into many types of mutual funds, explored in Chapter 8, their options will be wide open when given permission to transfer their accounts.

Growing criticism from higher education claims that TIAA-CREF has become monopolistic and paternalistic, since policyholders had inadequate investment options and were not able to decide how their money should be invested. As we enter the 1990s, more educated people will want to assume responsibility for their own financial destinies, and there will be more demand for a variety of investment choices. For example, neither a fixed annuity nor a mutual fund is the right investment for every participant. But in determining their own strategy for financial independence, participants choosing to transfer their "old money" will be able to do so only if their institutions agree to offer other options.

DEFINED CONTRIBUTION PLANS

Many colleges and universities now offer their faculty and staff plans under which the institutions contribute a fixed percentage of their employees' salaries. At some institutions employees are required to contribute to the basic plan, and employees are sometime allowed to contribute to voluntary or even supplemental plans. These offer extra retirement benefits in excess of those provided under the basic plan. A choice of investment options is common under a defined contribution program.

With TIAA-CREF, retirees can receive benefits in several ways. Annuity contracts allow employees to receive regular lifetime payments at retirement. TIAA-CREF policyholders can choose between TIAA, a fund that provides fixed-dollar annuities, and CREF, a fund that provides variable annuities based on the fund's market performance. In the past, many participants have split their contributions evenly between the two options. Under the new plan, transferability between the two would be unrestricted. However, a TIAA policyholder would still not be able to cash in his or her account at retirement and roll the distributions into an IRA.

A survey among educational institutions has found that the more employees know about retirement plans, the more likely they are to take advantage of alternatives. Competition will force many institutions to provide a much wider choice of retirement investment vehicles to their employees. Whether an institution decides to offer these alternatives or whether employees decide to take advantage of them, many pension officers agree that employees will have to take more responsibility for their retirement decisions. This, in turn, will lower the fiduciary responsibility of the employer and reduce his liability.

INVESTMENT CHOICES

The market for your retirement account will heat up in 1990. Not only will you be offered new investment choices from TIAA-CREF, but also you will be contacted by individual mutual fund groups, brokers, and custodians to move your account. Let's examine some of the alternatives to which you will be exposed.

1. TIAA-CREF may send a representative to your institution or have a retirement plan specialist in your institution explain the options of their new mutual funds. There will also be literature available to educate you on these retirement options. No matter how this information is disseminated, you should study the new alternatives available to you from TIAA-CREF.

2. Mutual fund representatives will contact you either directly by mail or through the brokerage community to explain the wide array of choices they have to offer. With the knowledge you gained in Chapter 8 on mutual funds, you will have a better understanding of their choices, and you should be able to decide on a family of funds that will best meet your retirement objectives.

3. Some individual companies will act as custodians so that you have the flexibility of choosing from a number of mutual fund families. Through the use of computers, there will be easy access to account information, speedy transfer of investment dollars from one account to another, and the generation of timely reports. If an employer signs up for this option, there will be even less fiduciary responsibility than with one single fund family.

COSTS

As of this writing, it has not been determined what TIAA-CREF will charge to transfer and set up an account in their new mutual fund group. But they are expected to be very competitive with other mutual fund families.

Most other mutual funds will have minimal fees ($10–$15) for setup and annual maintenance. However, as mentioned in Chapter 8, there are two types, load and no-load, which will be utilized for the new 403(b)(7) plans based on their past performance.

Individual custodians will typically charge the highest fees. For example, these fees might include a one-time setup fee of $25, an annual maintenance fee of 1.25 percent of the account balance, an asset allocation fee of 0.5 percent (optional), and a transaction fee of $15 for each buy and sell between funds of a different family.

SPECIAL TAX BENEFITS

Every qualified salary reduction contribution that you make to your 403(b)(7) account reduces the amount of your current income subject to federal income taxes. You pay no federal taxes on these contributions until you begin making withdrawals, usually after you retire—when you may be in a lower tax bracket. Some states allow you to exclude your contributions from state taxes as well.

Here are two examples of what these savings can mean to you today.

	Single Return		Joint Return	
403(b)(7) Plan	Taxable Income $30,000	Taxes $5,988	Taxable Income $50,000	Taxes $9,976
With 403(b)(7) Plan Salary Reduction Contribution of $250 Per Month/Per Person	$3,000		$6,000	
After 403(b)(7) Contribution	$27,000	$5,148	$44,000	$8,296
Savings on Current Taxes		$840		$1,680

"Taxable income" refers to the net amount subject to federal income tax after deductions and exemptions. "Taxes" are based on rates effective in 1989.

We would hope for an increase in taxable income. However, assuming tax rates remained the same, over the next 30 years a single person could save $25,000 in federal taxes and a married couple could save $50,400 in federal taxes.

The amount you contribute to your 403(b)(7) account goes to work for you right away. The earnings on your investment accumulate on a tax-free basis until your withdrawals begin. This can make a dramatic difference in the amount of money you have saved by retirement.

In our previous example, a contribution of $250 per month/per person, based on a 10 percent annual rate of return over 30 years, would grow to $569,831 (Standard Table of Compound Interest). This means you could plan on receiving an annual pre-tax income of $64,152 or $5,346 per month for the next 20 years. And, by keeping the balance of your savings in your tax-qualified 403(b)(7) account, your savings would continue to grow tax-free.

RECOMMENDATIONS

Now that you understand what is going to happen in 1990 regarding your TIAA-CREF retirement account, there are several logical steps you can take that will help you make the right decision and give you peace of mind.

1. Check with your employer to find out if participants will be allowed the option of transferring funds out of TIAA-CREF. If so, learn about the procedures (commencement date, time limit, paperwork involved, etc.) and what has to be done in case you decide to make a change.
2. Attend any special meetings or seminars regarding other investment options available for your funds. Before jumping into any new investment (mutual fund), however, study its track record, rate of return, how it performs in both good and bad markets, and whether it has a chance to help you actually achieve your financial goals. Don't be pressured to make a move until you're satisfied it's the right investment for you.

3. Since this decision will be one of the most *important* ones you will ever make regarding your retirement future, examine your current financial position entirely. This means taking the time to list all your investment assets, determining your current asset allocation structure (see Chapter 9), and setting your goals from now until retirement. This will also be a good time to determine what your income needs will be at retirement and from what sources they will come.
4. Based on the asset allocation structure you decide will be the most appropriate for your circumstances, you can make changes to the entire portfolio including those for your TIAA-CREF account. Just as in caring for your car, this realignment should balance your assets to give you a smooth ride into the 1990s to help prepare for eventual retirement.

Warning: Do not change your TIAA-CREF account until you study your entire financial position. A bad move could cost you dearly and lead you down the road to financial disaster! Don't hesitate to get professional help if you need to do so.

CHAPTER SUMMARY

1. A new law beginning in 1990 will allow TIAA-CREF participants the option to transfer their account balances to other mutual funds.
2. TIAA-CREF is currently the nation's largest pension fund with over $70 billion in assets.
3. Once the new plan is approved by individual institu-

tions, retirement accumulations will be eligible for transfer from CREF to other funding vehicles.

4. The transfer of funds from TIAA is expected to take place over a 10-year period.

5. TIAA-CREF plans to establish its own mutual fund family in an attempt to keep funds from leaving its pension fund.

6. Participants will have several investment choices, and the costs will vary with each one.

7. By accumulating pretax dollars in a 403(b)(7) plan, employees of nonprofit institutions not only can save a sufficient amount of taxes during their working years, but also can accumulate a larger capital balance to withdraw at retirement.

8. Do not change your TIAA-CREF account until you have made a thorough study of your retirement needs. Only after you know the sources of retirement income and your risk-tolerance level will you be able to evaluate a new investment opportunity and make an appropriate decision.

Practical Application: In order to help participating members, this author will conduct an educational workshop for associations or individual institutions on their specific TIAA-CREF plan, and will explain asset-allocation techniques that would be most appropriate for their individual members. Please contact the author for specific details (see Epilogue).

18

TECHNIQUES FOR MANAGING A LUMP-SUM DISTRIBUTION

Whether you are young and changing jobs, or are older and about ready to retire, you may be entitled to a lump-sum distribution. While it's always exciting to receive a large sum of money, it can become a problem for both actively employed people and for those ready to call it quits. Let's examine both situations to see how a potential problem can become an exciting investment opportunity.

LUMP-SUM DISTRIBUTION

A lump-sum distribution is one or more payments representing the entire balance of your benefits under your company's retirement plan. It must be paid to you within one taxable year when you leave your job or otherwise retire. Many plans pay out benefits in this manner and the burden falls on the employee to make both a tax and an investment decision.

The most important question facing lump-sum recipients is whether to take the money and pay taxes on it now, or to postpone the payment of taxes by rolling it into an IRA account. Most people would like to put off paying the taxes for as long as possible, but sometimes it may be to the advantage of the recipient to pay the taxes and use the funds for immediate personal purposes.

The recipient has only 60 days from the day payment is received to roll it over into an IRA account. If the 60 days elapse and the distribution is not rolled over into an IRA, the opportunity to defer taxes and receive tax-deferred growth is lost forever.

FORWARD-AVERAGING

If you roll your money into an IRA to avoid immediate federal income taxes, you must pay them when you withdraw the money from the account at a later date. As with a regular IRA, all earnings continue to grow in the account tax-deferred. However, it may benefit you to pay taxes on the distribution now using special forward-averaging techniques.

In order to qualify for forward-averaging, you must have attained age 50 prior to January 1, 1986. This will allow you to figure the tax on the lump sum using either 5-year averaging under current tax rates, or 10-year averaging under 1986 rates. In general, 10-year averaging yields a lower tax bill if the taxable lump sum is less than $473,700. Above this amount, 5-year averaging would yield a lower tax. Your financial planner or accountant can help you determine which method is best for your particular circumstances.

Let's assume a couple with $30,000 in other income

receive a taxable lump-sum distribution of $150,000. Under 5-year averaging, they would pay $30,398 in taxes (20 percent tax bracket) rather than $45,867 (31 percent tax bracket) under ordinary tax tables. However, with 10-year averaging, using the old 1986 tax rates, this couple would pay $24,570, an effective rate of only 16.4 percent. If, on the other hand, they elect the IRA rollover, the entire $150,000 would be available for reinvestment in a tax-deferred account.

Yet another option exists for people over age 52 who participated in their employer's pension plan before 1974. That portion of the distribution which is attributable to pre-1974 contributions can be taxed at a top rate of only 20 percent. The remainder can then use either 5-year or 10-year averaging, whichever generates the least amount of taxes. Ask your employee benefits department to furnish you with specific guidelines.

CHANGING JOBS

When you find yourself entitled to a distribution from your old employer's retirement plan as a result of a job change, your best bet is to roll it over into an IRA if you cannot take advantage of income averaging. By taking distributions before age 59½, you would have to pay regular income taxes plus a 10 percent early withdrawal penalty. This applies to the portion of your distribution that represents your employer's contributions plus earnings on your own after-tax contributions.

For example, if the taxable amount of your distribution is $30,000 and you are in the 28 percent tax bracket, you may have to pay as much as $11,400 in taxes and penalties on the money if you withdraw it prior to age 59½. Why get socked with this type of tax when you can avoid it with the IRA rollover? The general rule is that if you don't need to use the principal or income from the distribution, postpone the tax liability for as long as possible.

Likewise, a younger person needs to recognize future retirement needs and put the money to work in order to secure a financial future. Besides, there is no guarantee that a new employer will pay such handsome benefits. Don't be tempted to take the money and blow it on a frivolous item like a new sports car. This can come back in later years to haunt you.

RETIREMENT OPTIONS

When it comes time to retire, many people agonize over whether to convert their company retirement plan into an annuity or to take the distribution in a lump sum. Annuities promise a flat, predictable monthly payment for the life of the recipient. But this form of payment does not provide inflation protection. On the other hand, the thought of managing a large sum of money can perturb the inexperienced investor. Which choice is best? Let's examine the options with a specific example shown in Table 18.1.

Many corporate benefit-plan administrators advise retiring employees to consult a financial planner or an accountant before choosing between a lump sum and an annuity. This will help tremendously because the advisor

Table 18.1

Five Choices: Which Is Best? You and your spouse are both 65 and set to retire on Jan. 1. You can take a $2,000 check monthly for life or a $250,000 lump sum. What's a couple to do? Unless one of you is a math whiz, you might go to an accountant or financial planner, who would project both options for you. At MONEY's request, retirement planner Paul Westbrook of Watchung, N.J. has done just that. As the table below shows, the safe annuity course would shrink your annual income of $24,000 ($17,280 after taxes) to $10,608 in 1988 dollars by the time you reach 75 if inflation were to run at a modest 5% a year. By taking a lump sum instead, you would have four options, under which you would invest the $250,000 either in a tax-free bond fund paying 7.3% a year or in a taxable bond fund yielding 9%. In each case, you could withdraw $17,280 after taxes the first year and increase that 5% a year to keep up with inflation. If you needed income, you could pay income tax on the $250,000 right away using 10-year forward averaging, as explained in the accompanying story. Then you could put the remaining money in the tax-free fund, and it would last until you were 79. The next two options—using less favorable five-year averaging or rolling the money into an IRA with immediate withdrawals—would provide income until you were 78 and 80, respectively. The last course is best: roll the money over into an IRA and let it grow for five years untouched. Then the sum, invested in the taxable fund, would last to age 93.

Option	Initial Tax	Net Sum Invested	Income at Age 65*	Income at Age 75*	Balance at Age 75	Age When Income Ends
Pension (annuity)	$0	$0	$17,280	$10,608	$0	Death
Lump sum with 10-year averaging	50,770	199,230	17,280	17,280	87,552	79
Lump sum with 10-year averaging	60,110	189,890	17,280	17,280	70,053	78
IRA rollover with immediate withdrawals	0	250,000	17,280	17,280	148,759	80
IRA rollover with no withdrawals for five years	0	250,000	0	17,280	389,638	93

*In after-tax 1988 dollars, assuming inflation of 5 percent a year.

Source: Courtesy of Time Inc. Magazine Company, Money Magazine, December 1988.

can do the complicated math needed to project the financial results of each choice.

Sometimes, people prefer annuity payments because they know they won't outlive them or because they have assets from a personal investment plan to protect them against inflation. Also, some people can't sleep at night because they cannot deal with the responsibility of investing large sums of money. These people might be better off with the annuity option.

This problem often can be solved by the professional management that a family of mutual funds offers. For example, the distribution could be divided among conservative common stocks, high-yielding U.S. government securities, or a combination. This provides the portfolio with automatic diversification, the opportunity for growth of principal, and the peace of mind that comes with the ownership of securities backed by the U.S. government.

YOUR ANNUITY OPTIONS

There are three ways you can choose an annuity payout.

1. *Life-only* pays you a certain monthly amount until your death.
2. *Joint and survivor* assures that if you die first, your spouse will continue to receive a set payment for life.
3. *Life and period certain* pays benefits for your lifetime or for a specified period, whichever is longer.

Life-only annuities generally pay the largest amounts but cease once you die. The other two options provide checks for your beneficiary at the cost of reducing your income by 10 percent to 15 percent during your lifetime. One possible alternative is to select the life-only option and buy a life insurance policy on the beneficiary. Thus, when you die and the pension payments stop, the insurance proceeds will provide income for your beneficiary.

OTHER ROLLOVER INVESTMENTS

Once you have decided to roll over your lump-sum distribution into an IRA, the money is invested based on your age, risk tolerance, goals, and income needs. Younger employees who are switching jobs will want to concentrate on a balanced portfolio that can keep up with inflation. A reasonable allocation for a younger investor would be 15 percent in money-market funds, 25 percent in fixed-income securities that combine Treasury Notes and medium-grade corporate bonds, 40 percent in growth investments that include dividend-paying stocks and total return stock funds, and 20 percent in special equity vehicles, such as real estate limited partnerships.

An older recipient, on the other hand, will want to take a more conservative approach. A person ready to retire will not have the opportunity to make up for any losses should they occur in the portfolio. The allocation breakdown might be as follows: 20 percent in money-market accounts or cash equivalents, 40 percent in fixed-income vehicles such as shorter-term Treasury Notes and higher-grade corporate bonds, 25 percent in growth investments including blue-chip stocks and an international stock mutual fund, and 15 percent in special equity investments combining a real estate investment trust (REIT) along with an equipment leasing income limited partnership.

WITHDRAW PRIVILEGES OF IRA ROLLOVERS

In order to avoid the 10 percent penalty tax, you may begin distributions from an IRA rollover anytime after age 59½. You can decide on the amount to be withdrawn and when payments are to begin. When your monies are invested in a family of mutual funds, you can establish a periodic withdrawal plan in order to receive a monthly, quarterly, or semi-annual check. The money can be sent for direct deposit to the financial institution where you maintain a savings or checking account.

In the case of mutual funds, you are not locked into a particular withdrawal schedule. You may change the distribution amounts and even request a lump-sum payment to meet unexpected financial needs. Most mutual fund organizations also provide you with IRS life expectancy tables so that you can comply with the minimum distribution rules after you reach age 70½.

If you do not need to withdraw principal or interest from your IRA prior to age 70½, you must begin to withdraw it the year after you reach this age. The IRS requires that, at that time, a minimum distribution based on your life expectancy (or on the joint and last survivor life expectancy of you and your beneficiary) be made from the rollover IRA each year. But, you can also take out more than the minimum. These amounts will be taxed as ordinary income in your then current bracket.

HOW MUCH TO ROLL OVER

When people receive a lump-sum distribution, they automatically think the entire amount has to be rolled over. This is not necessarily so. Be sure to ask your employer for a breakdown to determine the portion that could be non-taxable. You need not deposit into the IRA any portion of cash that represents the return of your own after-tax contribution to a retirement plan.

Also, if you receive stock from a company plan, you can roll over only the shares that your employer and/or your reinvested dividends purchased. Those shares, which were bought with your own after-tax dollars, are yours to keep or to sell outside the IRA. You then pay tax only on any capital gain you might have made on them in your regular tax bracket.

CHAPTER SUMMARY

1. Receiving a lump-sum distribution is exciting, but what to do with the money can become a problem.
2. The recipient can either take it and pay immediate taxes on it, or roll it over into a special IRA in order to postpone the tax liability until funds are withdrawn at a later date.
3. People who qualify for income-averaging must compare between 5-year and 10-year averaging techniques. A financial advisor should be able to determine which method would yield the lower tax liability.

4. Sometimes, younger employees receive a distribution when they change jobs. Their best bet is to roll over the money from their qualified plan into an IRA in order to build future retirement savings and to avoid unnecessary taxes.
5. Retiring employees can take a monthly annuity payment for life or use income averaging. But the most popular method is to roll over the distribution into an IRA. Gradual withdrawals, although taxable, tend to yield the most payout during retirement.
6. Various types of investments can be used for an IRA rollover. Some of these include mutual funds (money markets, bonds, stocks), CDs, REITs, and equipment leasing income limited partnerships. Also, a self-directed account can be set up so the contributor can trade individual securities.
7. As with a regular IRA, distribution from an IRA rollover can begin anytime after age 59½. Distributions can be flexible to meet unexpected financial needs. The IRS requires that, at age 70½, a minimum distribution must be taken based on the recipient's life expectancy.

Practical Application: To help executives/employees, the author conducts educational workshops on preretirement planning for associations and corporations. Sessions are geared to their specific retirement plans, and a study is made at allocation techniques in order to prepare for the 1990s. Please contact the author for specific details (see Epilogue).

19

STRATEGIC INVESTING UNDER TAX REFORM

Many members of America's middle class tend to resent people who cut their taxes through legal means. They tend to take the view that anyone who earns more than they do but who pays less in taxes is cheating the system, even if this is done legally.

When taxes are due, most Americans pay dearly. Where do their taxes go? A good percentage goes to the nation's defense department, which many taxpaying citizens feel is necessary to keep America strong and safe. However, there will be more and more pressure on Congress in the 1990s to cut defense spending, especially in view of the treaty signed in late 1987 to reduce the number of nuclear missiles in Europe. Reducing the defense budget will also help to reduce our federal budget deficit.

Also, many people are angry with the wasteful spending that goes on in the defense department. In documented cases the Pentagon has spent $37 for a single screw, $243 for a pair of pliers, $435 for a hammer, $640 for a toilet seat, $2,043 for a nut, and $7,622 for a coffee maker.[1]

Most tax shelters were created to encourage investment in segments of the American economy that otherwise might not attract investors. Certainly, the likelihood of individual gain can be questionable with such investments as subsidized housing, but the likelihood of individual loss when it comes to paying taxes is 100 percent. It's not hard to beat those odds.

Furthermore, an investor knows where and how his or her money is going to be used, but a taxpayer does not. How would many taxpayers feel if they knew the government spent as much (if not more) for a coffee maker than the taxpayers spend for their cars?

Everyone should take advantage of any opportunity to lower his or her taxes through legal tax avoidance. Notice that I did not say "tax evasion." The IRS can get rough with people who are guilty of that. Al Capone pulled a stretch at various federal prisons for tax evasion. Although law enforcement officers were never able to show Capone that crime didn't pay, the IRS got its message across loud and clear by nailing him on federal tax evasion charges.

Don't mess with the IRS. There are many other lucrative and legal ways to build for your financial future. Both the novice and experienced investor can benefit from a review and application of new investment ideas under the Tax Reform Act of 1986.

[1] From *The Pentagon Catalog*, Henry Beard and Christopher Cerf.

STOCKS

As of late 1989, a proposal approved by the House of Representatives would slash the maximum rate on long-term capital gains to 19.6 percent from the current 33 percent. The rate would affect gains from the sale of assets held for one year. The new 19.6 percent rate would be in place until December 31, 1991. After that, capital gains would be taxed at 28 percent but be indexed to account for inflation.

While critics argue that this change would benefit only rich U.S. citizens, proponents insist that a lower tax rate on capital gains would encourage long-term investment and fuel economic growth. But many experts seem to agree that a lower capital gains rate would increase the volume of shares traded in the markets, which, in turn, would boost incoming tax revenues for Uncle Sam.

One thing is certain, there are many individual investors who are holding stocks and other assets that have appreciated in value over the years. Whether these assets were inherited, bought with hard-earned after-tax dollars, or acquired by some other means, their owners would stand to benefit greatly from a drop in capital gains tax rates. For example, let's assume that a stock purchased for $5,000 many years ago is now worth $13,000. A sale at the current market value would produce a capital gain of $8,000 ($13,000 − $5,000). Taxes to be paid at the 28 percent bracket would be $2,240. However, a tax under the new maximum rate of 19.6 percent would be only $1,568. This would result in a tax savings of $672 ($2,240 − $1,568).

BONDS

Income from corporate bonds and those issued by the government are still subject to federal income tax. But the municipal bonds picture is much brighter. On the positive side, very few other investments generate tax-free income. Congress has also severely restricted the supply of special tax-free bonds including those for private purposes used to fund housing or student loans. With fewer of these bonds on the market, buyers may bid up the prices of those that remain.

The law also contains some negatives for municipal bonds. For people who must pay the alternative minimum tax, private-purpose municipal bonds are now subject to that tax. Also, the lowering of tax brackets means the shelter feature is less important. Finally, more restrictive rules for financial institutions to hold bonds will reduce demand in that sector, possibly hurting prices.

To determine whether a municipal tax-free bond is right for you, check a tax equivalent table. From this, you can determine what you would need to earn from a fully taxable investment to have more after-tax income. For example, in Table 19.1 a couple in the 28 percent tax bracket, filing a joint return in the 1989 tax year, would need to earn a 9.72 percent return from a fully taxable investment if they could earn 7.00 percent from a tax-free bond trust. If they can find a taxable bond that earns more than 9.72 percent, they will have more after-tax money from that investment than from the municipal bonds. But before you jump into that type of investment,

Table 19.1
Taxable Yields Versus Tax-Exempt Yields

The tables below illustrate what you would have to earn on a taxable investment to equal a tax-exempt yield in your income tax bracket. Locate your income (after deductions and exemptions), then locate your tax bracket based on joint or single tax filing. Read across to the equivalent yield you would need to match tax-free income.

1988 Tax Year

Taxable Income ($1,000s)

Single Return	Joint Return	Tax Bracket	Tax-Free Yields						
			6.00%	6.50%	7.00%	7.50%	8.00%	8.50%	9.00%
$ 0– 17.9	$ 0– 29.8	15.0%	7.06	7.65	8.24	8.82	9.41	10.00	10.58
$17.9– 43.2	$29.8– 71.9	28.0	8.33	9.03	9.72	10.42	11.10	11.80	12.48
$43.2–100.5	$71.9–192.9	33.0	8.96	9.70	10.45	11.19	11.94	12.68	13.43
Over 100.5	Over 192.9	28.0	8.33	9.03	9.72	10.42	11.10	11.80	12.48

1989 Tax Year

Taxable Income ($1,000s)

Single Return	Joint Return	Tax Bracket	Tax-Free Yields						
			6.00%	6.50%	7.00%	7.50%	8.00%	8.50%	9.00%
$ 0– 18.5	$ 0– 30.9	15.0%	7.06	7.65	8.24	8.82	9.41	10.00	10.58
$18.5– 44.9	$30.9– 74.9	28.0	8.33	9.03	9.72	10.42	11.10	11.80	12.48
$44.9– 10.4	$74.9–177.0	33.0	8.96	9.70	10.45	11.19	11.94	12.68	13.43
Over 104.3	Over 177.0	28.0	8.33	9.03	9.72	10.42	11.10	11.80	12.48

check the credit risks of the taxable bond to determine the rating and amount of risk involved.

For a single person in the 33 percent tax bracket, and assuming municipal bonds are paying only 6.5 percent, Table 19.1 shows that a 10.45 percent return is needed to break even. There are investments that pay higher returns than this, but the risks associated with them must be carefully evaluated. The formula for taxable equivalent is a nontaxable rate of return divided by 1, less your tax bracket.

REAL ESTATE

If you have studied some of the implications of the 1986 tax laws, you undoubtedly know that real estate has been hit hard. Not only has the depreciation period been lengthened from 19 years to as high as 32½ years, but accelerated depreciation can no longer be used to increase up-front deductions on tax shelters. Lower tax rates also reduce the tax-saving benefits of large interest payments. As a result of overbuilding in many areas of the country, there has been a decline in new construction for apartments and commercial buildings. This could lead to an eventual shortage of quality properties as the economy grows in the 1990s. In some areas, where there is a glut of certain kinds of real estate, you can already buy attractive properties at much lower prices.

Real estate has probably been, and will continue to be, one of the best investments over changing economic cycles. Its value tends to rise with inflation but remains fairly stable during periods of deflation. Look at your own home. Would you sell it today for the same price you paid for it three, eight, fifteen, or twenty-five years ago? Of course not. The same holds true for high-quality, income-producing real estate offered as an investment, such as office buildings, shopping centers, business warehouses, and apartments.

The best way to take advantage of owning this type of high-quality real estate, other than your own home, is through one of two forms. The first is the **limited partnership**, where syndicated managers now emphasize income-producing properties that will actually pay a quarterly check to investors. The use of mortgage debt is lower in these newer structures, and limited partners (the investors) are liable for only the amount of their initial investment. Minimum investments are usually only $2,500 per subscription, and the net worth requirements are minimal. There is also potential for capital appreciation if the properties in the partnership rise in value. These profits are usually split between the general and limited partners. One small disadvantage to a partnership is its limited liquidity. The investor must be patient and hold on for five to ten years before the properties are sold. The big advantage to this is that the investment is not listed on a major stock exchange, so it will not fluctuate in value if stock prices plummet.

Another form of ownership is the **real estate investment trusts** (REITs). These are funds that buy either mortgages on commercial properties or the actual buildings themselves. By law, REITs must pay out 95 percent of their earnings to shareholders. Income is paid in the form of quarterly dividends, which are fully taxable. There is potential for price appreciation if the value of underlying mortgages or actual properties rise in the open market. REITs are usually traded on the major exchanges, and thus provide liquidity for investors. The returns (yields) can be very competitive with other forms of income-producing investments.

As an investment planner, I would highly recommend you hold some type of real estate (other than your own home) in your portfolio. Even a large percentage of your portfolio invested in real estate can give your net worth a chance to increase during inflationary times. If you do not believe inflation will remain at 4 percent for the rest of your life, remember that real estate is one of the few investments that will gain in value during rising inflation, while other fixed assets, like bonds, CDs, and money-market accounts are guaranteed to lose their purchasing power.

LIFE INSURANCE AND ANNUITIES

Both of these vehicles got a reprieve from the Tax Reform Act of 1986. The cash values that build up inside of both investments are still tax deferred until withdrawn. Both investments are issued by life insurance companies, but they can also be purchased at a number of financial institutions. There are various ways to plan with each type.

Single Premium Deferred Annuity

In the single premium deferred annuity, income builds tax deferred until withdrawn, whereas the interest on most fixed-income investments is fully taxable whether it is compounded or taken in cash. As with other cash equivalents, both principal and interest are guaranteed. Annuities usually allow their owners to withdraw 10 percent of the accumulated interest each year without penalty but impose a declining surrender fee on the balance. Unfortunately, withdrawals from annuities before age 59½ are subject to ordinary income tax as well as a 10 percent government penalty. This type of investment will become more popular because it does not fluctuate in value, as do other investment vehicles.

Single Premium Whole Life

Single premium whole life can be a very versatile planning tool. Your principal is fully guaranteed by a major life insurance company and interest rates are very competitive. Cash values accumulate tax deferred inside the policy, and a special provision allows for low interest loans against the cash value. Another special feature is that death benefits pass directly to the beneficiary without any tax liability and without going through probate. This could help a widow pay off a home mortgage or help fund a college education for a child or grandchild.

OLD TAX SHELTERS

What if you are an investor who had bought a tax shelter back in the early 1980s? If you're lucky, you have already used up most of your deductions for tax saving purposes and are now looking to receive income from your holdings. Unfortunately, the 1986 tax law hurt this form of investing by phasing out the deductions that could be used against ordinary income. You have three choices at this point: hold, sell, or make a gift.

Holding that old tax shelter could turn out to be a blessing in disguise. Even though passive losses are deductible only up to the amount of passive income from other partnerships, it might pay to evaluate ways of using these losses (investment in new partnerships or other products). Take for example, an all-cash equipment leasing partnership. During the next decade, leasing will still be a very attractive method for financing capital equipment. An investment that will give inflation protection and pay a high return to investors will continue to thrive. Most importantly, passive income from this type of investment can be used to offset unusable passive losses from some of your old tax shelters.

Another alternative is to *sell* your old tax shelter. This is probably the least attractive of the three choices. Many tax shelters are not publicly traded. Even though some companies now buy old shelters, obtaining a fair price for them is next to impossible. Sometimes, a sale triggers phantom income from which recaptured taxes must be computed and paid. You may have to give back many of the tax benefits you previously took.

The third alternative is to *give* your old partnership interest to a favorite charity. This method can generate a charitable tax deduction well in excess of possible recapture and may exceed cash that a vulture company would pay you. Depending on the partnership and the net tax savings from the gift, this strategy could be very beneficial for you. Charities are interested in this type of gift because tax reform dealt a heavy blow to their fund-raising abilities. Even though they might prefer cash, charity officials can afford to hold onto tax-shelter interests because they do not have to pay tax on income or on any gains realized in the future. Charities also do not have to worry about passive income and losses, as you do. Approach a favorite charity if it would benefit you to make the gift.

THE MONEY MANAGEMENT MATRIX

One of the most useful tools to help investors understand the portfolio management process is a "money management matrix," which is shown in Table 19.2. This illustrates how various investments are divided into four easy to understand categories:

1. Cash and cash equivalents
2. Debt instruments
3. Equity investments
4. Special equity investments

By examining each category, you can determine the scope of your knowledge with each type of investment. The most conservative investments, ones with the lowest average returns and lowest risks, are listed to the far left in the cash and cash equivalent section. Conversely,

Table 19.2
Money Management Matrix

Inflation →

Cash and Cash Equivalents	Debt Instruments	Equity Investments	Special Equity Investments
Checking accounts	Government bonds:	Stocks:	Equipment leasing: (all cash Ltd Partnerships)
Savings accounts	Treasury bills (up to 1 year)	Blue Chip	
Money-market funds	Treasury Notes and Bonds (1 to 30 years)	Secondary (OTC)	Real estate:
Certificates of deposit	Zero Coupon Bonds	Foreign	Personal residence
Annuity savings plans	Government agency bonds:	Special Industry:	Rental property
Life insurance policies	FNMAs, GNMAs, etc. (up to 30 years)	Utilities	Apartments
		Auto	Office buildings
	Corporate bonds:	Technology	Shopping centers
	Straight	Stock mutual funds	(All cash/leverage)
	Convertible		(Ltd Partnerships/REITS)
	Municipal bonds:		Precious metals:
	State		Gold
	Local		Silver
	Zero Coupon		Platinum
	Bond mutual funds		(Stocks/mutual funds)
			Antiques:
			(Various collections)
Average Return: 5–9%	Average Return: 8–12%	Average Return: 12% +	Average Return: 12–15%

the most volatile investments, ones with the highest average returns and highest risks, appear in the special equity investments section to the far right.

You will also note the inflation line which appears in the middle of Table 19.2. Investments listed to the left are subject to erosion by inflation, while the ones to the right have tended to outperform inflation in the past. Once you understand how each investment reacts to various types of risks, you can then develop a comfort or preference level which leads to the selection of individual investments in each category.

It is important for you to develop an investment game plan by allocating a certain percentage of your available funds to each category. If you are working with a financial planner in selecting various investments, you should become part of the decision-making process so that you better understand the reasoning behind any recommendations.

Some planners will simply refuse to use this method because they either lose control of the selection-making process or find that it is too simple or too conservative. On the contrary, you are the person with the money to invest, and since you will make the ultimate decision on how *your* money will be spent, you have every right to choose the investments with which you will feel the most comfortable. *Never* feel pressured into making a decision which may not be to *your* benefit.

Likewise, if an experienced investor has a portfolio that has been built up over the years, I will offer to analyze it, too. An analysis will show how an existing portis divided in the various matrix categories. Based on current needs and future financial objectives, a strategy can be worked out to bring the existing portfolio in line with a current, updated plan. These clients often remark how the matrix concept has helped them to make even better decisions, and to overcome the poor recommendations given to them by brokers or other inexperienced advisors.

In summary, you as an investor can make tax and investment decisions that will benefit you. An experienced planner may also be able to help you by pointing out opportunities that you didn't know existed. If it isn't your full-time business to keep abreast of the ever-changing tax laws and their relationship to the world of investments, talking to someone whose business it is to do just that on a full-time basis will be of tremendous help in making important decisions. You might even save some undetected tax dollars, and that is a gain we would all welcome with a smile.

CHAPTER SUMMARY

1. Most tax shelters were created to encourage investment in segments of the American economy that otherwise might not attract investors.
2. A lowering of capital gains tax rates to a maximum of 19.6% will benefit both the individual investor and Uncle Sam. These tax changes will also make in-and-out trading more popular.
3. Corporate and government bonds are still subject to

federal income taxes, but most municipal bonds are still exempt from all federal taxes.

4. The best way to take advantage of owning real estate is through the limited partnership and real estate investment trusts (REITs).

5. Both life insurance and annuities got a boost from the 1986 tax law. The cash values that build up inside of either investment are tax-deferred until withdrawn. Hopefully, tax laws won't change to eliminate this special benefit.

6. If you have an old tax shelter that is no longer profitable because of the revised tax laws, you have three choices: hold it, sell it, or give it away. Making a gift to charity may be the most lucrative option, but each one needs to be examined carefully to see whether it will benefit you.

7. Be sure to work out your investment program logically. Have your investment planner divide your funds into areas that will work to achieve your objectives. To avoid high risks, never put all your eggs into one basket—use diversification.

Practical Application: In order to aid investors in understanding the latest in tax law changes, this author will conduct educational seminars for interested groups or associations. Please contact the author for specific details (see Epilogue).

20

SPECIAL INVESTMENT STRATEGIES FOR SENIOR CITIZENS

If you are a senior citizen, you may live a longer, healthier life in the 1990s than your parents did in their retirement. So it's vitally important for you to get the most out of your financial resources. This will give you the freedom to make the choices you want to make. If you are also retired, you know how important retirement planning can be in establishing a comfortable and secure financial base.

Many retired Americans want to get the most out of life through community service, family involvement, and travel. In order to have the freedom to make these choices, you must make certain that your assets will produce enough income to give you both financial freedom and a comfortable lifestyle. These assets should also be structured to outlast your lifespan. For these reasons, post-retirement planning is just as or even more important than pre-retirement planning.

Prior to the Tax Reform Act of 1986, retirement planning for senior citizens was pretty straightforward. Medical expenses were fully deductible as itemized deductions on Schedule A of Form 1040, and Social Security benefits were tax-free to the recipient. But because of changes directly affecting itemized deductions and Social Security, senior citizens living on a fixed income in the 1990s will probably see their taxes increase and their net spendable income decrease.

One way to maintain or even increase net spendable income is to invest for tax-free income. With careful post-retirement planning, you may be able to lower your adjusted gross income to get the most out of itemized deductions, reduce your tax on Social Security benefits, and lower your federal and state income taxes in order to have more spendable income. There are several ways tax-free investing can work for your benefit.

THE SOCIAL SECURITY TAX

Many senior citizens have misconceptions about the taxation of Social Security benefits. They mistakenly believe that municipal bond income is taxed and investors would pay less tax on Social Security if they were not receiving tax-free income.

But, municipal bond income is not subject to federal income taxes, especially if it comes from a portfolio of professionally managed securities. And under no circumstances do retirees pay more taxes on Social Security benefits because they earn money from tax-exempt securities.

The law is set up so that certain retirees have to pay taxes on up to one-half of their Social Security benefits. It doesn't matter whether the income comes from taxable or nontaxable investments. The current rules are that, when "modified adjusted gross income" (total amount subject to taxation) exceeds $25,000 for single individuals or $32,000 for couples filing a joint return, Social Security benefits start to become taxable.

To determine the amount of your taxable Social Security benefits, use the lesser of Formula 1 or Formula 2 (see Table 20.1). The lower taxable amount used from one of these formulas is added to other taxable income and taxed at the investor's regular federal tax rate.

Some investors can lower the taxable portion of their Social Security benefits, plus earn more after-tax income, by switching from taxable to tax-free investment comprised of municipal bonds. The example in Table 20.2 shows how this works for a Medicare-eligible retiree filing a joint return.

Table 20.1

Formula 1
   Social Security benefits ÷ 2 = amount taxable

Formula 2
   Adjusted gross income
   plus tax-free income
   plus 1/2 Social Security benefits
   less base amount ÷ 2 = amount taxable
   The base amount is $32,000 for a joint return, $25,000 for a single return.

Source: John Nuveen & Co., Inc.

323

Table 20.2

Investor profile:

$100,000 to invest
$12,500 Social Security benefits
$29,000 other income (excluding $100,000 to invest)
$5,600 in deductions and exemptions

Investor choices (hypothetical yields):

9.00%	Taxable long-term bond:	$9,000 per year
7.25%	Tax-free municipals:	$7,250 per year

Adjusted gross taxable income:

Taxable bond:	$29,000 + $9,000 = $38,000
Tax-free municipals:	$29,000 + $0 = $29,000

	Taxable Investment	Tax-free Municipals
Other income	$29,000	$29,000
Taxable investment income	+9,000	None
Social Security benefits taxed (using Formula 2, Figure 20.1)	+6,125	+5,250
Adjusted gross income	**$44,125**	**$34,250**
(less deductions, exemptions)	−5,600	−5,600
Taxable income	**$38,525** **(28% Bracket)**	**$28,650** **(15% Bracket)**
(less federal income tax)	−6,764	−4,298
(plus tax-free income)	None	+7,250
After-tax income	**$31,761**	**$31,602**

Source: John Nuveen & Co., Inc.

As you can see from this example, tax-free municipal bonds yield more spendable income. And with tax-free income, the retiree pays taxes on only $5,250 of Social Security benefits, compared to paying taxes on $6,125. Also, compare the bottom-line benefits of these taxable versus tax-free investments. In this example tax-free income

1. lowers the amount of Social Security benefits taxed,
2. lowers the federal tax bracket from 28 percent to 15 percent, and
3. lowers federal taxes by $2,466.

Thus, with tax-free investing, your tax bill shrinks and your tax bracket goes down.

PORTFOLIOS FOR GROWTH AND INCOME

Senior citizens, just like younger adults, have special needs based on their ages and financial situations. The responsibility to invest funds wisely does not end at the time of retirement. On the contrary, it will continue to present a challenge as we enter the decade of the 1990s. Seniors must invest not only to preserve capital but to generate income they cannot outlive, while at the same time creating capital growth as a hedge against future inflation. Knowledge and experience will go a long way in helping to monitor financial stability during retirement. In order to illustrate some successful techniques, there follow some actual examples of clients who made wise decisions and are now benefiting from diversified asset management in their portfolios.

Case 1—Retired married couple, husband 79, wife 78. This couple first came to me in 1983 for counseling concerning their portfolio. The husband had been one of the top executives at a major St. Louis corporation. His wife also had business experience, mainly as a secretary. Both were retired and wanted to diversify their portfolio to generate more income and security. The husband had already done an outstanding job in building up a portfolio of individual stocks and bonds worth over $400,000. Since he had some extra cash to invest, he wanted to round out their portfolio with some high-quality mutual funds, special equities, and tax advantaged investments.

Over the past seven years, we have invested in a number of these vehicles, have made some switches in the portfolio to adjust for economic conditions, and have both reinvested dividends from some investments while taking cash income from some other ones. Their special portfolio is currently allocated as follows:

	Percent
Fixed Annuity Savings Plan	19.3
U. S. Government Mutual Funds	9.3
Convertible Bond Fund	15.5
Missouri Insured Municipal Trust	5.0
Growth and Income Fund	12.2

	Percent
Growth Stock Fund	14.0
Real Estate Investment Trust	7.6
Equipment Leasing Limited Partnership	17.1
	100.0

As you can see, the portfolio is divided into eight different vehicles, with heavy emphasis on income and security. The average yield from the income investments is 9 percent, while the growth investments have increased in value by 25 percent. Despite stock and bond market volatility over the past 7 years, the portfolio is performing admirably and should continue to do well entering the 1990s. Should their circumstances warrant future changes, this successful couple is in a position to withdraw more cash or make other flexible moves with a minimum of costs involved.

Case 2—Pre-retired executive (62) and wife (54). This couple first came to me in August 1986 with funds to invest for both themselves (at the time both were three years younger) and their two children, aged 17 and 13. The main objective of the family at that time was growth of principal to meet future retirement and educational (college) needs. The executive planned to retire at age 65 and was already contributing to an IRA account, along with his regular company pension plan.

He had received about $100,000 from the sale of an individual stock, and we invested these funds as follows:

	Percent
Treasury Reserve Account	25
Fixed Annuity Savings Plan	15
Convertible Bond Fund	15
Municipal Bond Fund	10
Growth and Income Fund	10
Growth Stock Fund	15
International Equities Fund	10
	100

As initially structured, this portfolio featured 40 percent security (Treasury Reserve and Annuity), 25 percent tax-advantaged (Annuity and Municipal Bond Fund), 25 percent growth and income (Convertible, Growth and Income Fund), and 25 percent growth (Growth Stock Fund and International Equities Fund). Despite stock and bond market volatility over the last three years, this portfolio has grown 30 percent in value.

Recently, this couple decided to liquidate three of the investments (Convertible, Municipal, and International Funds) and reinvest for higher income and security. We added three new investments to the portfolio which included a High Yield Bond Fund (rated BUY by Morningstar Value Services), a U. S. Government Bond Fund; and a special Fixed Annuity Savings Plan guaranteeing 8.3 percent for 3 years, with a special interest rate bailout clause over 6 years. The initial amount allocated to treasury reserves has been used for other purposes, so the revised portfolio structure now appears as follows:

	Percent
Equities	37.8
Corporate Bonds	12.2
Government Bonds	15.5
Annunity Savings Plans	34.5
	100.0

As the executive (now 62) approaches retirement, he will have more income and security, decrease his exposure to the volatile equity market, and increase emphasis on tax deferred benefits.

The children's assets were set up in 1986 under the Uniform Gift to Minor's Act (custodial accounts) and were composed of growth and income mutual funds. Unfortunately, the stock market crash of 1987 hurt the overall performance of these investments, and the client subsequently liquidated most of them at a breakeven point. However, we will see in the next case how "patience can be a virtue" and that sticking to quality investments, even during difficult times, can be rewarding.

Case 3—Retired executive (65) with IRA rollover. In 1985, this individual came to me with approximately $125,000 in taxable cash distributions from his company's retirement plan. In order to postpone the payment of taxes for as long as possible, we decided to roll over the entire amount into two different IRA Accounts. The portfolio, designed for growth and income, was structured as follows:

	Percent
Zero Coupon Government Bonds	16.4
Individual Stocks	4.1
Option Income Fund	40.5
Growth Stock Fund	15.5
Convertible Bond Fund	15.5
Real Estate Limited Partnership	8.0
	100.0

A self-directed IRA account was established to purchase the zero coupon government bonds, individual stocks, and all-cash, real-estate limited partnership. One mutual fund family was used to purchase the three types of funds listed above.

Despite the stock market crash of 1987, this portfolio

has shown outstanding results. As of October 1989, the status of the account was as follows:

Security	Cost	Current Value	Unrealized Gain (Loss)
Gators—Gov 0 Coupon Bds 11.9 percent due 5/91 Maturity value = $40,375	$20,168	$35,075	$14,907
Global Marine— stocks & wts	5,000	216	(4,784)
Money Market Fund	—	1,023	—
Real Estate Ltd. Partnership	10,000	10,000	—
Option Income Fund	50,000	48,521	(1,479)
Growth Stock Fund	19,053	63,385	44,332
Convertible Bond Fund	19,053	46,888	27,835
	$123,274	$205,108	$81,834

By not panicking after the crash and remaining confident that his selections would perform well over time, this gentleman has been rewarded with a 66.4 percent increase in the value of this portfolio.

In order to protect against a possible recession in the early 1990s, we decided to further diversify the portfolio, lock in some of its appreciated value, and take advantage of a possible decline in interest rates. Therefore, we executed the following changes:

1. Since the Option Income Fund did not perform up to our expectations and its outlook remained grim, we sold these shares and reinvested the proceeds ($48,521) to achieve more income and security:

   $18,521 into a U. S. Government Securities Fund (10 percent yield).
   $15,000 into a Real Estate Investment Trust (12 percent yield).
   $15,000 into an Equipment Leasing Income Partnership (12.5 percent yield).
2. The Growth Stock Fund has done an outstanding job and is expected to continue to do so in the 1990s. However, past performance is no guarantee of future results, and the fund could be highly volatile in a U. S. recession. Therefore, we took $22,000 out of $63,385 and diversified into a leading foreign stock fund in order to take advantage of worldwide economic growth in the 1990s.
3. The Convertible Fund has also done well and should continue to show positive returns as reflected in both the stock and bond markets. But again, no one has a crystal ball and can guarantee that this will happen. Therefore, we took $25,000 out of $46,888 and diver-

sified into a leading income fund composed of both government and high-quality corporate bonds.

By making these changes, the portfolio was modified as follows:

	Percent of Portfolio	Percent of Yield
Zero Coupon Government Bonds	17.0	11.9
U. S. Government and High Grade Corporate Bonds	21.3	9.5
Convertible Bond Fund	10.6	11.1TR
U. S. Common Stock Fund	20.0	20.8TR*
Foreign Stock Fund	10.7	25.1TR*
Real Estate (LP and REIT)	12.1	**
Equipment Leasing Limited Partnership	7.3	12.5†
Miscellaneous—individual stocks and money market	1.0 100.0	††

*TR = average annual total return (yield + price appreciation) over the last four years.
**The old real estate LP currently has no yield, but the new real estate investment trust will guarantee a 12 percent yield for the first two years.
†The goal of the equipment leasing limited partnership, although not guaranteed, is to pay 12.5 percent per year for five years and then to return all invested capital during years 6–8 when partnership assets are liquidated.
††The money market account is used to accumulate dividends and pay a yearly maintenance fee for the self-directed IRA Account.

In summary, this account is now structured for more safety and less volatility. Income from the special equity investments will continue to accumulate tax-deferred in the IRA. There will be more security with the increase in U. S. Government Bonds, yet an opportunity for more capital appreciation with the ownership of foreign equities. The profits which were generated as a result of our changes are all tax-deferred in the IRA. Income can be taken at any time the client wishes to do so, but must begin when he turns age 70½. We will continue to monitor results in the 1990s and to be in a position to make further changes should economic or personal circumstances warrant them.

CHARITABLE GIVING

Many seniors would like to make a gift to their favorite charity or nonprofit organization, but are deterred by their need for spendable income. If you are in this situation, you can make your gift and still collect tax-free income for life by establishing a charitable remainder trust (CRT) and funding it with tax-free investments. A lifetime flow of tax-free income for the donor can provide more spendable dollars than a gift of taxable securities. Because you continue receiving the income that your assets generate, the cost of making your gift with a CRT is generally lower than the cost of making a straight cash contribution.

Here's how a CRT can work for your benefit.

¶ When you transfer assets to a CRT, they are split into an income interest and a remainder interest. The income interest is paid to you (and/or other beneficiaries of your choice) on a regular basis for life. The remainder interest is held by the trust and passes to the charity or non-profit organization when the trust expires at your death.

¶ When a trust is funded with municipal bonds, tax-free unit trusts, or tax-exempt mutual funds, the interest income paid out by the trust can be tax free. These checks can be paid out on a monthly, quarterly, or semi-annual basis, whatever you desire.

¶ When you establish a CRT, you are also entitled to an immediate income-tax deduction based on the discounted value (remainder interest) of your gift. (Your legal or tax advisor can determine what this deduction will be, based on tables from the U.S. Treasury Department.)

Generally speaking, you come out ahead when making a gift through a CRT rather than making one with cash. Also, you have a choice of two types of trusts to use, the Charitable Remainder Annuity or the Charitable Remainder Unit Trust. You may wish to explore the benefits of both types of trusts with your legal or tax advisor before making your gift.

LOCKED INTO HIGHLY APPRECIATED ASSETS
Many retired people would like to unlock the value of their estate, but feel they are "locked in" to the ownership of appreciated assets, such as securities or real estate. They are reluctant to sell these assets to increase cash flow or diversify because they fear large capital

gains taxes, which currently run as high as 28 percent. Also, because traditional tax-shelter investments are under close IRS scrutiny, their tax benefits are limited under the new tax laws. As if these problems weren't enough, federal and state death taxes can consume more than 55 percent of family assets.

A popular solution to this problem, which will be used even more in the 1990s, is to make a gift of the appreciated asset to a Charitable Remainder Trust (CRT). This method unlocks appreciated property and provides additional tax and investment benefits to the donor as follows.

1. Because the trust is considered a tax-qualified charitable organization, it can sell appreciated assets and reinvest the proceeds into a more secure, diversified portfolio without paying capital gains taxes.
2. An immediate income-tax charitable deduction is generated by the gift to the CRT, and this gift also provides for significant death-tax savings.
3. It keeps these assets free from creditors' claims and increases spendable cash flow for new investments to be determined by the seller.

The trust is created to provide lifetime payments to the seller and/or other family members with the remainder, upon death, eventually payable to favorite charitable organizations. The lifetime payments may be in the form of an annual annuity usually equal to a fixed percentage (at least 5 percent) of the fair market value of the assets given to the trust, or in the form of a variable annual payment equal to a percentage (at least 5 percent) of the trust value each year. The creator's personal tax advisor must assist in making the computations for each particular situation. Finally, it is essential that an attorney be consulted, and that he or she approve any legal instrument before executing.

CHAPTER SUMMARY

1. Many senior citizens want to get the most out of their golden years. To do this, they must get the most out of their financial resources.
2. Retirement planning used to be pretty straightforward. But as a result of recent tax legislation, many senior citizens today will probably see their taxes increase and their spendable income decrease.
3. There are many misconceptions about the taxation of Social Security benefits. But municipal bond income is not subject to federal taxation, and retirees do not pay more taxes on Social Security benefits because they earn money from tax-exempt securities.
4. Portfolios should be structured to meet the individual needs of each retiree. Some desire growth, others income, and yet others a combination of the two.
5. Sources of income at retirement may come from years of personal portfolio accumulation, the sale of a major asset, or a company pension distribution.
6. The income generated in a retirement account,

whether subject to immediate taxation or tax-deferred within an IRA rollover, should come from conservative investments designed for security and low volatility.

7. A charitable remainder trust (CRT) can be utilized to generate tax-free income for the life of the donor when funded with municipal bonds.

8. A CRT can also be used to unlock the value of highly appreciated assets, thus avoiding a big tax liability for the donor.

Practical Application: This author frequently speaks to senior citizen groups on solving their financial problems. If interested, please contact the author for specific details (see Epilogue).

21

ESTATE PLANNING—PRESERVING YOUR ASSETS

You've spent a lifetime acquiring various possessions to further the cause of life, liberty, and the pursuit of happiness. Perhaps you own a home, an automobile, a recreational vehicle such as a boat or a motorcycle, a musical instrument, a coin collection, or an assortment of books and various other items that have value to you. If you couldn't care less what happened to your worldly possessions (not to mention your money) when you die, then you may not need a will. But most people who fall into this category have precious little to bequeath anyway. On the other hand, if there are people in your life whom you would like to receive any or all of your property upon your death, you need a will. This is something you must get when you don't need it, because by the time that you realize your car is going off the cliff or a bus is about to run you over, it will be too late to act.

MAJOR AND MINOR POSSESSIONS
Of course you want your spouse, child, or parent to inherit your home and other major possessions. But what

about your musical instrument, coin collection, and assortment of books, in which your child or parent may have no interest? Perhaps your cousin, who is a book collector, would be pleased to inherit your library. Although your next-of-kin may not be at all musically inclined, your good friend and neighbor down the street might feel gratified indeed to receive your guitar, once he or she knew that you were finished with it permanently. Perhaps a young niece or nephew would delight in receiving a collection of coins that were minted years before even his or her parents were born. If you leave it up to the state to decide, your immediate next-of-kin might receive and liquidate these possessions at fire-sale prices just to be rid of them.

If you want your property to go exactly to the people you want to receive it, you must have a will that details your desires. Otherwise, Uncle Sam may decide for you.

STATE LAWS

Unfortunately, many people feel that state laws will adequately provide for proper disposition of their properties. For example, a married person may believe his or her spouse will automatically inherit his or her possessions. Actually, state laws vary. Some states provide for distribution of a decedent's property among his or her spouse and children. This could become a financial problem for the spouse, if he or she is responsible for supporting minor children. The surviving spouse's share of the estate can be consumed by the purchase of essentials for the surviving family, while the children's property might remain tied up in a guardianship until they attain legal age (usually 18 or 21 years of age), at which time they may dispose of the property in any way they see fit—on a college education or a frivolous life in the fast lane.

On the other hand, some states permit spouses to inherit any and all property. This may or may not be in the children's best interests, especially if the deceased had children from a previous marriage. The surviving spouse would be under no obligation to distribute any of the funds to the children, whether they be his or her own or from the deceased spouse's prior marriage. As a result, any plans you may have had for your children, such as college, fall totally into the hands of your spouse, who may or may not share your plans.

Even if state-mandated asset disposition meets with your approval, if you and your spouse die simultaneously, such as in an automobile accident or house fire, your asset distribution is divided among your next-of-kin, including family members whom you may or may not want to inherit your goods. Furthermore, your minor children will be appointed wards of the state, and a guardian will be assigned. This guardian may or may not be someone you would select yourself, and could be someone with whom the children themselves wouldn't prefer to reside.

If you're married, have no children, are both fatally injured in a car crash, and neither one of you has a will, state laws again come into play. The property owned by the first to die very likely will pass to the survivor, even though he or she may only survive by minutes. Then the family of the second spouse stands to inherit the entire estate, and the family of the first spouse inherits nothing.

To illustrate the heartbreak that dying without a will may cause in certain circumstances, consider the case of a bachelor who died intestate (without a will). His closest survivors were his sister and mother, who counted on her son for financial support. Other survivors included four half-siblings from a marriage between the bachelor's father and a woman for whom the father had abandoned his first family. As a result, the bachelor and his father, also dead, had experienced a falling-out. Consequently, there was never any type of caring relationship between the bachelor and his half-siblings. The law of the state specified that half-siblings were entitled to as much of a deceased's estate as full siblings. As a result, the bachelor's assets were divided among his five siblings, each of whom received one-seventh of his estate, and his mother, who received only two-sevenths. This unfortunate distribution of property could have been avoided had the bachelor taken the time and trouble to draw up a will.

Death is not something that most people enjoy thinking about, especially when they or their loved ones are dying. But an even worse thought is that your loved ones will suffer financially as well as emotionally upon your death. With a will, a person can die in peace (as much as that is possible) knowing that his or her spouse, minor children, parents, and siblings will be provided for in the manner he or she would prefer, and that his or her property will go to those people or organizations that he or she personally selects.

Spare your loved ones the hassle of fighting over your property. Make sure they're provided for as you see fit. After all, it's your property, and you are entitled to have some say over it.

GENERAL POWER OF ATTORNEY

A power of attorney is a legal document naming another person to act on your behalf in business or financial matters when you know you will be away. This document should be drawn up as part of your estate plan. It becomes useless, however, if you become incapacitated. Therefore, it does not guard against life's unpredictable setbacks. In order to protect yourself more fully, you need a durable power of attorney.

DURABLE POWER OF ATTORNEY

Even if you have a will, a durable power of attorney (DPA) is an important legal document. It enables you to name the person or persons you want to handle your affairs in case you are unable to do so because of serious illness, incompetence, disappearance, or even kidnapping. While a will defines how matters will be handled in the event of death, the DPA becomes effective immediately or at the time of disability. It remains in effect as long as you live, unless you decide to revoke it.

For example, many people have found themselves handling the affairs of elderly parents. Through a DPA, the parents can appoint the person of their choice to sign checks, buy and sell securities, or even run a business should they become disabled. If a person becomes disabled without a DPA, the court will appoint the person who will be in charge of the affairs of the disabled person. The danger here is that the court could select a person other than the one that the incapacitated person may have selected. The most often named are trusted relatives, friends, or the family lawyer. Likewise, you can protect yourself by choosing a backup person just in case your first choice becomes incapacitated.

A DPA can also provide

1. a means for handling tax-related matters;
2. income and maintenance for the grantor's dependents;
3. the transfer and management of stocks, bonds, personal property, real estate, and commodity or options transactions;
4. the right to enter the grantor's safe-deposit box;
5. the power to continue litigation for the grantor;
6. the power to make decisions concerning housing, physical care, the payment of medical bills, and business decisions in the case of a closely held business.

THE GOVERNMENT WILL GET ITS SHARE
Even though it is your property, Uncle Sam will want what he feels is rightfully his. But federal inheritance laws give people with small to average estates a break. Starting in 1987, a person may bequeath an estate of up to $600,000 without being subject to inheritance taxes.

This amount is subject to change by Congress at any time in the future. The estate may be left to anyone or any organization the benefactor chooses. Estate taxes generally do apply to the portions of estates valued above $600,000, unless these are sheltered by such vehicles as marital or charitable deductions.

While $600,000 is a long way from an insignificant figure, that figure can be quickly reached when some estates are totaled. Consider the value of a home, other property such as a vacation home or rental property, and the value of various investments, all subject to increases in value because of inflation. In addition, life insurance proceeds may be included in the taxable estate, as well as wrongful death benefits, which are payable to the estate of a person whose death is caused by another's negligence. The combined worth of these holdings may easily surpass $600,000.

If you have such an estate or if you plan to amass one in your lifetime, you probably would like to find a way to leave as much of your assets to your heirs as possible.

A person may bequeath his or her entire estate to a spouse without being subject to federal estate taxes unless the spouse is not a U.S. citizen. So many people whose spouses are still alive believe that they don't need a will. But if both spouses die simultaneously the state determines who their heirs are and how much each will receive after appropriate taxes are deducted. So protect your estate through estate planning. In addition to maintaining an updated will, you might want to check out a number of trusts designed to protect your property from unnecessary taxes.

BYPASS TRUSTS

Suppose you are married, have two children and own an estate valued at $1 million. In the event that you are the first in your family to die, you might prefer for your estate to go to your spouse and, after the spouse's death, to your children without having a considerable amount of estate taxes taken from it.

A "bypass" or "family" trust can accomplish this end. Taking effect upon the founder's death, this trust may include a maximum of $600,000 worth of assets and still totally avoid estate taxation. The surviving spouse may receive all, part, or none of the income generated by the trust, depending on the desires of the founder. The spouse also may be entitled to some of the principal in the trust, as much as 5 percent or $5,000 per year, whichever is greater, without jeopardizing the tax benefits. The trust continues to exist until the spouse dies. At that point the trust dissolves, and its assets are distributed to recipients designated in the founder's will.

With this arrangement, you can provide for your surviving spouse's needs and still protect the assets for your children or other beneficiaries. The trust assets are not subject to inclusion in your spouse's taxable estate; they have effectively escaped taxation in both estates. In addition, the remainder of your spouse's estate, which might consist of the $400,000 remaining from a $1 million estate after $600,000 had been placed in trust also completely escapes taxation, because it does not exceed the separate $600,000 exemption. This bypass trust still permits the passing of $1,200,000 through the estates of both spouses without the imposition of any federal estate tax. The bypass trust also is an ideal place to put assets that are likely to appreciate in value, because they will not be subject to federal estate taxes on the death of the surviving spouse.

MARITAL DEDUCTION TRUSTS

Instead of bequeathing the remaining $400,000 directly to your spouse, you could form a marital deduction trust, which requires that all trust income be paid to the spouse. This type of trust might be favored by someone whose spouse is a poor money manager. Such an arrangement also protects the source of income in the event of remarriage: With this trust, the new spouse cannot abscond with the trust funds.

There are two types of marital deduction trusts. One is a general power of appointment trust. A person who establishes such a trust for his or her spouse allows the spouse to determine who will ultimately receive the trust assets upon his or her death. The other type is a qualified terminable interest property trust (QTIP), a fairly new creature of statute. With this trust, the founder selects the beneficiary who will inherit the trust assets upon the death of the spouse. Such trusts are popular with parents of children from a previous marriage. The QTIP trust provides for a spouse while preserving the principal for the founder's children or other selected beneficiaries. With this trust, the surviving spouse has absolutely no control over the assets and cannot prevent their eventual distribution to the beneficiaries selected by the founder.

GENERATION-SKIPPING TRUSTS

Suppose that your spouse is already dead or, at least, out of your plans for post-life disposition of your assets. Perhaps you have children for whom you'd like to provide, but you know that in the hands of your spendthrift children, the family fortune is likely to decay before you do. If this adequately describes your situation, you might resort to a generation-skipping trust. With this trust, a child or children receive the income from the trust while the assets remain protected. When the child or children die, the assets go to the founder's grandchild or grandchildren. In larger estates, substantial estate tax savings can be achieved by the use of such vehicles, because these assets can totally escape taxation in the children's generation. Remember, the marginal (highest) estate tax rate is currently 55 percent and is not scheduled to drop below 50 percent in the near future.

LIVING TRUSTS

When an estate is set for disposition, the process of probate (determining whether the will is valid and inventorying the assets) can take months, if not years. In the meantime, the heirs do not get possession of bequeathed property. Furthermore, probate costs and legal fees can require as much as 5 percent of a $200,000 estate. With smaller estates, the percentage can be even greater.

If you wish to avoid the costs and delays of probate, you may establish a living trust. This trust takes effect immediately, in contrast to the testamentary trust described above, which does not take effect until death. The founder of the trust can transfer his or her property to the trust, act as trustee, receive any or all income produced by the trust, and dissolve the trust, if he or she so desires. Upon the founder's death, the trust can remain active, generating income for the founder's beneficiaries, or the trust can be dissolved and the assets divided among the beneficiaries, depending on the desires of the founder.

There are two types of living trusts: revocable and irrevocable. With a revocable trust, a founder can change his or her mind about the disposition of assets at any point in time. For example, a revocable living trust founder who has provided for someone to receive the trust assets upon his or her death could simply amend or dissolve the trust if he or she decides to dispose of the assets in a different manner. Of course, the founder would still have complete control over trust assets and income, and would be taxed according to his or her marginal individual tax rate upon receiving the trust income. Remember, the value of the trust assets remains fully subject to estate tax upon the founder's death.

With the irrevocable living trust, property placed in trust must remain there. Once the beneficiaries of such a trust are named, they can't be disinherited. Assuming no retention of income or other incidents of ownership, an irrevocable living trust founder isn't taxed on property placed in such a trust, because it has been removed from the founder's control and, thus, his or her estate. Hence, income can be effectively shifted to lower-bracket taxpayers, such as children or dependent parents, and estate taxes can be avoided.

If your estate is large enough to be taxed significantly, you might consider an irrevocable living trust, because it offers both probate and estate-tax avoidance benefits. If it isn't, a revocable living trust may be to your advantage, because you can maintain control over its assets, retain all income and lifetime benefits, and still escape a probate administration of all trust assets upon your death.

GIFTS

If all else fails, you may give your money away. A person may give up to $10,000 per year (or $20,000 annually, with consent of a spouse) to each of his or her children, nieces, nephews, siblings, or even family friends. This is a terrific way to reduce your taxable income and minimize estate taxes while gaining favor with the recipients.

A competent financial planner can review your estate's value and inform you as to whether such a strategy would be of as much benefit to you as it would be to your recipients. After all, depending on your estate, you may not get to keep it anyway. If it doesn't go to your loved ones, it might go to Uncle Sam.

The few dollars you invest in a planner's fee may be recouped dozens of times over in what you leave behind. Remember, you must always contact a qualified attorney to draw up your will and help advise you in estate matters. Oftentimes, the attorney and the financial planner will work together to draw up the best estate plan for your particular situation.

CHAPTER SUMMARY

1. Wills are good for distribution not only of major possessions, but of minor possessions as well—possessions that may be of intangible value to people who would love to have them.
2. If you leave distribution of your assets to the state, they may be distributed to people you wouldn't want to have them. If you have minor children and they are orphaned, the state may place them with a guardian of whom neither you nor the children approve.
3. Although the government allows a person to bequeath the first $600,000 of his or her estate tax free, people with estates of greater value must take precautions to minimize, if not eliminate, the tax consequences of dying. Some precautions include bypass trusts, marital deduction trusts, generation-skipping trusts, and revocable and irrevocable living trusts.
4. A person can reduce his or her taxable income by giving money to heirs. A person may give away up to $10,000 per year to each of his or her children,

nephews, nieces, siblings, parents, or friends, without reducing the $600,000 estate tax exemption.

5. Don't let the government inherit your estate. If the value of your estate significantly exceeds the tax-free limit of $600,000, consult a financial planner and/or attorney to draw up a plan that would best suit your needs and the needs of your heirs.

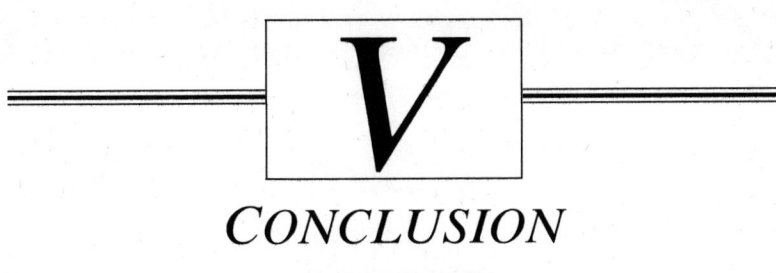

CONCLUSION

22

TAKING ACTION TO BE SUCCESSFUL IN THE 1990S

Imagine long-term Treasury bonds yielding 6 percent or the Dow Jones Industrial Average crossing 5,000 within five years. Practically applied, you can make an excellent case that this will happen, if not within five years at least sometime during the 1990s.

Demographic, political, and economic factors converging in the next decade could lead to sharply lower interest rates. For example, the baby-boom generation, 76 million strong, will get older and become more conservative. They will spend less and save more in order to educate their children and grandchildren, and to plan for retirement. Because the bulk of their house-buying will be behind them, the demand for new mortgage loans will drop. The additional savings means that more money will be available for fewer loans, which could lead to lower interest rates and lower inflation.

This excess savings will find its way into U.S. government securities, as will the burgeoning surpluses in the Social Security trust fund. This will be a bonanza for bondholders, with very positive effects for stock buyers as well. However, if there is a recession during the 1990s, the holders of lower-rated junk bonds may be in for a real disaster.

To cash in on plunging interest rates, the safest investments will be long-term Treasury bonds, assuming they meet your specific objectives. For example, if you are 55 years old and know you will need cash to buy a retirement house when you turn 65, you might buy a U.S. government bond fund or zero-coupon government bonds with an average maturity of only 10 years.

Generally speaking, in planning for the next decade, you will find that the longer the bond maturity, the bigger will be your total return. If you buy a 10-year bond yielding 9 percent, and five years from now rates have dropped to 5 percent, your average annual total return would be nearly 14 percent. However, if you buy a 30-year bond, the average return would be much higher at 21 percent per year.

What about the equity markets? As bond yields decline, stock prices will zoom as the cost of borrowing drops for businesses. This means rising corporate earnings and higher dividend payments to stockholders. So investors will realize there are better total returns in the equity markets.

With the decline in the number of shares available resulting from leveraged buyouts, and companies repurchasing their own shares in the open markets, more demand for fewer shares from both institutions and individuals will push stock prices much higher for quality, blue-chip issues. Foreign investors will also add fuel to the fire as they view the U.S. stock market as being grossly undervalued. Therefore, the Dow Jones Industrial Average could easily hit 5,000 by 1995.

To get yourself in a position to benefit from the trends of the 1990s, you can structure your portfolio with an asset allocation model (see Chapter 9). This combines only the highest quality investments in the areas of cash, fixed-income, equities, and special equities.

CAUSE FOR OPTIMISM

We are constantly being bombarded with negative stories through the news media. If we are not careful, these can actually have a negative effect on our way of thinking and on how we conduct our daily lives. Not excluded from all this chaos are events that take place in the financial community, such as the Ivan Boesky scandal and the Michael Milliken junk-bond debacle.

Despite fears that the market's historic reversal in October 1987 would tip the U.S. into a recession, as of today's writing, the economy remains very strong. In fact, there's been a lot of good news which the media has not told us about lately. It's time for hesitant investors to look around and marvel at what's been taking place in our dynamic economy.

¶ Corporate profits are surprisingly good. In fact, estimated 1988 earnings for the S&P 500 were up 37 percent over 1987.
¶ Dividends are expected to grow a healthy 10 percent per year over the next decade.

¶ Stocks are much better bargains today. The current price-earnings ratio for the S&P 500 (based on estimated 1988 results) is 11.5, well below the 1957–1987 average of 14.

¶ Interest rates are currently in the 9 to 10 percent range, down from 18 to 19 percent in the early 1980s.

¶ Faith in American enterprise is being renewed. Real gross business and personal investment has risen more than 30 percent since 1981.

¶ The federal budget deficit, despite what everyone thinks, has fallen sharply. It was running at about $150 billion in fiscal 1988, down from $215 billion in 1985.

¶ The trade deficit is also better than anticipated. It's expected to shrink to roughly $140 billion in the early 1990s down from $170 billion in 1987.

¶ The price of oil (as of this writing) has dropped dramatically. It's now $18 a barrel, down from nearly $34 a barrel in early 1981.

¶ We are currently witnessing peace and prosperity. The largest arms reduction treaty in history was signed by Reagan and Gorbachev in 1987.

¶ American industry is running at 83.5 percent of capacity as of July 1988, the highest level since March 1980.

¶ The "Rust Belt" has become the site of economic revitalization in industrial America. For example, the steel industry cut operating costs 35 percent

while boosting labor productivity 38 percent since 1982.
¶ Renewed competitiveness of American manufacturers in export markets has led to a healthy upswing in nearly every sector of manufacturing.
¶ The ownership of common stock among individuals and corporate pension funds is lower than at any other time over the last quarter century. This may set the stage for a huge upswing in stock prices as investors begin to move back into the market.

These are some of the reasons that a few years from now stocks of many strong, growing companies may be much higher than they are today!

THE PRESENT

Whether you read this book in 1990, 1991, or even 1992, does not make any difference. Where we are and what we are doing with our lives will still be the same. Everyone will continue to strive for more comfortable lives and to take advantage of our democratic system. We have been blessed by being able to live in a land of such great opportunities and to better ourselves through hard work.

But along with these advantages come disadvantages. More freedom to enjoy life means more spending on consumer goods and services. This leads to a demand for higher wages which results in higher prices. In order to enjoy living in our great country during the 1990s, we must pay for the privilege. This makes it a must for every perceptive American to plan for the future.

PLANNING LEADS TO SUCCESS

Financial planning is just the first step. The person who fails to plan is heading for disaster, but many people who do plan still fail because they postpone putting their plans into practice.

A road map can show you how to drive to any place in this country, but you won't get there if you don't start your car and go the distance. Your plan can show you how to obtain financial security. But if you don't implement it, your plan is nothing more than words on a page.

Money is expensive. No matter what you do for a living, you work hard for your money. It's only fair that, in the end, your money work hard for you. To accomplish this, you must set aside regular amounts of money and put it into lucrative investments.

Each of us is ultimately responsible for the support of an old, unemployed man or woman. Whether this elderly person eats beans or steak is up to us, depending on how much we contribute to this person's well-being. That elderly person is you. Just how well you eat depends on how well you planned for your future when you were younger.

Take care of this responsibility while you can. If you do, when you become old and no longer work for a living, you'll have the time and the money to do the things that you had neither the time nor the money to do before. Therefore, while retirement is a punishment for the people who never planned for it, it can be your reward for following a well-planned financial strategy.

CHAPTER SUMMARY

1. We are privileged to live in the United States of America. We can look forward to many exciting changes which will take place during the 1990s, many of which will affect us directly.
2. The outlook is for interest rates to decline and stock prices to rise. It will not happen overnight, but will take place slowly as we progress into the next decade.
3. Don't let negative events get you down or lead you to postpone planning for your financial future. These events come and go quickly and will not stop the trend of rising prices or dynamic economic growth.
4. Prepare yourself for the 1990s and beyond by taking charge of your future destiny. Don't let procrastination lead you to disaster.

Epilogue

I hope this book has done several things for you. First, I hope you now have an excellent understanding of techniques you can use to build financial security in the 1990s and beyond. Second, I hope you are motivated to meet the financial challenges that will confront you during the next decade. Finally, I hope you are educated about the field of financial planning so that you will not only become more successful in your future financial endeavors, but that you will share your knowledge with friends and relatives so that they can also become successful.

This reminds me of my 13-year-old son, Eric, who was in the Boy Scouts. Whenever his troop engaged in a project or sporting activity such as swimming or canoeing, they used the buddy system: they had backup support and each scout shared his experiences with a friend. In the same way, as you strive to achieve financial success in the future, I hope you will share your ideas and experiences, both good and bad, with a spouse, friend, or "buddy." Therefore, you can learn together how to travel the path to success.

Even if it's not possible for you to share your adventures with a "buddy," you should be able to "wing it" by educating yourself as much as possible. Through your increased proficiency in the field of financial planning, you will be able to make some excellent decisions. But don't forget, an understanding, competent professional can give you support and advice in your quest for financial freedom. My final wish is that God will be with you during all of life's challenges and help you to find success in all your future endeavors.

I hope you will use this book often as a reference. If you benefited from my book, please share its wisdom with a friend. If you belong to an organization, association, or corporation, I am available to conduct an educational seminar/workshop on a particular topic that would help to solve a specific problem. Please call or write me for an informational packet. Also, I would appreciate receiving your comments on my book. You may send them to me at this address: 1044 Medoc Court, Chesterfield, MO 63017; home phone (314) 394-0107.

Glossary of Terms

The word *jargon* is defined in most dictionaries as "unintelligible speech; gibberish" as well as "a technical or specialized vocabulary used by members of a particular profession," because jargon defeats, rather than increases, understanding.

The financial industry is awash in gibberish. This glossary is designed to help you understand terms you might read in this book that would be otherwise confusing. Don't hesitate to refer to this glossary to increase your knowledge of investment principals.

After-tax return. The yield to an investor after all income taxes have been deducted. Only by comparing after-tax returns can an investor determine which investment makes the most sense based on his or her tax bracket.

Aggressive. A bold investment approach that takes higher risks in return for potentially higher rewards.

Annual meeting. A shareholder meeting held to vote on matters of importance to a company or mutual fund. Shareholders who can't attend vote by *proxy*.

Annualized rate of return. The average return over a period of years taking into account the effect of *compounding*. Also called the compound growth rate. For example, a 100 percent return over five years is equivalent to an annualized rate of return of 18.2 percent per year.

Asset allocation. A way to diversify a portfolio into certain classes of investments based on the economic outlook and the objectives of the investor. Percentages are assigned to certain classes of assets in order to reduce risks and increase the potential for reward.

Automatic cash withdrawal plan. A withdrawal plan that sends the investor a check for the same dollar amount every month or quarter, deducted from the balance of the investor's mutual fund account.

Backup withholding. An IRS regulation requires registered owners to certify the Social Security or tax ID numbers on their financial accounts or have 20 percent of all dividends and redemptions withheld for taxes. Mutual fund shareholders certify tax ID numbers by signing an account application or W-9 form.

Balanced fund. A mutual fund that seeks growth and income, with stability of principal, through a portfolio that includes both stocks and bonds.

Bear. A large four-legged animal with teeth and claws that causes investors to quake in their boots; an investor who believes stock prices will decline; a pessimist.

Bear market. A prolonged period of declining stock prices, the bottom of which may offer courageous investors (and investors using *dollar-cost averaging*) very attractive values.

Beneficiary. A recipient of proceeds from a qualified retirement plan or insurance policy upon the death of the registered owner.

Blue-chip. A well-financed company with a position of industry leadership, a proven record of profits, and a long history of dividend payments. The term comes from poker, in which blue chips have the highest value.

Bond. A long-term debt security, or IOU, issued by a government or corporation that generally pays a stated rate of interest and returns the *face value* on the *maturity date*.

Breakpoint. The dollar level of mutual fund purchases that qualifies an investor for a reduced sales charge. There are usually three ways to reduce sales charges; the *combined purchase privilege,* the *right of accumulation,* and the *statement of intention.*

Bull. A male bovine; an investor who believes stock prices will rise; an optimist; advice that you need a shovel to wade through.

STRATEGIC FINANCIAL PLANNING FOR THE 1990S

Bull market. A prolonged period of rising stock prices.

Business cycle. The recurrent rise and fall of a country's economic fortune over time, characterized by fluctuating employment levels, industrial productivity, and interest rates.

Callable. A bond or preferred stock that the issuing company can redeem before maturity. By calling a bond when interest rates fall, a company can issue new bonds at lower interest rates.

Call option. An *option* in which the buyer has the right to purchase a specified number of shares of common stock (or other financial asset) at a specified price on or before the *expiration date* of the option.

Call protection. A provision in a bond's *indenture* setting a certain period during which the bond cannot be called away by the issuer.

Capital appreciation. A rise in principal value. Also used to describe the investment objective of a *mutual fund* when the primary criteria for choosing securities is the potential rise in value rather than generated dividend income.

Capital gain (loss). A profit or loss on the sale of a security. Under the Tax Reform Act of 1986, capital gains are taxed as ordinary income and capital losses can be deducted up to a maximum of $3,000 against ordinary income. Capital gains and losses can also be used to offset each other for tax-planning purposes.

Certificate. A document of security ownership. Mutual funds do not issue certificates unless requested, because most shareholders find it is more convenient to have fund shares held on deposit.

Certificate of deposit (CD). A short-term debt security issued by a commercial bank or savings and loan association.

Certified tax identification number. The IRS requires a certified Social Security or tax ID number on all investment accounts. The investor certifies the tax ID number by signing an account application or a W-9 form. See *backup withholding*.

Combined purchase privilege. Allows an investor and his or her family to qualify for a reduced sales charge by combining individual mutual fund purchases made at the same time.

Common stock. Units of ownership in a public corporation, usually with voting rights on important company matters. If a company is liquidated, the claims of secured and unsecured creditors and holders of bonds and *preferred stock* take precedence over those of common stock owners.

Compounding. The effect of interest previously earned earning additional interest and increasing an investor's return. For example, reinvesting mutual fund distributions takes advantage of compounding.

Conservative. A cautious approach to investing that allows only prudent risks to seek a reasonable return.

Consumer price index. The change in consumer prices determined monthly by the U.S. Bureau of Labor Statistics, often cited as a general measure of inflation.

Contingent deferred sales charge. A fee assessed when shares are redeemed from certain mutual funds sold without an initial sales charge. This fee usually decreases the longer an investor holds the fund's shares.

Convertible security. A corporate bond or preferred stock that can be exchanged for shares of a company's common stock. Allows an investor to participate in a company's growth while receiving a higher yield than is paid on the company's common stock.

Debt securities. General term for any security representing money loaned that must be repaid to the lender at a future date. Bonds, notes, bills, and money-market instruments are all debt securities.

Deflation. A decline in the prices of goods and services; the opposite of inflation.

Discount. 1. (*n*) Selling below par; *e.g.,* a $1,000 bond selling for $900. 2. (*v*) Anticipating the effects of news on a security's value; for example, "The market had already discounted the effect of the labor strike by bidding the company's stock down."

Distribution. A payment of income and/or capital gains from a mutual fund's earnings, paid either monthly, quarterly, or annually. Shareholders may take their distributions in cash or reinvest in additional shares of the fund.

Diversification. Investing in a large number of securities or various classes of investments to reduce the risk of any one investment going bad. A basic premise of good portfolio management.

Dividend. 1. A payment of cash from net profits of a business, made at the discretion of the board of directors. 2. A payment by a mutual fund derived solely from net investment income (dividends or interest).

Dollar-cost averaging. An investment strategy based on making investments of equal amounts in a mutual fund at regular intervals. Because the investor buys more shares at lower prices and fewer shares at higher prices, the average cost of the shares is lower than the average price over the period in which they were bought. It is a conservative method of investing in fluctuating markets, but cannot guarantee a profit in a prolonged down market.

Dow Jones Industrial Average. The most widely recognized stock market index, consisting of the average stock prices of 30 of the largest American corporations.

Equity security. A type of security representing proportional ownership in a corporation. *Common stock, preferred stock,* and *convertible securities* are all equity securities. *Debt securities* do not represent ownership.

Equivalent taxable yield. A comparison of a nontaxable yield on a municipal bond or tax-exempt mutual fund with a taxable yield at an investor's own tax rate. The tax-exempt yield divided by the tax rate equals the taxable equivalent yield.

Exchange Privilege. A service that lets an investor move money from one mutual fund to another in the same family in order to respond to changes in the financial markets. Exchanges are generally made at net asset value (bid price) without a sales charge.

Expiration date. The day on which an option ceases to have value.

Face value. The value of a bond stated on the bond certificate; thus, the redemption value at maturity. Most bonds have a face value, or par, of $1,000.

Federal Reserve System. The central bank of the United States, which has regulated credit in the economy since 1913. Includes the Federal Reserve Bank, 14 district banks, and the member banks of the Federal Reserve, governed by the Federal Reserve Board.

Financial pyramid. A strategy many investors use for spreading their money among low-, medium-, and high-risk investments. The pyramid shape ensures that most assets will be secure while still allowing an investor to take advantage of a wide range of opportunities.

Fixed-income security. Any security that pays an unchanging rate of interest or dividends. Bonds, notes, bills, money-market instruments, and preferred stocks are all considered fixed-income securities. When interest rates decline, fixed-income securities increase in value because of their higher return; when rates rise, their value decreases.

401(k). A corporate retirement plan that allows employees to contribute pretax dollars to a company pool invested in stocks, bonds, or mutual funds. Because money taken out of an employee's salary is not taxed until withdrawn, and all earnings are likewise tax deferred, a substantial amount of capital can be accumulated.

403(b). Qualified retirement plans for public school teachers, named for the section of the Internal Revenue Code authorizing their use.

Ginnie Mae pass-through. A security backed by a pool of mortgages guaranteed by the Government National Mortgage Association (GNMA), with principal and interest payments made by homeowners "passed through" to the investor. Ginnie Maes are usually the highest-yielding government-guaranteed securities.

Government security. Any debt obligation issued by the U.S. government, its agencies, or its instrumentalities. Certain securities, such as Treasury bonds and nie Maes, are backed by the government as to both principal and interest payments. Other securities, such as those issued by the Federal Home Loan Mortgage Corporation, or Freddie Mac, are backed by the issuing agency.

Indenture. The formal contract governing a corporate bond that explains the bond's maturity, coupon rate, call privilege, and other rights.

Individual Retirement Account (IRA). A tax-deferred savings plan to which employed individuals can contribute up to $2,000 a year. Recently, Congress limited the IRA deduction to couples earning less than $40,000 a year (or individuals earning less than $25,000 a year) and employees not covered by a corporate pension plan. Others can still make nondeductible contributions and benefit from tax-deferred compounding of earnings.

Inflation. A rise in the prices of goods and services caused by too much money chasing too few goods; often equated with loss of purchasing power.

Internal Revenue Service (IRS). Created in 1913 to administer the collection of federal income taxes.

Investment-grade. Term describing bonds suitable for purchase by prudent investors. Standard and Poor's and Moody's Investors Service designate bonds in their top four categories (AAA/Aaa, AA/Aa, A, and BBB/Baa) as investment-grade.

Investment objective. The goal an investor or a mutual fund seeks to accomplish. An investment objective may be current income, capital appreciation, or a combination of the two.

Joint account. A shareholder account that is registered in two or more names. Transactions on joint accounts generally require the signature of all registered owners.

Jumbo CD. A certificate of deposit issued by banks in amounts of $100,000 or more, paying higher rates of interest than smaller denomination certificates. The ability to participate in jumbo purchases is one of the advantages of investing in a *money-market fund.*

Leverage. The use of borrowed money to increase funds available for investment in order to achieve a greater rate of return.

Liquidity. A characteristic of an asset that enables it to be converted into cash quickly. Mutual fund shares are liquid investments because they can be redeemed quickly and easily.

Long-term investment strategy. A strategy that looks past the day-to-day fluctuations of the stock and bond markets and responds to fundamental changes in the financial markets or an investor's life.

Lump-sum distribution. A single withdrawal of an account's entire value. Upon retirement, participants in an IRA or other qualified retirement plan can choose to have a lump-sum distribution of the proceeds from their account. Certain lump-sum distributions qualify for special tax treatment.

Market timing. A strategy of buying or selling securities in anticipation of changes in market or economic conditions.

Maturity date. The date on which the principal of a bond must be repaid.

Money-market fund. A mutual fund offering a stable principal value, high liquidity, and market rates of return through a diversified portfolio of short-term, high-grade, money-market instruments.

Municipal bond. A *debt security* issued by a state or local government, the interest from which is free from federal income tax and may be free from state and local taxes as well. Munis usually yield less than taxable bonds because of their tax advantages. For convenience and liquidity, most investors like to own munis through a trust or mutual fund.

Mutual fund. An *open-end investment company* that pools the assets of individuals to invest toward a common goal. Generally offers an unlimited number of shares and will buy back shares at any time. The major advantages of mutual funds for individuals are professional management, portfolio diversification, convenience, and ease of record-keeping.

National Association of Securities Dealers (NASD). An industry organization charged by Congress with standardizing investment practices and establishing high ethical standards in the financial community.

National Association of Securities Dealers Automated Quotation System (NASDAQ). A computerized system provides prices for securities traded *over the counter* as well as on the major stock exchanges.

Nest egg. Money put aside for future needs such as retirement or a college education. An investment in an *IRA* or other qualified retirement plan would be part of a nest egg.

Net asset value. The market value of a mutual fund share, calculated daily by adding the value of all of the securities in the fund's portfolio, subtracting liabilities, and dividing by the number of shares outstanding. Often abbreviated as NAV and referred to as the "bid price."

Open-end investment company. A *mutual fund,* so called because it continuously offers new shares to the public.

Option. A contract giving an investor the right to buy or sell a specific security within a specified time at a fixed price. An option to buy a stock is known as a *call option;* an option to sell is called a *put option.*

Over-the-counter market (OTC). A market in which securities transactions are conducted through computer and telephone networks rather than on the floor of a jor stock exchange. The *NASDAQ* is the main clearinghouse for over-the-counter stocks.

Par value. The nominal or *face value* of a debt security; the value at *maturity*. Par value of a bond is usually $1,000.

Portfolio. Any combination of more than one security. A mutual fund's well-diversified portfolio lowers investment risk.

Preferred stock. A class of stock with a fixed dividend that has preference over a company's common stock in the payment of dividends and liquidation of assets.

Premium. The amount by which a *bond* sells above its *par value*.

Prepayment risk. The chance that a homeowner will pay off a mortgage loan early, resulting in early retirement of mortgage-backed *Ginnie Mae* securities. Prepayment risk increases during periods of declining interest rates, when many homeowners refinance their mortgages.

Price/earnings ratio (P/E). A commonly used method of valuing stocks, calculated by dividing the price of a company's stock by its earnings per share. A P/E ratio, also called an earnings multiple, reflects investors' perceptions of a company's growth prospects. The higher and more predictable a company's earnings are, the higher its P/E ratio will usually be.

Prime rate. The interest rate a bank charges on loans to its most creditworthy customers. Frequently cited as a standard for general interest-rate levels in the economy.

Professional management. The investment selection, analysis, and review performed on a full-time basis by individuals working to achieve specific investment goals for their shareholders.

Profit-taking. Selling securities after they have risen in value to realize a gain.

Prospectus. The legal document that describes the investment policies of a mutual fund or limited partnership and provides key financial data and other essential information. By law, it must be furnished to all investors before they invest.

Proxy. The process by which shareholders who cannot attend a fund's annual meeting vote by mail.

Public offering price. The price of a mutual fund share including any *sales charge*. Often abbreviated as POP.

Put option. A contract that gives the buyer the right to sell a security at a specific price at any time before the *expiration date*.

Qualified retirement plan. A retirement program such as an *IRA, Keogh, 401(k),* or employee pension and profit-sharing plan that qualifies for tax deferral and other benefits by meeting standards set by the *Internal Revenue Service.*

Real rate of return. The return on an investment after it is adjusted for the effects of *inflation.*

Reinvestment privilege. The right of mutual fund shareholders to use income and/or capital gains distributions to purchase additional shares of their fund without paying a *sales charge.*

Return of capital. A distribution that includes a portion of an investor's original principal.

Right of accumulation. The right of shareholders to combine the value of shares already owned when purchasing additional shares to qualify for a reduced *sales charge.*

Risk/reward ratio. An investment principle that states that the greater the investment risk, the greater must be the potential reward.

Rollover. A transfer of a *lump-sum distribution* from a *qualified retirement plan* to an IRA. Once a rollover is completed, no additional contributions should be made to preserve the investor's ability to transfer the assets to another pension or profit-sharing plan in the future.

Sales charge. A fee added to the price of some mutual fund shares, paid to brokers to compensate for their services. Sales charges vary from fund to fund and decrease as the size of the investment increases.

Securities and Exchange Commission (SEC). The federal agency that administers the laws governing the securities markets.

Sector fund. A specialized mutual fund that invests exclusively in a related group of industries, designed for investors who believe these industries offer better opportunities for capital appreciation. Sector funds are usually more volatile than funds that invest in a more diversified range of industries.

Self-directed retirement account. A retirement account offered through an investment dealer that can include stocks, bonds, and mutual funds. So called because the investor is free to make his or her own investment decisions.

Signature guarantee. A protection against fraud that assures the authenticity of a signature on a sale or transfer of mutual fund shares. Most mutual funds accept signature guarantees from commercial banks or member firms of a major stock exchange. The institution guaranteeing the signature assumes liability for the signature's authenticity.

Simplified Employee Pension Plan (SEP). A retirement plan that allows small businesses to contribute to IRAs for their employees.

Spousal IRA. An Individual Retirement Account for a married couple when one partner has less than $250 in income. A couple filing a joint tax return can contribute up to $2,250 each year (or 100 percent of the working spouse's income, whichever is less) divided between two IRAs in any combination as long as they do not exceed the $2,000 limit in either account.

Statement of intention. A way to qualify for a reduced sales charge by declaring in writing that you will invest at least $25,000 within 13 months in any mutual fund or funds.

Super bowl indicator. A superficial stock market index based on the theory that a Super Bowl victory by a National Football Conference team foreshadows a strong year in the stock market.

Systematic investing plan. A mutual fund investment plan that deducts money from the investor's checking account each month to invest in a fund of his or her choice.

Tax deferred. A term describing an investment in which the earnings are free from taxation until they are withdrawn by the investor. Most qualified retirement plans, including IRAs, are tax-deferred investments.

Tax-exempt security. Generic term for a municipal bond.

Tax loss carryforward. A tax benefit that allows an individual or a mutual fund to offset past losses against future profits.

Torpedo. A stock that sinks as if hit by a torpedo. One of the principles of successful investing is to avoid such stocks, which can have a devastating impact on overall portfolio performance.

Total return. The return on an investment taking into account the change in price plus dividends or interest received.

Treasury bill, bond, note. Negotiable debt obligations issued by the U.S. government and backed by its full faith and credit. Treasury bills are short-term securities with maturities of one year or less. Treasury notes are intermediate-term securities with maturities of one to ten years. Treasury bonds are long-term securities with maturities of ten years or longer.

Trust. A legal arrangement through which title to property (such as real estate, mutual funds, or stocks) is given to one party to manage for the benefit of others.

12b-1 plan. A mutual fund distribution plan under which a certain percentage of fund assets, usually 1 percent or less, can be used to pay distributions and marketing expenses. These funds usually do not levy an up-front sales charge to the investor, but do levy a back-end sales charge if the investor withdraws money over a specified number of years.

Uniform Gift to Minors Act (UGMA). State laws that allow any adult to contribute to a custodian account in a minor child's name without having to name a legal guardian or establish a trust. Each person can contribute up to $10,000 a year per child without incurring any gift tax liability. UGMAs allow parents to shift income to their children, who may be taxed at a lower rate. Recent legislation has reduced the tax advantages of a gift to children under 14.

Volatility. The tendency of a security to have rapid and wide price swings in a short period of time. Mutual funds strive to minimize the volatility of fund shares, although different funds have different acceptable levels of volatility.

Wall Street. The financial district in New York City where the New York and American Stock Exchanges and many other financial institutions are headquartered; also a nickname for the entire investment community.

x. Appears next to a mutual fund's listing in the newspaper to indicate that the fund recently paid a capital gain or dividend. Because this amount was previously included in the fund's net asset value, it is deducted from the net asset value when it is paid out. The "x" stands for "ex-dividend."

Yield. The rate at which an investment pays out interest or dividend income, expressed in percentage terms and calculated by dividing the amount paid by the price of the security and annualizing the result.

Yield to maturity. The difference between the price initially paid for a bond and its value at maturity or, simply, the return on the investment.

z. Appears after a fund's name in the daily newspaper if the price isn't available in time to meet the *NASDAQ* reporting deadline. It reflects an extremely tight reporting schedule.

Zero-coupon bonds. A special type of bond that pays no interest until maturity. Zeros are purchased at a deep discount from face value and are redeemed at par at maturity. Interest accrues over the life of the bond. Although zeros don't pay any interest currently, the IRS taxes them as if they do (except for zero-coupon municipal bonds for which all income accrues tax free).

Zzzzz. What you should never do when you drive a car or invest your money.

INDEX